WOMEN IN THE LAW

Strategic Career Management

General Editor:

Elizabeth Cruickshank

The Law Society

Women in the Law

Related titles by Law Society Publishing

Becoming a Partner
Young Solicitors' Group
1 85328 841 1

Employment Law Handbook
Daniel Barnett and Henry Scrope
1 85328 716 4

Equal Pay
Sara Leslie, Sue Hastings and Jo Morris
1 85328 827 6

New Partner's Guide to Management
Simon Young
1 85328 776 8

Titles from Law Society Publishing can be ordered from all good bookshops or direct from our distributors, Marston Book Services (tel. 01235 465656 or email law.society@marston.co.uk). For further information or a catalogue, call our editorial and marketing office on 020 7320 5878.

Dedication

In memory of my father, Alexander Watt Taylor, who felt that girls deserved as much education as boys.

Elizabeth Cruickshank, June 2003

Contents

Foreword

This year's annual report from the Law Society shows that more and more women are becoming solicitors. At the last count, they constituted just over a third of those holding practising certificates.

In the workforce as a whole, there are now double the numbers of women compared to 25 years ago, making up nearly half the working population. Projections show that in 10 years' time, there will be two million more jobs in the economy – 80 per cent of which will be filled by women.

This is good news. As this timely publication from the Law Society Publishing points out, women lawyers have come a long way from the days when marriage meant an end to a career. Literally. You now have some inspiring role models, highlighted in this publication, in Dame Elizabeth Butler-Sloss, Helena Kennedy and Eileen Pembridge.

Despite the progress that's been made, the labour market is still not functioning as well as it should. There is still a 'glass ceiling' that holds too many women back, and in the legal profession there are not enough women at partnership level.

I know that in the legal profession – as in many other commercial environments – there is intense pressure to work long hours. As a senior woman in my own profession, I am aware of just how intense that can be.

It's not surprising, therefore, that when asked by this Government a few years ago what would make the biggest difference to their lives, women said they wanted to strike a better balance between their work and home lives.

We have made it a priority to encourage a working environment that is more family friendly. For the first time mothers and fathers now have the right to apply to work flexible hours, fathers can take paid paternity leave, parents who adopt can take paid adoption leave, and the arrangements for maternity leave and pay have been improved and simplified.

But as lawyers just starting out, you also need guidance that is specific to your career. And *Women In the Law* will help to show you how others have been successful in pursuing both their careers and their family lives. In particular, it will give you advice on how to achieve a healthy work-life balance.

Whatever you decide – whether to work in the private or public sector or to set up your own firm – I hope that you will find *Women in the Law* of great value in helping you make the best decisions. I wish you all every success in your future careers.

Patricia Hewitt
Secretary of State for Trade and Industry
and Cabinet Minister for Women

Acknowledgements

First of all my thanks go to Judith McDermott who always has interesting little projects in mind, to Jane Withey, my commissioning editor and to the committee members of the Association of Women Solicitors for their interest and encouragement. Finally, I always wondered why authors so often acknowledged the contributions of their partners and spouses. Not any more. This book would not have left the pen of a very fledgling author without the support, encouragement and forbearance of my husband, Don.

Elizabeth Cruickshank
June 2003

About the Contributors

Jayne Buxton is the author of *Ending the Mother War: Starting the Workplace Revolution* (Macmillan, 1998), which argues for a radical overhaul of workplace norms and practices to make balanced working lives genuine possibilities. She has provided work/life consulting services to a number of organisations, is a regular contributor to UK television, press, radio and conference discussions on the topic of workplace flexibility and the workplace of the future, and is a core member of the UK's National Work Life Forum. Until December 1999, Jayne was a strategy consultant with Gemini Consulting, where she had been employed for 12 years. She co-founded Flametree in 2000, a work/life consultancy that was later acquired by the human resources services group of PricewaterhouseCoopers.

Dianna Keel, a solicitor, is a director of FutureVisions^SM, the professional learning and development practice, and author of two e-courses on 'soft' (actually 'critical') skills. Future Visions^SM provides leadership, management, career and outplacement support, practice/business development coaching/consulting, coaching skills training, group and team programmes, culture change programmes and one-to-one coaching for organisations of all sizes. Visit **www.FutureVisions.org** for a wonderland of tips on time and stress management, EI, career planning, and much more, including several free e-newsletters.

Tania Martin is a dual-qualified (Australia/England) solicitor who commenced practice in Sydney before moving to, and practising in, London. After years in legal practice, Tania assisted in the development of a legal recruitment consultancy in London, and became a trainer in interview techniques, legal practice and networking strategies. Tania has since returned to practice in Australia where she specialises in government and commercial contracts with the Australasian law firm Phillips Fox. Tania has written articles about legal recruitment and legal practice for English and Australian legal journals.

Richard Payne is managing director of BSPS Training Consultancy Limited. Richard is a learning and development specialist with 12 years' experience of training design and delivery in both the public and private sector. He has a special interest in assisting lawyers to improve their business development and pitching skills. Richard regularly lecturers on academic staff development courses at a number of universities and has contributed articles and quotes to various journals and newspapers. His website is at **www.bspstraining.co.uk**

Penny Terndrup is a director of leading recruitment specialists EJ Legal, having joined in 1997 after practising as a solicitor at a medium-sized City firm. The company covers recruitment into private practice and commerce and industry at all levels of qualification, from newly qualified to partner or head of legal, nationwide. Penny specialises in partner and team moves in private practice, primarily in London. EJ Legal is a member of EJ Group, which covers tax, human resources and mergers recruitment.

Sally Woodward is a founding member of Sherwood PSF Consulting and specialises in change management, knowledge management, training & development strategy and programme design, and facilitation. She also provides coaching and mentoring to senior professionals. Sally is also Professor of Legal Professional Development at the Centre for Law Firm Management at Nottingham Law School, and, with its Director, Professor Stephen Mayson designed the first MBA in Legal Practice Management, which was launched in 1995.

Sally is a solicitor, having qualified and practised in intellectual property and media law, and has an Executive MBA from London Business School (1992). In 1986, she joined Freshfields to initiate the development of a full range of professional support services. In 1997 she set up her own consultancy, working mainly with lawyers and insurance brokers, before joining with six others in 1999 to set up Sherwood, which offers a range of integrated consultancy services to the professional services sector.

Introduction

This book is in three inter-related parts. The first part gives a brief history of women in the law, then focuses on the career options that are open in the legal profession, concluding with a chapter on work-life balance. The third part contains good advice from experts on how to acquire skills that will enhance a legal career. I am very grateful to all those who have written these contributions for giving of their time to produce material which will benefit women at all stages of legal life.

In the middle is the main part of the book, for which I have been responsible, and which is about the achievements of women lawyers. It is not an artificial merit list, but a celebration of what women of various ages who qualified as solicitors or barristers have achieved since they qualified. As someone who trained as a teacher, re-trained as a solicitor and somewhat late in life has fallen into magazine editing and writing, I have been fascinated by the diverse routes that many of these women have followed to attain public prominence.

Overview

There is a great temptation to look at successful people, and in our case successful women lawyers, and to assume that it has all been easy, and that they have moved along a smooth road through school to university and professional training to arrive at some public pinnacle of achievement. For those at the start of their careers this can sometimes be discouraging, because all they can see is success and not the struggle behind it. A few of my interviewees certainly appeared to find a fairly straight path, knowing very early on that they wanted to be lawyers, aiming for it and moving forward. But there are others for whom success has been reached through a much harder road, and I am very grateful to my interviewees for sharing their difficult experiences with me as well as their successes, because they appreciated that the purpose of this book is to encourage young women, not to daunt them.

The majority are the daughters of professional men, teachers, lawyers or doctors. Although, perhaps not unsurprisingly very few had mothers who were in professional occupations, all of them had the backing of their parents. Indeed the parental influence was very noticeable and ranged from a desire to see a daughter able to support herself in an uncertain world, to suggesting a positive choice between medicine and law and helping with subsequent career decisions. At a time when many men were regarded as being anti-women, there were clearly some fathers who valued the abilities of their daughters just as much as those of their sons, and many mothers who wanted their daughters to have the opportunities not available to them. In addition the majority of those interviewed had the good fortune of finding a supportive partner who actively encourages them and does not resent their success. The importance of this cannot be underestimated.

Home and work

One interesting point made by many of these women concerns 'the financial imperative'. If money is required either because they are the sole breadwinners or because additional money is necessary to keep their families comfortable these women just get on with it, and eschew what someone aptly called 'the tyranny of choice'.

The majority of my interviewees are mothers, some are grandmothers. In some cases they have combined work and bringing up children because their income was necessary and in others they loved their work and their family so much that they could not imagine giving up either. But nearly all feel that there needs to be some alteration to the way that legal work is organised, particularly in City firms. Not one of them suggested that because they had survived, accommodation should not be made for today's young mothers. Their feeling was rather that everyone would benefit if flexible working were available to all parents and not just to women.

Many have found a renewed energy to devote to work once their children have become more independent and even more so when they have left home. There is still so much of the day-to-day domestic organisation that falls to women; when that burden is lessened they are able to use the considerable managerial and administrative skills that they have acquired through years of balancing child management and client management for the benefit of the organisations in which they operate.

A whole life

The older members of the group have a calm sympathy for today's young women lawyers and feel that life may well be more difficult now than when they were first qualified and a rarity in the profession. This may be because they had lower expectations, merely to get a job until they married or had children, or because legal life is harder now and the competition for jobs is more intense. Many women made the point that looking after a child is a very intense experience but that it occupies only a very short part of a career, and it is wrong that that short part should be so influential in determining the rest of a woman's life.

This ability to see beyond their own particular situations, not just to the situations of their own daughters or their own colleagues but much wider to the family situation as a whole, was what in a sense most impressed me, and which made the interviewing experience a great privilege.

Another theme widely expressed was the benefit of a legal training generally. An ability to analyse, work hard, understand legislation, assess information quickly, explain that information to clients in a clear and concise manner, to chair meetings, to market oneself and one's firm are all attributes we assume in a good lawyer, but are transferable skills to be highly valued in any occupation.

The pleasure that so many expressed in being asked to consider their past came as a great surprise to me, but on reflection should not have been, because their lives are so focused on the future and the next challenge. Goals do not exist in the past, achievements do. If you are always looking forward to the next goal you can easily discount what has happened in the past. A quiet sense of adventure is obvious, as is a willingness to take on new cultures, whether ethnically, socially or geographically different. Emblematic of this is the fact that 'retirement' in the traditional sense was not something that any of the older women were considering at the present time.

Indeed the phrase used most often when they talked to me, and which was a clear message to the younger generation, was 'Go for it!'.

Elizabeth Cruickshank
June 2003

Part One
Background

Women lawyers have come a long way from the time that flexible working could on the whole be summed up as career followed by marriage and no career at all. This section briefly summarises the progress that women have made over the last 80 years from total exclusion to now producing more than half of the newly qualified members of the legal profession.

It is also concerned with the notion of a legal qualification being for life. Penny Terndrup and I set out the different ways that women can qualify into the profession, the relative advantages and disadvantages of qualifying as a solicitor or a barrister and some of the alternative opportunities that are subsequently open to those with a legal qualification.

The final part recognises that there may be times when it is impossible to pursue an onerous full-time career at the same time as undertaking considerable outside responsibilities. The recent Flexible Working Regulations of 2002 and 2003 have granted employees the right to request flexible working but not necessarily to receive it. Jayne Buxton gives advice on how to analyse the work situation and then to present a case which is more likely to persuade employers that flexible working will not be detrimental to their business.

Chapter 1.1
A Short History

Elizabeth Cruickshank

Although Frenchwomen had been able to practise as barristers since December 1900, it was not possible until 1919 for women in the United Kingdom to become solicitors, barristers or magistrates. In 1861, it was recorded that over 72 per cent of teachers were women and approximately 200 women had become doctors by 1900, but prior to 1919 the Law Society and the various Inns of Court steadfastly resisted all efforts by women to enter their hallowed but exclusive halls. The Scottish Society of Law Agents refused Margaret Hall permission to take their entrance examination in 1900, Gray's Inn refused the application of Bertha Cave in 1903 and the Law Society had a long history of refusing to permit women to register for its examinations or to enter into articles of clerkship. They rejected 'a young lady' in 1879, and most famously four female university graduates who in 1913 took them to court in the case of *Bebb* v. *The Law Society* [1914] 1 Ch 286.

They lost on somewhat spurious grounds (the Court was not influenced by the notion that the Solicitors Act provisions could be interpreted using the Interpretation Act 1889), and it was not until women had quietly proved their capability in traditional masculine occupations during World War One that they were enabled through the Sex Disqualification (Removal) Act 1919 to hold any office or to enter or carry on any civil profession or vocation. Very soon thereafter the Lord Chancellor appointed more than 200 women magistrates, but it took 14 years before the number of women solicitors reached that number. Magistrates may have been unpaid but they were not required to pay for their training as solicitors and barristers were. As premiums payable to principals and pupilmasters were at least as much as a newly qualified lawyer could hope to earn in the first year or years of qualification and salaries were rarely paid during training, it is not surprising that most of the early women solicitors came from families with legal connections.

The first women lawyers

Carrie Morrison was the first woman to be admitted as a solicitor in December 1922 and Maud Crofts was the first woman to take out a practising certificate. Mrs Crofts set up in practice with her husband and brother, Miss Morrison with her husband, and many women went into practice with their fathers who had trained them. There were also a few all women practices, or practices which appeared to be women friendly and trained more than one female articled clerk in the period between 1922 and 1962. If that seems a very minimal criterion, reflect that there were fewer than 500 women in the whole of England and Wales who had qualified as solicitors during those 40 years.

Ivy Williams, who had taken all her Law examinations in Oxford in 1903, was the first woman to be called to the Bar in England in 1922. As she immediately returned to an academic life at Oxford, it was Helena Normanton who in fact became the first woman to practise as a barrister, notably at the Old Bailey. Normanton was a remarkable woman who fought to become the first married woman to be able to travel on her own passport under her maiden name in 1924. In 1949 she and Rose Heilbron were the first two women to be appointed as King's Counsel, and Heilbron went on to become the first woman judge to sit at the Old Bailey in 1972.

In the early years women joined the Bar in roughly the same numbers as they became solicitors. In the 20 years post 1922 on average 13 women a year qualified as solicitors and 13 women a year qualified as barristers! Because the Bar in total was much smaller this meant that a higher proportion of the total number of barristers were women as opposed to the proportion of women who were solicitors. In both cases many women lawyers found themselves, despite their undoubted intelligence, university degrees and high qualifications subject to the same social constraints as other women. The general social expectation of those decades was that women should work only until they married or at the very most until they had children. Many of those who continued in practice were therefore single or childless.

Social attitudes

Although women had helped to keep the country going during World War Two they were not in career terms the immediate beneficiaries of peace in the way that they had been after World War One. There was an assumption that they would step aside, that university places and jobs would go to returning ex-servicemen and that women if they worked at all would give up as soon as they had a family. The explosion in the number of women solicitors holding practising certificates has taken place mainly since 1987. As recently as 1967, only 619 women, or 2.7 per cent of the total profession held practising certificates, and in 1977 there were only 336 women barristers in the whole of England and Wales.

Simply fighting for what might be regarded as basic institutional freedoms has been a distraction for women in both branches of the profession. One reason given by the Law Society for not wishing to admit women members was its lack of suitable 'cloakrooms', women could not use the Law Society's Reading Room until 1974 and women were not permitted to address the court wearing trousers until 1995, it being a favourite ploy of some judges who did not like the way that a female lawyer was dressed to indicate that she 'could not be heard'.

Up to the present

Until fairly recently, given the very low numbers of women at the Bar and given the number of years' practice required to qualify for senior appointment (in 2002 only 10.6 per cent of new silks were women), it is perhaps not surprising that there have been few women at senior level in the judiciary. Sybill Campbell became the first woman stipendiary magistrate in 1945, but it was not until 1962 that Elizabeth Lane was appointed as the first woman county court judge. At present there are only four female judges in the Court of Appeal, the first being Dame Elizabeth Butler-Sloss who was appointed in 1988.

Partnership in solicitors' firms has been available to women from the start, and they have even formed their own all female partnerships like Beatrice Davy who went into partnership first in 1931 with Edith Berthen and then in 1937 with Madge Easton Anderson, who first qualified in Scotland in 1920. The percentage of partners who are women has gradually increased but over the past few years has remained static at around 25 per cent of the total number of law firm partners.

The abolition of the partnership limit by the Companies Act 1967 gradually made it more likely that women would be elected to the partnerships of the largest firms, but it took until 1972 for Rosalind Bax to be elected as the first female equity partner at a major City firm, Coward Chance (subsequently Clifford Chance). More than two decades later Lovells elected Lesley MacDonagh as their managing partner and by the turn of the century first Diana Parker and then Janet Gaymer had become senior partners of their firms, Withers and Simmons & Simmons, respectively.

Perhaps we shall feel that we have achieved true equality when we no longer note when a woman lawyer is the first one who . . . but as I write this in the year of office of the first female President of the Law Society, Carolyn Kirby, that day has clearly not yet come.

Careers in the Law for Women

Elizabeth Cruickshank and Penny Terndrup

Nothing stands still – the first women who entered the profession in 1922 wouldn't recognise the career possibilities available for women today. Well over 50 per cent of those qualifying as solicitors and 49 per cent of those qualifying as barristers are female but somewhere along the way, by their mid-30s, the balance changes. Much of this is just the way of society, and even human nature. But perhaps there are some basic considerations early on that could maximise the chances of a woman having a career in the law with longevity (if she wants it) and satisfaction.

Career options

A legal qualification provides many career options. The five most common are:

- ○ Private practice in a solicitor's firm.
- ○ Private practice in barrister's chambers.
- ○ Employment as an in-house solicitor/barrister.
- ○ Employment in the Government Legal Service.
- ○ Teaching and research in academic institutions.

This chapter deals in outline with some different options, but because more women qualify as solicitors than barristers, and indeed more women practise as solicitors than pursue any other legal career, it focuses initially on career options for solicitors.

Private practice as a solicitor

The training route is an initial degree, either law or non-law, law school (either Legal Practice Course (LPC) only for law graduates or Common Professional Examination (CPE) plus LPC for non-law graduates) followed by a two-year training contract with a firm of solicitors, leading to qualification, and the lofty title of 'newly qualified solicitor'. Large City firms usually require their trainees to have at least a Class 2:1 degree but may also provide them with financial assistance during Law School. Salaries in private practice vary hugely. As a trainee in 2003 you could be earning anywhere between the Law Society minimum of £14,600 (£13,000 outside London) and £28,000–30,000 in the City. On qualification again the range is huge, but newly qualified lawyers in the City earn up to £50,000, although salaries in High Street practices are considerably less.

The career path here is slowly widening beyond purely fee earning work for clients, but essentially the big decision is still 'partnership or not'. The perception is that partnership status brings increased remuneration; this can be true, but the profitability of firms varies hugely and although the average amount paid in a firm will probably be greater than that available in-house or in academia, you need to look closely if money is your motivation here. Put simply if you're just in it for the money, think carefully. Partnership brings other pressures and a careful weighing up is vital. If making your way up the partnership ladder is not for you then there are other options such as being a professional support lawyer, a career associate, a pro bono coordinator or even finding a niche in business development or training.

Recent research conducted by EJ Legal has shown that 48 per cent of partners and 47 per cent of assistants felt that the traditional career path for solicitors (trainee, junior assistant, middle assistant, senior assistant, partner) was increasingly inappropriate. Of those, 86 per cent of female partners and 70 per cent of female assistants felt it was increasingly outmoded or should be changed.

Private practice as a barrister

Historically barristers are the 'other branch' of the profession, although in some ways the training route is similar. A degree, whether law or non-law, is required followed by the Bar Vocational Course (BVC) for law graduates or CPE plus BVC for non-law graduates, followed by pupillage in chambers. For many years there has been talk of fusing training for solicitors and barristers, but this has not happened yet! Many people choose the Bar in the belief that it offers a more pure practice of the law. Some say it can be lonely as there is less client contact especially in the early years, and initially it can be harder financially as newly qualified barristers, being self-employed, do not have the healthy salaries of newly qualified solicitors. Some chambers, but by no means all, have addressed this issue, and pay their pupils a living salary during pupillage and guarantee fees up to a reasonable level for the first year or so after qualification.

Employment as a solicitor or barrister

Employed solicitors or barristers are often known as 'in-house' lawyers or counsel. An in-house lawyer, whether solicitor or barrister is the legal resource for one client – the corporate employer. Depending on the size of the company and the job description, an in-house lawyer may operate much like a solicitor in private practice, with a specialism, time sheets, and a variety of sources of instructions. Alternatively an in-house counsel can be a trouble shooter who is more commercially involved with the business. The pluses often associated with this path are more flexibility in lifestyle and a greater 'say' in the actual business of the employing organisation. On the other hand, the salary for an in-house lawyer may be marginally less than the equivalent in private practice, and certainly levels out earlier while partnership profits in practice just seem to keep rising. However there are prospects to move upwards through management to board level, and the salary package may include bonuses and share option schemes not available in private practice.

Employment in the Government Legal Service

The Government in various forms is a substantial direct employer of lawyers. There are very few opportunities for training with the Government Legal Service (GLS) itself; the GLS usually recruits lawyers who are already fully trained, either newly qualified or with several years' experience. Their work covers statute drafting to rent review, preparing papers for judicial review to the CPS and a multitude of other things in between! Those drawn to this branch are attracted by making a difference, by dealing with real people and issues and by being at the cutting edge of new legislation. The financial rewards may not appear so attractive as those in other branches of the law, but there is greater flexibility in terms of hours and family-friendly working policies, and in most areas there is the opportunity to move both between government departments and into higher management roles. Local authorities also offer training as well as employment opportunities.

Academic teaching and research

Universities in England and Wales and other institutions such as the College of Law offer opportunities either to conduct research in or to teach law or related subjects. Subjects range from the entirely academic to the largely practical. Law without any consideration of practical application, of how it might be used in the context of a legal practice is called black letter law, and in recent years the emphasis in educational institutions which prepare students for training contracts or pupillages has been towards more practical skills such as drafting, advocacy and client care. Usually an Upper Second is required for the lowest echelon of tutoring, and a higher academic degree is required to enter the lectureship ladder proper.

Solicitors in private practice

Typical career progression:

- ○ Training contract, during which the trainee experiences work in several different legal departments. It is a Law Society requirement that practical experience should be gained in at least three different areas of the law. At the end of the contract often trainees are kept on, depending on the economic climate, but there is not usually any obligation on either side. At this point you may want to consider moving on, although probably the majority of newly qualified solicitors stay put.
- ○ First two years of post-qualification experience (PQE). This is a time to reassess your position. Are things going the way you want? Where do you want to go from here? Are you in the right place to get to where you want to be?
- ○ Five years' PQE. If you want to be a partner, are you doing all the right things? (see below)
- ○ Partnership! Even when you have attained this you should still ask yourself whether your firm continues to offer you everything you need. Are you performing there as well as you can?

This is the 'traditional' career path which pre-supposes that you will continue as a fee earner (a solicitor doing chargeable work for clients) after qualification. But alternative career paths in professional support, business development or pro bono all have their own considerations.

Alternative positions in private practice

In EJ Legal's recent research we found that 60 per cent of all partners interviewed and 56 per cent of assistants thought that the availability of an alternative career path would have some impact on any decision whether to stay with or leave their present firm. Eighty-six per cent of female partners and 65 per cent of female assistants felt that there should be more options. One third of the more senior assistants (six to nine years' PQE) compared to 50 per cent of those at three to five years', thought that this would help them to stay in the profession.

Professional support lawyers (PSL): In the past, this role mainly involved precedent bank maintenance and general quasi-librarian type skills. However, this growing and increasingly recognised discipline offers more and more responsibility and status. PSLs usually focus on one legal discipline, although they are occasionally multi-disciplinary. In some large firms their role can also be managerial, and there are now several City firms which have appointed PSLs as partners.

Business development: This is strictly a marketing function. Because what is required is an understanding of the industry and culture, and the needs and stresses of the fee earners and partners, often an ex-fee earner is the most suitable candidate for such a role. The work includes exploring new business lines, preparing pitches for new and existing clients and being on top of market intelligence.

Pro bono: Many commercial firms now recognise that pro bono work is an important way to give something back to the community in general through allowing their fee earners to staff Law Centres, and have begun to appoint fee earners to manage and co-ordinate the efforts of other, usually more junior, fee earners.

Knowing what's right for you

Although things are changing and the old adage 'you can do anything if you put your mind to it' is worth holding on to, private practice is still a relatively inflexible profession. It is never too early to try to work out exactly what you want, and what will make you happy – as once you're set on a path it becomes very much harder to try out different options. Although this section is nominally concerned with solicitors, much of it is equally relevant to barristers.

There are as many considerations as there are graduates, but you should consider the following:

- ○   Type of work, discipline or practice.
- ○   Location.
- ○   Money.
- ○   Work-life balance.
- ○   Status.
- ○   Environment.

How do you find out?

Of course, you can't see into the future, but you should do what you can to maximise the chances of finding the right situation. The best practical way of doing this is through work experience. Most large firms now operate formal 'summer placement' schemes, which you must apply for, and for which there is a formal selection process (often with interview). You may already have an idea what sort of law you want to work in – but do try it out, find out for sure that you like the look of it in practice (I wonder how many pupil barristers were inspired by *Kavanagh QC* on television only to be disappointed with the reality . . .).

If you are unsuccessful in obtaining a paid summer placement, and as usual more people apply than there are places, then try to obtain other relevant experience. Your local High Street firm may be willing to take you on as a general dogsbody (paid or unpaid) and having keyboard skills will increase your chances of obtaining this type of work as well as being useful during your training contract. And you can learn a great deal by using your own personal research skills.

Most firms have a website from which a great deal of information can be gleaned, but speaking to as many people as possible at all levels of the profession, including your local solicitors and your lecturers, will also be very productive. Private practice firms in the UK can be roughly categorised as follows:

'High Street': Although it is a huge generalisation, High Street firms, which is a term applied to firms which are situated anywhere but in the centres of major cities, are general practices usually involved with conveyancing, criminal, family/divorce, civil litigation (personal injury, etc.), and private client work (wills and probate). There is a huge variety in the size of these firms, in the quality of the work and training they offer, and in terms of the possible career progression, remuneration and quality of life available This is where most legal aid work is done.

'The City': This is a geographical description of the financial heart of London, which to some extent can narrow the type of work available. The type of work undertaken is centred on business, is mainly transactional and concerned with areas such as banking, corporate finance, commercial litigation, commercial work, perhaps involving intellectual property (IP) or information technology (IT) and special projects. With the increasing importance of international work, especially in the EU, this is where solicitors would obtain most advantage from any language skills that they have. Several highly regarded firms do have private client departments and most have large commercial property departments.

The hours tend to be the longest, the standards of admission highest, and the money best. At worst, you may be asked to 'sell your soul for your salary', at best it can be stimulating and remunerative work in a supportive and understanding environment. Moving out of the City is easier than moving in. American firms with London offices – mostly City or West End based – form a sub-set of large London firms. Their chargeable hours tend to be higher and the salaries they offer can be at least double in extreme cases.

Commercial firms: These are firms whose primary client base is business. The areas of work here are more likely to be transactional or litigation-based, and include corporate finance, banking, IP and IT, property and dispute resolution. The hours are perceived to be longer than in High Street firms but the money usually better. Many excellent commercial firms are based outside London, so if the smoke is not for you, don't ignore other cities. However, there is still a perception, although diminishing, that 'the best training is in London'. This can be a bit like comparing silk with potatoes; again the most important thing is to find a firm which provides good training in what you want to do.

Small firms and large firms: The size of a firm is an important consideration on its own as it has both culture and lifestyle implications. A small firm may offer a wide variety of disciplines or it may be 'niche', specialising in only one particular discipline or industry such as shipping. Accepting a training contract in such a firm can limit options and may well be unwise if you are not fairly sure that this is what you want to do on qualification. Another thing to ask is whether you would mind being one of a 100 plus trainees or whether you would prefer being one of two or three?

Transactional versus private client work: There is a general division between what is regarded as transactional work and what is lumped together as private client work, although many firms do offer both.

Transactional work: This type of work is focused on business deals: corporate, banking, IT, commercial litigation, etc. It offers remuneration and commercial insight, but can be repetitive or narrow depending on the firm and its location. This type of work is often accused of being harder on the hours and lifestyle fronts. The hours can also be unpredictable with peaks and troughs in activity – one month all nighters, and the next struggling for chargeable hours to record.

Private client/family work: For those people who like dealing with individuals this type of work can be very satisfying, because they will be dealing with clients who see the direct result of their work. It can also be traumatic or frustrating for lawyers who become too personally involved. The lifestyle will generally be better, although there are lots of overworked private client and family lawyers out there!

It is important to experience as many different legal specialisms as possible whether through placement, talking to people or by reading and surfing the Internet. If you want to be an IP lawyer, handling copyright disputes or dealing with patent law, there is little chance of finding the ideal job if your training contract work has been restricted to conveyancing and divorce. Even placement choices may enhance or limit available options for training contracts. Be aware – be informed.

Getting the right training contract

Think about it. There is fierce competition for jobs which means that at each stage you have to justify why someone should give you a chance. Having relevant experience to prove you know what you are talking about and that you are committed to achieving your goals will go a long way. It is almost certainly vital to have gained relevant experience during training in the discipline you wish to qualify into. Do *not* take a contract with a firm that does not provide you with at least a variety of options, unless you are positive that it is right for you. If you really don't have a clue what you want to do, general commercial firms with a varied client base are your best bet. It becomes increasingly difficult to move between disciplines the more senior you become. If you are sure of the specialism you would like to work in post qualification, find out what would be relevant experience and then try to obtain it (e.g. trusts work for share schemes, commercial contracts for IT). Choose your seats during training carefully.

It can also be difficult to move between the different ways of working as a lawyer. Although a generalisation, it is still hard to move from being a solicitor to practising as a barrister (until more senior) or from in-house only experience to private practice, unless you have acquired practical experience in a legal specialism that has scarcity value at that time, for example shipping or IT. However, it is generally easier to move from private practice to in-house, and from being a barrister to practising in a law firm, and academic institutions which specialise in the LPC or the BVC often welcome solicitors and barristers with practical experience.

Career progression in a legal firm

The first decision point in private practice is on qualification, deciding whether to remain with or leave the firm which trained you. Remember that the choice may not be yours. Do not take it too personally if you are 'rejected'; your firm may simply have no need of another newly qualified lawyer at that time, especially in your chosen area. After two years of trying out different discplines, you may find that only moving to another firm will enable you to obtain the career that you want. Make sure you get good advice about the legal marketplace at this point, and see as much of it as you can before making a decision, because once you have moved, it is wise to keep your head down in your new firm for a couple of years. It is still the case that a 'serial mover' as they are termed in the law, is frowned on – plan each move carefully and be able to justify, not excuse.

After two years ask yourself whether you are getting what you want from your job in terms of the type and quality of work, amount of responsibility and possible prospects. You might also consider whether the geographical location of your firm is making it difficult for you to have a decent life. Do you need to consider a new firm to address any of these issues? Or do you need to move house?

After five years or so – you will probably be considering partnership if you haven't already ruled it out. The reality is that not everyone can become a partner these days. How likely is it that you will be made up at your current firm? How many people are there in front of you? What noises are being made? What business case is there for another partner in your team? If you do want to be a partner be realistic about your position in your present firm, and plan ahead. If you're 'passed over' where you are, and wake up at 10 years' PQE, the first question any other firm will ask is 'why didn't you get made up by X & Co?'. Have you done what you need to do to get partnership?

Many people would have you believe that the business case is complex, but the bottom line is – do you make the firm money? It is never too early to bring in your own clients. Team work is essential and no one likes a show off, but you should make sure that the right people are aware of your victories.

Partnership

This can happen at any time after around five years' PQE, or even earlier if there are special reasons. But, even when you've made it, you can't rest on your laurels. Never forget that law is a business. Although some firms are more driven by the bottom line than others, in all of them your profitability is your security blanket. Your ability to add value to your fellow partners will ensure your success. Except in certain very niche areas such as some areas of tax where your expertise is vital for the firm's credibility, being a 'good lawyer' is just not enough anymore.

With the growth of the lateral recruitment market has come restrictive covenants on the 'ownership' of clients by individual partners as opposed to firms. Although track record in adding value is often good enough, most recruiting firms will expect partners on the move to have loyal clients who will want to move with them, unless they have an under resourced skill set. Careful consideration of covenants, adequate support for clients at their current or new firm, and the old 'ratio' of following (or track record of fee generation) to remuneration (generally one to three being the starting point) come into play. Are your clients growing? Will they be looking for more high powered advice in the future? You need to think ahead.

EJ Legal recently undertook a survey of partners and assistants at the top 100 firms. When we asked existing partners how they felt about being a partner, 57 per cent of women compared to 75 per cent of men were very happy, 43 per cent of women compared to 22 per cent of men were satisfied, and only 3 per cent of men were unhappy. Seventy-four per cent of male assistants but only 55 per cent of female assistants felt that their career plan included becoming a partner. Forty per cent of women rejected the idea completely compared to only 17 per cent of men. When they considered partnership assistants as a whole said that they were worried about stress, responsibility and hours in descending order of concern. An overwhelming 46 per cent were worried about stress, and only 33 per cent were attracted by the money!

With partnership (and even before) comes management – running a team and responsibility for some part of the business. It is rare at partnership level to be able to maintain a 100 per cent fee-earning role.

Lifestyle

When plotting your progress through the legal landscape lots of issues may be relevant, and an awareness of what is important to you is vital. Different disciplines can offer pluses and minuses, but there are other factors to be taken into consideration. Where do you want to live? Do you mind commuting for an hour each way every day? Is it important to you to be able to drive to work? How are your stress levels? Do you take things personally? Do you get a kick out of finishing a deal? Is work satisfying enough for you to be happy to have less free time? How does your family life fit into your work patterns? Deciding what balance you need is important – as there is no doubt that while employers in private practice are becoming more 'family friendly', some disciplines are inherently pressurised and others suffer from seasonal pressures to get things done. Property clients want things done before Christmas and private client lawyers are always busy when tax returns are due.

Some firms are more 'family friendly' than others. It can be illuminating to compare the ratio of female to male partners at the firm you're considering joining or considering staying with. When asked how family friendly they thought their firm was, 55 per cent of male partners compared to 14 per cent of female partners thought that their firms were very family friendly, but 35 per cent of female assistants thought they were not at all good. Only a small majority (53 per cent) of firms had formal family friendly measures in place, according to the human resources managers questioned. Of those with no measures in place, 65 per cent said that they were considering their introduction. This is fortunate given that over half (55 per cent) of human resource (HR) managers considered a family friendly environment very relevant to retention and a further 30 per cent said it was relevant.

Hours are a big issue – the research showed that 71 per cent of female partners compared to 33 per cent of men thought that their hours were excessive. When asked what factors would influence them to leave their firm, 30 per cent of women overall said working excessive hours was the most important factor, with lack of recognition following close behind at 25 per cent (20 per cent said quality of work). Forty per cent of men on the other hand cited quality of work, followed by low remuneration.

Moving around

The legal marketplace is now a fluid one. While it is still not acceptable to move too often, there are often times when it's the right thing to do. There are various ways to find a new position.

Internet: This is a great resource for research, but the more senior you become the less useful it is for recruitment. There are an increasing number of recruitment websites but remember that they are just another method of advertisement.

Headhunters: They usually operate at the high end of the market and they will contact you. Real headhunters will have only one client whom they are talking to you about. The advantage is that they will often have very detailed information about that client and the role, and let's face it – it's flattering. The downside of dealing only with them is that you will not know what else is out there for you. You need to ask yourself whether this is the best role or firm for you? However, maintaining a relationship with one or two headhunters over the years may be of benefit in developing your future career at a senior level.

Recruiters: Interview a few reputable recruiters to find one that you get on well with, who listens and understands what you're saying. Look for someone who knows the market and knows you as this can be invaluable. When considering a move don't use every agent under the sun, and don't be too prescriptive about the firms that you will talk to. Good recruiters should also be able to help you with specific issues – family friendly policies, work-life balance issues, career options, and insights into each firm and each team they represent.

Barristers

Education

The BVC differs considerably from the LPC course that solicitors undertake. The emphasis is on practicality, and tuition is carried out mainly in small groups to enable interaction and role play. Because barristers will spend at least part of their working lives in the court room, students are frequently videoed and their performance discussed with their peers. The skills on which the course focuses are opinion writing, advocacy, negotiation, drafting and interviewing clients, whether lay or professional; in addition, students are given a thorough grounding in civil and criminal court procedure.

It is essential that students have a good grasp of basic legal principles, and particularly of contract law, criminal law and the law of tort before they embark on the course, whether gained from a law degree or the CPE, because even more than in the LPC the emphasis on practicality precludes teaching 'black letter' law during the course.

Assessment methods also differ from the LPC. The rules of procedure and the rules of evidence are tested mainly through multiple choice, and advocacy and negotiation are assessed through observation. As barristers must be able to think on their feet and to give clear answers this method of testing has been designed so that students cannot 'pick' only part of the syllabus for examination and cannot easily fudge their answers. Decision-making skills are at a premium.

Whereas both courses are expensive BVC fees are slightly higher than those for the LPC. It is also much harder to obtain external financing for the BVC. In contrast to solicitor's firms, hardly any chambers offer financial support during study even if they have committed to giving pupillage after a student has completed academic training. Some scholarships are offered by the Inns of Court.

Career progression

Although a barrister's career path is perhaps not so certain as that of a solicitor, it can be considered as follows.

Mini-pupillage

This is not strictly speaking part of the training process, but in some ways it is an essential pre-cursor to consideration of a career as a barrister. A mini-pupillage lasts for two to five days during which a would-be barrister spends time in chambers gaining an insight into the work of that chambers. As the quality of this experience varies greatly (some chambers ask students to do photocopying while others give students files to read preparatory to shadowing a barrister in court) it is recommended that as many as possible should be undertaken. Having had 10 mini-pupillages prior to pupillage is not unheard of.

Mini-pupillages are free but unpaid, and may be applied for from the age of 16. It is wise to experience as many different types of chambers as possible, but if you are sure which type of work you want to do on qualification, try to obtain as many mini-pupillages as possible in those chambers which specialise in that type of work. Things to look out for are the general attitude and work ethos of the chambers, and whether you get on with the chambers' clerk.

Pupillage

Pupillage lasts for a year, or rather two sets of six months each. There are approximately two applications for every pupillage, but of course there will be relatively more applications for the most highly regarded chambers. Application is usually through an Internet clearing house (called OLPAS) plus interview. This screening process is fairly tough and each set of chambers sets its own criteria for acceptance. The Bar Council has recently insisted that chambers may not take on pupils without payment, so that even this minimum requirement of £10,000 per annum may mean that smaller chambers will not be interested in taking on pupils; some chambers are willing to pay considerably more than this, but the competition for these places is obviously stronger.

It should be noted that not all chambers use the OLPAS system and that application should be made to them direct. Other chambers will offer students pupillage on the basis of what they have seen during a mini-pupillage.

Pupils are taken on by pupilmasters, who are experienced barristers; the pupils are in effect apprentices who conduct research, prepare initial drafts, sit with their pupilmasters in court or at 'cons' (conferences for most barristers, or consultations if the pupilmaster is a Queen's Counsel (QC)). They also carry the books.

Tenancy

At the end of the year's pupillage, those pupils who are kept on become tenants. Tenancy entitles the newly qualified barrister to have her name on the door of chambers, and also to pay her share of chambers' expenses. In general there is no guarantee of work or of any income, although some chambers do now guarantee their junior tenants income from work for a period of up to three years post qualification.

Work is dispensed by the chambers' clerk, who is an administrator and not a qualified barrister. The clerk allocates the work, negotiates fees with the clients, subsequently bills the clients for the work done and manages the chambers' finances. By law barristers cannot sue for their fees, so that a sympathetic and effective clerk is essential to the financial existence of the young barrister. The clerk has traditionally taken a percentage of all fees earned by his barristers, although in many chambers he now receives a salary rather than a percentage of fees.

Even though the newly qualified barrister may earn little or nothing at the beginning of her practice she will still be liable for her share of chambers' expenses, comprising rent and all the other expenses of running a small business. The amount payable will vary depending on the way that the established tenants have decided that expenses will be divided. Some chambers ask for a fixed fee per month which bears hard on the newly qualified but others take a percentage of fees earned which is easier, and some operate on a combination of these two methods.

It might be sensible to clarify the expenses position when choosing chambers in the first place, but this may be a difficult question to raise at interview. Some informal research might be more advisable.

Provided that the more senior members of chambers have good work, there will usually be 'feeder' work in the form of research and drafting for the junior tenants; they may also be offered minor court hearings which are necessary, but may not be cost or time effective for the senior barrister. The junior tenants can start to build up their own practices and relationship with solicitors who will become the main source of their work. Remember though that most work is channeled through the clerk with whom it is vital to maintain a good relationship.

Things to bear in mind

For a woman one of the most important things to bear in mind is that being at the Bar means being self-employed. There is no maternity pay, and the maternity and flexible working legislation does not apply. The most that a female tenant can expect if she is pregnant is that her chambers will give her a 'rent holiday' of about three months when she has her baby; after that she will still be liable for chambers' expenses even if she is not earning. Flexible working is not really possible because much of the work is geared to court appearance, which cannot be scheduled to coincide with the days that the barrister wants to be in attendance.

Potential earnings will depend totally on the type of law that is practised. Earnings should rise much faster for commercial law barristers than
for family law (child protection, divorce, care orders), and although very
hard-worked, criminal barristers will earn quite a lot less. On the other
hand a barrister who has a reputation for handling big money divorce cases
will reach a high income much sooner, as will barristers who practise in
the specialised areas of tax and shipping.

Bear in mind that although most practising barristers are based in
London, they will have to travel often quite long distances around the country to attend court, they will have to pay travelling and other expenses,
which fortunately are tax-deductible, out of their fees and a large amount
of time is required for preparation of a case and de-briefing afterwards.

At the Bar the law of supply and demand is very much in operation. It
requires stamina and a quick mind as well as an ability to get on with
clients and to perform in court.

Squatting

If the newly qualified barrister is not able to obtain a tenancy either in the
chambers where she was a pupil or in another set, she may be permitted
to 'squat' in chambers. This has more or less the same connotations as
squatting in unoccupied housing. The barrister is not liable for a share of
the chambers' expenses, but her name is not on the chambers' door, she
is not included in any of the marketing literature and the clerk has no
obligation to send any work her way. She will literally get the leftovers
that nobody else wants or can do at that time, on which she will be liable
to pay the clerk the usual percentage.

Taking silk

Becoming a QC or taking silk is not an option open to all barristers.
Although the manner by which partners in solicitors' firms are chosen
can be equally shrouded in mystery, there is a perception that because
the Department of Constitutional Affairs (formerly the Lord Chancellor's
Department) appoints silks, the selection process should be more transparent. Barristers apply for silk, but are not given reasons for refusal. Very
few people obtain it on the first application, but if someone has been
refused three times it is generally accepted that there is little point in
applying further.

There are very few silks. Barely 10 per cent of qualified practising barristers take silk, and the proportion of women is naturally much smaller,
although recently there has been an increase in their numbers. Becoming a
silk is an entrée to greater recognition, higher fees, possibly more interesting cases and the main route to the judiciary. The whole system of appointing silks is under discussion at the time of writing and it is possible that
those appointed in April 2003 will have been the last to become QC.

The judiciary

There are various levels in the judiciary, but generally speaking the higher ranks are open only to QCs. QCs usually take a substantial reduction in remuneration when they become judges but it is regarded by many as not only a less strenuous occupation but also a way of building up a government pension before retirement. Now that solicitors have more rights of audience in the courts they also have more access to junior judicial posts thus providing more competition for barristers.

In-house counsel

Very few in-house counsel are actually trained 'in-house'. Usually they are already qualified barristers or solicitors moving out of private practice. What they have in common is that they are employees of a non-legal organisation, usually a company. The 'clients' of in-house counsel are their fellow employees usually at a senior level. Their function is to take instructions from their internal clients and to manage the provision of legal services to those clients, whether by providing the services themselves or by instructing and managing external barristers and solicitors. They may also act as company secretaries.

The nature of the work that they do will vary from company to company, but as a generalisation most in-house counsel will have to consider, at least in the first instance, matters of employment law and property law and have a sound understanding of contract law. The significance of additional specialisms will depend on the nature of the business. Property developers may require specialist property expertise, and IT companies will require strong commercial skills in the negotiation of licences. Newspapers and television and radio companies have a requirement for libel lawyers to vet copy before it is published or transmitted. In-house counsel pop up everywhere.

In-house legal departments are not usually large, so that the opportunities for promotion in a strictly legal capacity are restricted. Promotion to general management in the company and ultimately to the board is possible but again this depends on the business of the company, and the nature of the decisions that the directors in that organisation are required to take.

In-house counsel may appear less well-paid than their counterparts in solicitors' firms, but they are likely to have more regular and predictable working hours than most solicitors and barristers. In addition, they will as employees have access to benefits generally available to the other employees of their organisations, but which are not usually offered to solicitors in private practice and certainly not to barristers in private practice, such as share options and company cars. International travel may well be a feature of this type of work, but again this will be dependent on the company's business.

The Government Legal Service

About 1,700 lawyers, both barristers and solicitors, work for the Government Legal Service (GLS) in about 40 government organisations. They work in teams ranging from a single lawyer to more than 200 in some of the larger departments such as the Treasury Solicitor's Department. The main thing to remember is that the employer is the Government so that there will always be some sort of political aspect to the work, whether it is directly drafting legislation or implementing government policy in departments such as the Inland Revenue or the DTI. The work itself is varied and ranges from interpreting existing UK and EU legislation for ministers and possibly then assisting in drafting new or amended legislation to being directly involved in civil litigation.

Only a few departments, such as the Land Registry, the Charity Commission and Customs and Excise have offices where GLS lawyers work outside London, and by far the majority of GLS lawyers work in London. Although some lawyers would prefer to remain within one government department, there are opportunities to move around different government departments.

Lawyers join the GLS because of the intellectual challenge and the ability to acquire expertise in a particular practical area such as VAT, agriculture or EU issues. Salaries are often regarded as being inferior to those available in private practice, but there are certainly other compensations such as flexible working, index-linked pensions, a high emphasis on training and an element of job security higher than in many other law-related occupations. However, unless you are going to make partner or build up a considerable practice at the Bar the potential salaries on offer for some GLS positions are not completely out of line with private practice.

It should be noted that Parliamentary Counsel, lawyers in the Foreign and Commonwealth Office and the Crown Prosecution Service (CPS) are not part of the GLS (although of course they are employed by the Crown). But the Serious Fraud Office lawyers are. Confusing!

Joining the GLS

There are several routes into the GLS. The least common is to enter as a trainee solicitor, and to actually qualify into the service. Usually qualified solicitors or barristers enter much later. The GLS in common with many other government departments employs people on the basis of 'competitions'.

Vacation placement scheme

In common with solicitors' firms and barristers' chambers, the GLS offers a number of vacation placements to university students who have completed at least part of their degree course or who have already graduated.

These last for two to three weeks and are paid at the rate of £150 per week. Several departments each year offer placements and decide on the basis of a written application whether or not to award a placement.

Legal trainee competition

The GLS offers about 30 training contracts and pupillages annually all of which are based in London, although not all departments offer training places every year. The GLS does pay sponsorship for LPC and BVC courses but does not pay for the CPE course unless a student is considered to have outstanding potential. Legal trainees and pupil barristers are paid salaries in the region of £17,000–£21,000 during training. Legal trainees spend their whole training contract with the GLS although possibly in more than one department to satisfy Law Society requirements. Pupil barristers on the other hand spend part of their time in chambers and part in the government department to which they are assigned.

Qualified solicitors or barristers

The majority of GLS lawyers are already qualified when they come to work for the service. Individual departments do their own recruiting although posts are advertised on the GLS recruitment website. All departments use the same method of selection by a written test and a short interview. Qualified lawyers come in at all levels of qualification, even from a very senior level of private practice, because what they are making is a life-style choice, from long hours and high earnings to possibly lower remuneration but more manageable working conditions.

Promotion

GLS lawyers may be promoted within their departments, but there are many posts which are advertised across the whole of the service so that interested lawyers with the right mix of skills and experience may apply for lateral or upward moves to other departments. Obtaining wide experience of several departments, especially in the Attorney-General's Department or the Treasury Solicitor's Department is usually seen as being a sensible way to move to a very senior post.

There is also some opportunity to move outside the strictly legal field into more general civil service management.

Academic teaching and research

There are two routes into academic life. Entry can be either straight from a first degree or after qualification and experience as a solicitor or barrister. In general a First or an Upper Second Class degree in law or law-combined subjects is required to commence work as a legal academic. A doctorate is also becoming a more common requirement for formal appointment as a lecturer in universities although not for institutions such as the College of Law which provide tuition for CPE, LPC or BVC courses, and for which practical experience as a solicitor or barrister is a more likely qualification.

There are two separate but related aspects to academic life – research and teaching – and the balance between them will depend on the particular academic institution involved.

Research

Research continues throughout and is an essential part of the life of any university lecturer. It is essentially private study where you establish an area of knowledge which you want to investigate more thoroughly in order to publish your findings in academic journals or books. Conducting research efficiently requires clarity of thinking and controlled imagination, and an ability to use modern computerised research tools in an efficient way. It is easy to spend time on unfocused discussion and reading, so some degree of self-discipline is necessary. Pure research can also be a lonely undertaking at times, particularly if the topic chosen is not of general interest.

Postgraduate university research requires approval by a university for the research proposal and some sort of funding for the research. The first needless to say is usually easier to obtain than the second. Universities charge fees for postgraduate degrees such as a one-year or two-year Masters or a three-year course of postgraduate study leading to a doctorate, so that the cost of obtaining a higher degree may equate to the cost of professional legal training. Many universities have only limited research funds available for junior staff. Although grant-giving bodies such as the ESRC, the British Academy and certain educational charities can provide funds these are also limited, and it may prove necessary to borrow the full cost of the course and associated living expenses.

Some universities offer Master's degrees on a fully taught basis, while others assess on some combination of tuition and personal supervised research. Doctorates are awarded after at least three years of supervised but independent study on the basis of a substantial dissertation plus a viva voce, where students are examined on their dissertation by a panel of senior academics. It can prove very difficult to complete a doctorate in the theoretical three years allotted to it, especially if you undertake tutoring as well to supplement your income.

As a Ph.D student you may be able to take tutorial classes for undergraduate or even postgraduate students; these usually take the form of leading structured discussions on set questions arising out of lectures given by departmental lecturers. Because these sessions are paid for, there is a great temptation to undertake too much of this type of work just to ease the financial burden. This can actually be counter-productive in the long run, as the amount of time required to prepare tutorial sessions combined with the time taken by the sessions themselves will reduce the time available for personal research and thus prolong the time it takes to obtain a doctorate and a permanent teaching post.

The difficulty is compounded by the fact that the subjects you are supervising will probably bear no relation to the subject area you are studying for your Ph.D. You may be considering a narrow area of property law for your dissertation but may be required to supervise a range of subjects as diverse as civil procedure, human rights law, trusts and equity and employment law.

If anything the pressure to continue research is even more keen after you have obtained your doctorate, because you are paid to produce research results as well as to teach. However as you become more senior the opportunities to discuss your findings with other academics will expand through attendance and speaking at conferences and being able to involve more junior colleagues in aspects of your research.

Teaching

Teaching is a very different sort of activity from research. Lecturing to large groups, running seminars for smaller groups and conducting tutorials for small groups all come under the heading of university teaching and different skills are required for each one. This is not the same as school teaching where teachers spend at least one year in formal study and practical experience designed to help them in the classroom. Although more guidance is available through structured presentation courses and packages than previously, much will be learned on the job.

The whole process involves mastering the material to be delivered or discussed and anticipating students' questions, plus considering, trying out and often discarding because unsuccessful, different methods of delivery, maintaining interest or provoking discussion. It is important to be able to be objective about your own personal performance in the teaching situation. Teaching is not just a performance art, and at university level requires extensive preparation, writing of lecture notes for publication and assessment of students' work during term-time by means of essays, tests and formal examinations.

Lecturers usually teach at least two 'main' subjects, which must fit in with the university's teaching requirements. In addition they are expected to publish research on topics of interest to them and their university, and as with Ph.D students this may be on an area completely different from those which they are required to teach.

Promotion

After you obtain your doctorate and if you want to remain in academic life you will apply for a lectureship. These are usually graded in some way. Universities traditionally have classed their lecturers as Assistant Lecturer, Lecturer or Senior Lecturer, although many now use a numerical classification instead. You will normally only be appointed to even the most junior grade once you have already obtained a doctorate or you are in the final stages of Ph.D assessment. Some universities may offer an assistant lectureship to someone who already has a good Master's degree and has registered an intention to complete a Ph.D.

There is also a third component in an academic's life, that of administration. This 'catch-all' phrase covers arranging courses and conferences and also work placements in those universities which offer sandwich degree courses as well as interviewing and advising students on subject choice and future careers. A lecturer's life can be very diverse and certainly very different from the student life it seems to develop from. Some universities have a mentoring approach to their new young teachers and this is something that you might look out for when looking for your first lectureship, because otherwise it can be all too easy to be swamped by administration and a badly-organised teaching load which you have taken on in an effort to oblige.

It is wise to remember that universities exist for two purposes, to teach and to research. Traditionally some universities have been big on research and low on teaching. But now in order to procure government funding they must usually reach certain minimum standards in both and are graded on how they perform in each area. However each university law department is different in its allocation of emphasis, and in some universities lecturers will have written into their contracts precisely how many articles they are meant to write and how many books they are meant to produce over a defined period of time.

Promotion will come as the result of publication of research results and opinions, good examination results from the students and also coping well with administrative responsibilities, but the main emphasis is on publication. It is usual to start with writing case notes for legal journals, and then to move on to more substantive articles. Not all legal journals pay their contributors as they know that publishing is essential to an academic's promotion prospects. It is wise to contact the editors of the journals to ascertain their requirements before submitting a carefully crafted article, which is either not suitable for them or which they have already commissioned from someone else. What most academics are aiming for is the publication of a book. This is paid for by the publishers and can be very lucrative if it turns out to be the standard student text on a topic. However the main purpose of book publication is to enhance academic credibility and thus promotion prospects.

It is usual to remain as an assistant lecturer for three to five years, but progress can be accelerated by taking on more responsibility, by designing and running new courses, by increasing the profile of the department externally or, crucially, by obtaining sponsorship for a project or a course. The immediate rewards of success at this level can seem almost intangible, sometimes merely the removal of one or two classes, but the freed up time can be used for more research whose publication will facilitate promotion to senior lecturer and eventually, and perhaps, a professorship.

Senior lectureships become available traditionally after eight to ten years as a lecturer, although some universities, particularly those which offer CPE, LPC and BVC courses are believed to offer senior lectureships immediately to qualified solicitors and barristers with a few years of practical PQE.

There is one interesting difference between academic life and being a barrister or solicitor when it comes to promotion and that is the requirement for mobility. Academics do tend to move around from one part of the country to another and even from country to country in order to obtain promotion. University law departments can be quite small compared with many solicitors' firms thus making it less likely that there will be a precise match between those ready for promotion and the promotion prospects available. And if you equate a professorship with being appointed as a QC or becoming a head of a decent-sized department in a solicitor's firm you will get some idea of the possibilities of promotion to that level.

The academic life

Academic life can seem almost schizophrenic. During term-time it is intense with student contact, discussion and assessment and during the long vacations university campuses can be silent places. This is when academic staff are meant to prepare teaching materials, write articles and conduct research. For those who like variety, and within the broad structure of university terms, a certain flexibility of approach, this can be a very attractive life.

You do need to have the ability to compartmentalise your time so that you treat all parts of your job, research, teaching and administration with equal respect. You really must also love your subject and the process of thinking, analysing and formalising your own point of view, regarding it as a great privilege to be paid to pursue it.

The academic life is in many ways a very suitable way for a mother to use her legal skills. It is not necessary to be 'on the job' all the time. Work can be done at home, late at night, or early in the morning provided that the basic requirements of being present at lectures, departmental meetings, etc. are met. There is also clearly less difficulty with school holidays, and many of the practical CPE, LPC and BVC courses are taught by erstwhile solicitors or barristers working part-time.

As far as promotion is concerned women sometimes find themselves doing proportionately more teaching than men, which of course leaves them less time for the public profile work of publication. Remember that publication is necessary for promotion.

Finally

Most importantly, and this is not necessarily something that you will be considering when you set out on a legal career, remember that a legal training gives you a great many transferable skills. To be a successful lawyer you will need to acquire skills in analysis, writing, persuasion, advocacy, training and management of others and above all self-discipline. These are all qualities that other employers will value.

Taking Control of Your Work-Life Balance

Jayne Buxton

This chapter is adapted with permission from a chapter in *Ending the Mother War: Starting the Workplace Revolution* by Jayne Buxton (Macmillan, 1998) which looks at the experiences of many people (primarily women) working across a wide variety of organisations and their efforts to juggle and then balance their family and working lives.

Think about it

Many of us work for organisations which, though cognizant of the difficulties that many working parents face, have yet to develop the will to change the work culture and practices that contribute to those difficulties. An increasing number of law firms offer flexible working packages or say that they will listen sympathetically to requests from their employees to work flexibly. But there does not appear to be an overwhelming rush to take advantage of this – a recent survey of large firms found that while the firms offered flexible working only 25 per cent of women and 10 per cent of men had taken advantage of the packages. We are not all in positions of leadership which would allow us the latitude to begin to affect the working culture and practices of such organisations. Even those of us who are managers of small teams or even substantial departments, may feel ourselves as much the prisoners of the corporate culture as the people we manage.

But perhaps we should be asking whether we really are powerless to instigate change? Or have some of us sufficient authority and influence to be able to affect, if not the wider corporate culture, then our own working lives and the working lives of those around us? The answer is, undoubtedly, yes. Many of us are acknowledged as people whose experience and talent are of value to the organisations we work for. We already manage projects, small teams or large departments. We could in fact have some capacity to start the workplace revolution, even if it is only one that brings change to our own working life.

Most organisations are likely to begin their work-life experiments with individuals or small groups rather than with abstract strategies, because individuals will be unable to wait patiently for a systemic approach to take root and the impetus will initially come from them. They need some form of work-life balance immediately, however imperfect. The only way to do this is to capture some of the principles of systemic organisational change within a strategy for accommodating individual needs. What this means in practice is that, rather than negotiating part-time working hours that leave job responsibilities and performance expectations intact, arrangements need to be put in place that involve some fundamental restructuring of that individual's personal priorities and/or work responsibilities. It also means that, in crafting individual solutions, it is important to generate managerial support for and commitment to not just the merits and mechanics of a particular arrangement, but to the principle of work-life balance.

Developing a personal change strategy

Developing a personal change strategy which acknowledges the importance of organisational change and commitment to work-life balance means focusing on changing your own working life while keeping one eye on the big picture. There are five principles to keep firmly in mind as you embark on your pursuit of a more balanced life.

Choose your time

Timing, while not being everything, is important. Women who have taken steps to restructure their working lives have often waited until they have achieved significant professional success and standing before doing so. In part, such advice acknowledges the fact that intense and uninterrupted experience and learning in the early years may be necessary for individuals to amass the knowledge, skill and confidence to succeed at managerial levels. It also reflects an appreciation of the realities of corporate politics, which are such that requests made by seasoned, highly valued employees will be looked upon with a good deal more favour than those coming from junior and, to some extent, more easily dispensable, employees. This is borne out by the survey of law firms which found that flexible working was most likely to be offered on a discretionary or performance-related basis rather than length of service.

But timing cannot protect you entirely from negative consequences. There is simply no way of attempting to restructure your working life without accepting some risk to yourself and to your career in the process. Restructuring your working life means taking a risk. But in choosing to jeopardise nothing in your work environment, you are likely to jeopardise things far more precious in your personal life – family, relationships and that all-important source of strength – the opportunity to be comfortable in your own skin.

Take personal stock

Transforming your working life is impossible without the transformation of yourself and your values. A failure to grasp the depth of the change required is likely to lead to a half-hearted and ultimately unsuccessful attempt at restructuring your work life. Many women cling to their original life agendas – agendas formed during years of education within traditional institutions and male-dominated work environments, and, for some, years of unbridled commitment to the feminist vision of equality. Creating a balanced life, one in which work and personal life exist comfortably alongside one another, is impossible without this stock-taking process. Our own definitions of personal identity, success, power and career need to shift as much as the organisation's definitions of them.

If you are serious about creating a better balance between your work and your personal life you must establish a vision that includes a new definition of professional competence and how it is built and demonstrated, as well as a different perspective on your career, what it looks like, how it is to be built, and over what period. You need to redefine the desired pace of your life, as well as its goals. Unless you develop a clear sense that there is such a thing as enough – enough money, status, professional recognition – as well as a sense of what your own personal level of 'enough' is, you will be forever trapped by the doctrine of 'more, better, bigger, faster, richer'.

Many people are reluctant to change their working lives for fear of relinquishing power – the power to make decisions, economic power, even the power to command dinner reservations that comes from a prestigious business title. Those of us who wish to achieve balance will have to trade off some career success and power as we have traditionally defined them. We will need to accept that our careers will look different from those we once might have imagined – slower paced and with a flatter trajectory, more disjointed, punctuated with unforeseen breaks, twists, turns and foregone opportunities. Re-designating your life as a marathon rather than a sprint is not tantamount to an endorsement of what the Americans have termed the 'mommy track', a slower career path running parallel to the mainstream track, effectively preventing women from ever reaching positions of seniority. When jobs are genuinely restructured to make part-time working possible, performance can be assessed relative to new objectives and strong performance records can be maintained leading ultimately to a rejoining of the traditional career track.

Job-sharing, for example, can enable you to keep a foot on the career ladder and keep choices open for the future. But it demands new values, as is illustrated by the experience of two job sharers in the position of chief executive at Barking and Havering Health Authority. They point out that there have been significant changes to their ambitions and the desire for power that once drove them. 'You've got to share power and you can't worry about accreditation or individual recognition. We are task-oriented and motivated by the satisfaction of a job well done.' A job-sharing appeals lawyer in the Lord Chancellor's Office says that she is now motivated by her ability to keep in touch with the 'real world', having an income to call her own and the self-esteem that comes from making an impact in a case.

Understand what you need

Not all efforts to change working life require the same degree of personal transformation to inspire and sustain them. For some, the smallest amount of change could make a difference to their lives. It is important to be honest with yourself about what it is you really need. Only you know what is not working in your life, and only you can decide what is necessary to fix it. Understanding and accepting your needs – whether they be for change at the margins, fundamental job restructuring, a new work environment or total independence – is the first crucial step to meeting them.

Adopt a systemic approach to getting what you need

Systems-thinking recognises that there are interdependencies within any system and that any action taken in one part of the system will have an effect somewhere else. A systems-thinker will acknowledge the wider system of which she is part and the influence that system will exert upon her ability to work differently, and will steel herself against the inevitable organisational pressure to revert to old habits; she will seek a fundamental change, rather than the quick fix represented by a boss's proposal that she solve her 'time problem' by working from home once a week; most important of all, she will attempt to change, not just the structure of her working life, but the behaviours and attitudes – particularly her own – that underlie the structure. Thus, it is vital to do your homework before approaching your management team about making a change. If taking personal stock gives you the strength and conviction to embark upon and sustain an effort to change your work life, doing the necessary homework will enable you to take the first practical steps towards it.

Doing your homework is all about making a strong case for change. That case needs to respond to these three key questions. What sort of flexibility do you need? How can that be achieved? How will it impact your immediate manager and the firm as a whole? Answering the first question is not as simple as it seems. Though you may be certain that your existing working arrangements are making you miserable, you may have difficulty envisioning exactly what sort of flexible arrangement will make you happier. Is it fewer hours, different hours, less work, different work or less travel that you want? Or is it all of these things? However difficult it is to be precise about the sort of flexibility you are asking for, you must form some view of it. Simply saying to your manager that you need something different, and placing upon him or her the onus of figuring out what sort of arrangement will work, and how, is a sure-fire way of maximising resistance to your suggestion.

Parents at Work's 'Employee Guide to Flexible Working' (**www. parentsatwork.org.uk**) lists various options for getting your life and your work in balance – flexible hours (flexitime), part-time working, job-sharing, working from home, term-time working, annual hours (that is, so many hours a year) and employment breaks. As you consider which of these options might best suit your needs, you should simultaneously think about the way in which each option could be implemented. If you decide, for instance, that you need to work a three-day week, you must think about how your existing job could be restructured to fit in with this schedule.

When you analyse your present job, you may find that it could be divided into a series of projects, some of which could be carried out by you and some by another part-timer. Or, you may find that by employing a talented deputy with your foregone salary you could retain oversight of most of your existing responsibilities while hiving off some day-to-day responsibility to the deputy. Some jobs require nothing as complicated as 'projectising' or deputising to make them doable on a part-time basis. They can be made to fit a reduced-hours' schedule simply by halving the targets normally set for full-time employees. Conversely, some jobs cannot be made to fit within a reduced-hours' schedule. Some require an all-or-nothing commitment for a definable period. For jobs like these you may need to propose a different sort of flexible arrangement, one based upon working every other project or case, rather than being obliged to work them back to back. This way, a part-time schedule would be achieved in the form of a month off for every two or three months on. For example, a barrister specialising in clinical negligence could work part-time attending court in connection with one or two cases per year and otherwise advise her clients while working from home.

If you have trouble envisioning how your job could be restructured to fit in with a reduced weekly-hours' or yearly-hours' schedule, look for examples of how similar jobs have been restructured in other firms, or even other industries. Tapping into the available evidence that flexibility works is an essential part of your homework. Providing examples from other firms within or outside your industry builds your confidence and credibility, and will help to dispel your manager's scepticism; after all why should she want change? However and wherever you find the relevant parallels – whether through your own networks or by contacting organisations like Opportunity 2000, Parents at Work, or New Ways to Work – the key is to go to your manager armed with as much information as possible.

The case for change that you present should not be just about you and your job. It should also take into account the organisation and its needs. In addition, it should address the needs of your immediate manager, and how these might be affected by a restructuring of your job. You need to construct a business case for change that highlights on several levels the potential benefits of your flexible working.

Benefits to the organisation might include: lower recruitment costs, higher staff-retention levels, lower costs of absenteeism and stress, higher morale and productivity, and greater individual and organisational creativity. You need to draw on data specific to your firm to describe these benefits in a way that is convincing and relevant. And most importantly you need to identify a hook for your own request for a new working arrangement. Find a problem that it will help to solve, or a way in which it will enhance business performance. And depending on who your manager is and how she feels about flexibility, you may need to spell out what she specifically has to gain from it – what her own personal hook is. It may be that your manager has been having trouble filling particular vacancies, and that the possibility of flexible working would help attract more and different applicants. Or perhaps there has been a problem with training and preparing new talent to fill more senior management posts, in which case the creation of deputy positions to support part-time roles like the one you are proposing would represent a way of managing the promotion process. The extent to which you can create a hook based on your manager's particular problem or needs will greatly influence the likelihood of your crafting a work arrangement that suits you.

But remember that despite all the benefits that flexibility may represent for you and the organisation, it will also create some difficulties. Organisations are systems and, as already noted, a change in one part of a system usually has repercussions elsewhere within it. You cannot foresee and solve all the complications that might be created by a change in the way you work, but do consider the possible repercussions in your immediate working environment, and propose some initial ideas on how these might be dealt with. If a change in the way you work will necessitate changes in the way those around you work, do some research into what might be their likely response. Identifying and addressing potential complications in advance can only strengthen your case. If you fail to anticipate them, or sweep them under the rug, they will end up sabotaging your efforts to create a sustainable new working life.

Build support

If you take all the old corporate baggage with you to your new work situation – the work ethic which equates long hours with commitment, the assumption that clients need you to be available 24 hours a day, the association of success with an ever-increasing salary – it is unlikely that you will gain much flexibility or freedom from your new arrangement. But the perceptions and responses of other people may be as much of a threat to your ability to work flexibly as your own inability to shed conventional assumptions and behaviours. Support for your case for working differently is something that you must build, from the outset and continuously.

The quality of the thinking you put into your proposal for a different working option, and into the business case in particular, will go a long way towards building that support. But you need a relatively sympathetic and supportive ear to put that case to. If that ear is not your immediate boss, it may belong to the manager of another division, or the firm's human resources manager. You need, somewhere in the organisation, a mentor – someone who will listen to you, support you, and assist you in persuading the organisation to give you what you need. If you cannot find someone willing to fulfil this role, then the chances are that you face greater problems than that of having to propose a new way of working.

For some, putting a proposal to a mentor may be a simple matter. For others whose mentor may be organisationally remote or less well versed in the rationale for flexible working, the proposal may need to be leaked gradually and subtly before it can be made formally. A number of factors will aid you in making your case. First, being able to demonstrate that a certain percentage of firms in your sector have official flexible policies may mean that your job is easier. As importantly, the Employment Act introduced in April 2003 requires that firms consider all requests for flexible work made by parents of children under six and parents of disabled children under 18, and sets out a required process for doing so. This means that requests for flexible working cannot be easily dismissed, and must be given due consideration. However, you may still run into conservative attitudes and judgments about your commitment to work within your department or management team that will make it difficult to take up any policy on offer or to negotiate the specific terms of your arrangement.

Only you can judge how gradual should be the process of convincing someone to support your case. One lawyer claims that she spent several years building up the support of a couple of key partners within her firm for her part-time working proposal. She did it during informal conversations, by exposing them to new information that would serve as a rationale for change, and finally through a formal proposal for a 'trial run'. The trial run was successful, and she continues to work a nine-to-four day. Not all of us could afford to wait so long for a change in the way we work, but we can learn from her experience the importance of a carefully planned and paced persuasion strategy, which tests the waters and prepares the ground with one or two key individuals before placing the formal case on the table.

Seeking a mentor to champion your cause, and working with that mentor to persuade the organisation to accept your proposed working arrangement, is only the first step in building support. As important, in the long run, will be the extent to which you build support in the organisation at large, not just for your particular case, but for the principle of flexible working and work-life balance. Here is the point at which individual action meets systemic organisation change: you can leverage your individual arrangement to further the cause of work-life balance in general by, first, continuing to do the job well and, second, by being seen to be both an example of flexibility and a spokesperson for it.

I always have mixed feelings when a manager tells me that an employee is so good that people really aren't aware that she works part-time. Good for her, I think, but too bad for everyone else. For unless the link between strong performance and flexible working becomes more obvious to people, flexibility will forever be viewed with scepticism by large parts of the corporate world. Worse, the barriers to work-life balance will remain entrenched within the corporate culture. The assumption, particularly, that people should give priority to their work life over anything else, will remain intact.

If the working world is really going to change, then the individuals who are beginning to change it need to be honest. This doesn't mean that at every opportunity they need to shout from the rooftops about their three-day week. But it does mean that they should not attempt to hide it. The more comfortable a person becomes being perceived as a part-timer who also has talent, adds value and is committed to her career, the more readily others will associate flexible working with those qualities.

Getting out and moving on

If you work for an organisation that is completely antagonistic to the balanced-life philosophy and refuses to be persuaded by your business case, you have two choices. Take your case to court or leave.

The chances are that even if you do fight your case in court and win, you will end up leaving the firm because the legal battle will have injected such a level of discomfort into your relationship with the firm that it will be impossible to stay. Even if you work for a relatively flexible firm, you may find that the degree of flexibility you want is too great for it to accommodate. Getting out may be the best or only option open to you.

With another firm

If going it alone is unappealing or impossible, you need to direct your job search towards firms with a reputation for being more family-friendly. Despite the availability of various directories, such as the membership lists of Opportunity 2000, Parents at Work, and Scarlet MacGwire's book *Best Companies for Women*, this is no straightforward matter. These directories, in addition to the informal lists you may acquire through your personal networks, can only be a starting point for your job search. And once you have identified family-friendly firms that you could and would like to work for, you need to set about investigating just how work-life friendly they are in practice.

The only way to establish how well a given firm might accommodate your needs is to ask questions. Prospective employees should begin asking questions at the first interview stage; if you are serious about wanting some form of flexible or part-time arrangement, you should make this clear at the outset, and convey confidence in your ability to contribute on those terms. Initially, however, you can ask relatively safe questions, such as how women have progressed within the firm, what the general benefits are, how the review process works and the extent to which the firm is involved in the community. Questions like these can give you a sense of the firm's attitude to its employees, and the extent to which it feels responsibility to its stakeholders.

If you and the firm decide to proceed with further interviews, you can then ask some tougher questions. Ask to see the employee handbook, request details about flexible policies and the number of people who make use of them, and ask whether you can talk to a few employees about what it is like to work for them (of course, you may have already done this through your own personal networks). When putting this kind of question about the opportunities for flexible working, continue all the while to express interest in other aspects of the firm's strategy and operations; your aim is to come across as someone who will be interested in the intrinsic values of the job and in contributing to the success of the firm, but who is also committed to a balanced life. It can feel uncomfortable and risky to ask questions such as these in the early stages of an interview process, and indeed it often is. But if you are serious about changing your working life you need to steel yourself to take the risk. Otherwise, you may find yourself landing the job but not the life you want.

Your own firm

Setting up your own firm is one option that may be available to you if you have the funding to get it off the ground, some loyal clients and an entrepreneurial spirit. It is almost certain to demand more of your time and energy, particularly during the early stages, but can provide you with a greater sense of freedom and control. So you may end up working more hours and thinking about the business almost constantly, but you will have more control over when and where you do those hours. If you want to spend a morning at home with a young child, then work late into the evening on a client or product proposal, that will be your choice. Before you embark on this it is important to decide whether you are not satisfied in your present position because you have a deep-seated need for independence or whether you have an immediate need for very flexible working.

Portfolio careers

Increasing numbers of people opt not for a flexible arrangement within an enlightened firm, but for total independence. They start their own businesses, or become what Charles Handy calls 'portfolio careerists', people who exchange full-time employment for independence, amassing a collection of different bits and pieces of work for different clients.

Going portfolio is one way of starting your own business when access to funding is limited. Portfolio workers build their careers around a strategy for finding the work that needs doing in order to provide what a customer wants or to enhance a client's ability to provide what a customer wants. Your market can, and often does, include some part of the organisation you already work for. It may not be necessary to break all ties with your employer in order to create a new working life for yourself. Understand what you have to offer, look for a market need for it within your firm, and write a proposal for how you could go about meeting that need.

One lawyer says the concept of employees marketing their own particular sets of attributes and abilities within a firm is an accurate reflection of how many firms operate, although they may be unaware of it. Law firms in reality are made up of individuals who apply their talents and experience to solving problems. They are, essentially, free agents. Yet so many of the top firms persist in hanging on to the idea that they 'own' their employees, and that unless these employees are working flat out, all the time, for them, there is something wrong. If we could convince senior people to accept the notion that they are buying services from individuals, some of whom may do only three assignments a year for them, others of whom will work back-to-back assignments as per the traditional model, there would be a lot more scope within the profession for working flexibly.

Remember though that a portfolio career can have its drawbacks. Income can be insecure and the various parts of your portfolio may sit uneasily alongside one another, creating periods of stress and chaos. As with the owner of a small business, the link between income and time spent is so direct for a portfolio careerist that some feel compelled to work most of the time. But for others, the portfolio career affords them a welcome, and even necessary, opportunity to control their working lives.

Whatever your personal circumstances and factors requiring balance in your life, there are many more options open to you today than a decade or even five years ago. Achieving balance will not likely be easy or without some sacrifice, and may mean that you have to change roles or jobs, but it is entirely possible. The first all-important step is to define what 'having it all' means to you, and then devise a strategy for getting what you want.

Part Two
Interviews

Elizabeth Cruickshank

This section contains interviews with many successful women lawyers. Some of them are household names and some are known to only that limited circle of people who have had the good fortune to be taught or advised by them.

What they have in common is a considerable amount of determination and reading their stories, much of it in their own words, can give a good idea of the skills and attributes that are required both to become a good lawyer and to make a success of life generally. Some have had to overcome considerable disappointment, some have made a new life in England after growing up in another country. Most have thought carefully as to how they would advise today's young women entering the professions. All are worth listening to.

Florence Baron

Florence Baron QC, the Head of Queen Elizabeth Buildings Chambers is a family law specialist. She is also a Recorder and a Deputy High Court Judge.

From Jersey to London

Florence Baron has no real idea why she decided to pursue a career in law other than 'I suppose that I liked the sound of my own voice, and advocacy appealed to my theatrical side'. She participated in both debating and drama while at school in Jersey and still enjoys the theatre and opera in London. Born in London she spent her early years in Africa, before her family moved to Jersey when she was ten. There were no legal connections in her family.

The explanation she gives for not being able to recall the reasons for her decision to become a lawyer is that the idea 'was always there. I think that I had had a sense of what was right and wrong almost from the outset'. Her school, Jersey College for Girls, did not particularly encourage girls to excel in any academic way, 'they had not sent any girls to Oxford within living memory'. But when, after a discussion with a peripatetic careers adviser, Florence decided that she wished to go to Oxford to read philosophy, politics and economics (PPE), her school did what it could to help by providing additional lessons supervised by her English teacher. She recalls sitting her entrance exams in a waiting room adjacent to the corridor where juniors lined up for lunch – it was very noisy – but she passed and was accepted by St Hugh's College Oxford, certainly an early tribute to her powers of concentration.

PPE she thought would be 'an interesting way' to spend her university years before embarking on law, but it did not take her long to decide that, although it was undoubtedly intellectually challenging, she was just 'marking time'. She switched to law, and encouraged by her excellent tutor at St Hugh's, Ann Smart, she later applied to Middle Temple. Florence has a very strong sense of gratitude to all those who have helped her. 'The States of Jersey not only supported me with a full university grant at Oxford but also gave me additional assistance while I was at Bar School. Even with that and the minor entrance scholarships that I had won, I had to work during vacations to earn money, but without it I should have found it almost impossible. My parents would have tried very hard to see me through but it would have been difficult for them. I owe Jersey a great debt of gratitude.'

Pupillage

Apart from her first six months' pupillage the whole of Florence's career as a barrister has been spent at Queen Elizabeth Buildings (QEB). Her first six months were spent with Stella Hydleman at Dr Johnson's Buildings 'because I wanted to see how a woman operated at the Bar'. Her main ambition, however, was to spend her second six at QEB because 'it had such a high reputation and was well known for the quality of its training. What I did learn from Stella was how hard she had had to work to get where she was and what a very tough time she had had initially'.

Despite being accepted for pupillage at QEB she was constantly told by others that 'you will be extremely lucky if that chambers ever accepts a woman as a tenant'. The only woman, Lord Denning's step-daughter, who had ever been accepted was a door tenant (i.e. non-practising). Florence took the pragmatic view that this was a risk worth taking as she would receive excellent training, and that QEB's high reputation would ensure that she would have less difficulty obtaining a tenancy in another chambers thereafter. Many judges, several Appeal Court judges and even a Law Lord had come from QEB so that to a young Oxford graduate it seemed like an exciting place to be even if for only a very short time.

She began as a pupil to Sir Edward Cazalet, 'a most fantastic teacher, erudite and really shrewd, who taught me the strategic and tactical way to deal with cases. He was an extremely nice man, and his pupils are littered all over the Temple from the Law Lords down'. He was also a 'workaholic, he loved the law and he loved to work', and his example set the standard for her later career. Whether or not she follows him into the judiciary remains to be seen.

In 1976 when Florence was called to the Bar, QEB was a general common law chambers, but as with so many chambers over the years it has specialised and is now best known for its high value ancillary relief work. Florence started out as most young barristers do, accepting anything that the clerk could put her way. For the first year after call with no permanent place in chambers she was literally 'squatting and working as a "devil"', doing research and basic drafting for other barristers and picking up any work that they did not have time to do. At the outset she worked for families with little money where people had nothing very much to divide between them. She also did cases for the Official Solicitor.

The greatest challenge in ancillary relief is not in acting for those with the most money, although these are the cases which hit the headlines, but with the very poor, because they have so little money with which to craft a solution. So the early years of practice call for a great deal of wisdom. It might seem trite to say that Florence is someone who 'enjoys dealing with people', but in her case it is true. She would not enjoy spending her time solving purely intellectual commercial problems, although such problem-solving forms a central part of her work. She is primarily interested in practical solutions that enable two people to continue to be able to communicate and get on with their lives. 'It is one of the great strengths of our system that someone can be the weaker party and yet the law protects them.'

The interaction of barrister and solicitor

'The barrister is always one step removed from her client and that is how it should be. The solicitor absorbs the emotion, in fact many of the solicitors that I deal with give their clients their home telephone numbers for weekend crises, and that is how it should be. Solicitors are the ones who take the initial instructions and who may build up lasting relationships with clients over many years. This is not what barristers are about. As a barrister I need to be dispassionate so that I can be objective and give my clients the often tough advice that they need. And that is why we need a dual system.'

The barrister is not there to sympathise in a partisan sort of way but to understand and communicate and advise on the approach of the courts, 'because in financial cases the court is not interested in the underlying emotions. They are not interested in the conduct of the parties or in the reasons for the marriage breaking down and judges are not interested in punishing a "wrongdoer". Of course this is not necessarily what the general public feels and certainly not what the wronged party in a divorce feels, but the court wishes to achieve a fair financial outcome and it is a great deal fairer in this area than it was.'

Florence explains that for a long time the allocation of assets on breakdown of a marriage was based on the concept of 'reasonable requirements', which in most cases meant that once the court had decided what was 'reasonable' for the wife's needs, the husband would be left with the substantial part of the assets built up during the marriage. The law since *White* v. *White* [2000] 2 FLR 981 and *Cowan* v. *Cowan* [2001] FLR 192, where she acted for the wife, has changed and now the court has to be 'fair' and then check any award against the yardstick of equality. This has made the outcome of some cases more uncertain, 'because fairness, like beauty, is in the eye of the beholder'. Indeed the result may be influenced by factors such as the contribution made by one party to the financial success of the marriage or the amount of wealth, whether through personal endeavour or inheritance, possessed by each party at the time of the marriage.

Florence is more interested in preventing the disappointment of her clients by not raising false hopes. 'I am not a gambler by nature, and most of my predictions as to outcome are normally fulfilled. Touch wood.' Such certainty comes not just from her estimate of having a cautious nature, whether or not justified, but from the distillation of years of experience in her field, enhanced by her present position where as a leading silk she takes responsibility for up to 100 cases a year.

Taking silk

It has become clear that Florence must have been one of Sir Edward Cazalet's aptest pupils, and has imbibed his advice about strategy and tactics not only in the conduct of her cases but also in the planning of her own professional life. Florence took silk in 1995, which she considers was a 'natural progression at the right time'. The 'right time' is not merely a matter of age or of years of call but of examining the overall position to ascertain whether there really is room for another silk in the field.

'I decided to apply because as a junior, even a senior one, I was still having to do a lot of drafting and I was drowning in paperwork and court appearances. I was also coming up against silks in court and beating them.' The economics of the decision also require careful scrutiny. 'If you apply too early you may have several lean years, if there are already a sufficiency of silks in your area of law. People would ask themselves quite rightly why they should pay for a new QC when they could have someone else who has been in the position for many years. If you were having an operation you'd probably choose a consultant surgeon who had been operating for 20 years and knew what he was doing over someone who had just been appointed a consultant. So you have to time your application for silk just right, there is a sort of natural wastage as people are appointed to the Bench. Being a silk is a very stressful occupation and people do not on the whole want that level of responsibility for years and years.'

Florence says quite unassumingly that she chose to apply when there had been a general upward movement to the Bench in her area of law. To her mind the controversial process of so-called 'secret soundings' is a reasonable way of assessing a barrister's suitability for public promotion. 'The whole list of applicants is sent to all the judges who would see you in court, and all the judges in your Division are asked to comment on you, because they are the ones who know what you and your practice are like. Of course the Lord Chancellor's Department also know what your income is because they ask that on the application form as a guide to the viability of your practice. It is right that the opinion of the judges who see you every day should count. If they say that you are a decent hard-working advocate who prepares her cases and takes sensible points then that will count for you, but they could equally say that you are incompetent and should not be appointed. The judges are the right people to have a view as to whether you are worthy of promotion.' Florence points out that the same process is adopted in industry. 'Your superiors will sit round a table and decide whether you are the right person with the right qualities to be promoted into a particular job, and for senior positions they will call for reports from all sorts of people.'

Being a silk and responsibility

When she took silk the nature of Florence's professional life changed. She tends to talk about being a QC in terms of responsibility, but this is not in terms of it being a burden rather in terms of what it is that you have to do on an ongoing basis to warrant the privilege of that particular position. 'The main responsibility that a silk has for a case is strategic. I have a meeting with the solicitor and my junior at the outset of a case to decide on strategy, and then the junior and the solicitor develop the case by assembling evidence, doing research and drafting, but we shall all get together on several subsequent occasions to reconsider our strategy and negotiating tactics.'

Florence's aim is to try and keep her clients out of court, because court is a distressing experience for them as well as being expensive. In matrimonial proceedings there is court-led mediation called a Financial Dispute Resolution (FDR). She will represent her client at that application. This, she explains, is a hearing in front of a judge where all the paperwork and submissions are presented on a without prejudice basis. The judge, whose intention is to make it easier for the parties to resolve the litigation, will then indicate 'this is what I would say were there to be a trial'. Armed with this opinion, the parties are counselled to go off and negotiate in the hope that they will come to an agreement which the court can then approve. 'And 90–95 per cent of cases settle at this point.'

If there is no settlement, it is the 'responsibility' of the silk to run the trial, but this is an outcome that Florence does not seek, 'because apart from anything else I don't want to take people into court unless we are going to win'. This might sound like an egocentric motivation, but it is really concerned with recognising and wanting to protect clients in vulnerable positions. Eschewing emotional involvement does not mean that she does not understand or that she lacks sympathy with that client's predicament. Indeed 'I always prepare people for a court appearance and make sure that they understand what is going to happen. I always want to treat people as I would want to be treated myself, and I explain that that is also what judges wish to happen. It is important that the client realises that the judge is just another human being trying to be fair'.

Certainly the responsibility of being a silk is extensive. 'If I am not in court I will usually have a consultation every day of every week, of course if I am in court I cannot prepare for a meeting, so I suppose that I handle about 100 cases a year.' That means that she has to read all the papers, 'and if it is a big case with 17 files that may take a whole week or more, but it is important to master all the details because how otherwise can you give good advice to a client'.

She is very clear that in order to deal with her area of law, 'you need to understand human beings. I advise equal numbers of men and women. I may have to advise a very clever businessman, who is used to making decisions quickly or an emotionally scarred indecisive wife. I deal with a whole gamut of people and to make sure that each one understands the process I have to find the right words and take the right amount of time to explain it'. Her examples may appear stereotyped, but they are chosen to indicate that a good family barrister must be aware not only of the law, of the chances of success and of the correct strategy to be adopted but must also be able to win the confidence of clients in a short space of time by understanding and speaking their language, and by engaging their respect not just for her intellectual competence but for her understanding.

This emphasis on psychological understanding will not be the same for those barristers who operate in more commercial sets because their clients will tend to come from the business community, so that there will be less emphasis on finding the correct voice for explanation and exposition.

Judiciary

As well as managing her own practice Florence is also a Recorder and Deputy High Court judge. 'This is part of my way of giving something back to the system and it is also part of the whole learning process of how to give a better service. I have realised that there is nothing like sitting on the Bench and being irritated by advocates, whether because of bad preparation or because they have some annoying mannerism, like keeping their hands in their pockets while addressing the Bench.' Being a judge requires different skills. 'A good lawyer should always try to see both sides of an argument so that she can assess the other side's argument and work out how to counter it. But a judge not only has to be able to see both sides but must be fair to both sides. This can require sensitivity in a courtroom situation, especially in childcare cases. In a family court you have to be responsive, keep a nice atmosphere, be fair and maintain a balance. Instead of giving advice you have to give a judgment and sometimes the decision is very difficult. I do not worry about decisions in the sense of being kept awake at night, because that would indicate that I could not make my mind up and that I was indecisive, but I am concerned to get the right result. Because you are the one who has to make your mind up about a case and to give the judgment it can feel very lonely being a judge. Whereas in chambers there is a great sense of camaraderie.'

Head of chambers

Feeling lonely is not something that she ascribes to her position as head of chambers, which she clearly regards as a great privilege as well as a responsibility. 'We have never had an election strictly speaking in our chambers, although other chambers may conduct matters differently. I always say that in about 2000 we had six members of our chambers lost to the High Court, so that only the tea-boy and I were left, and as the tea-boy was more important, there was a general movement to choose me as the new head.'

Whatever the process by which she has arrived in her light office overlooking the Thames and Middle Temple Gardens, she is prepared to work very hard at being head of her group of barristers. 'This job is what you make of it'. When she was first appointed she worked every morning from six a.m. until nine a.m. dealing with the head of chambers' part of her work before getting down to client work. 'It involves a lot of man management, I spend a lot of time working with the Clerk's Room, which is headed up by Ivor, who has been with us since 1979, almost as long as I have. It is essential to have a really good working relationship with your senior clerk.'

Otherwise Florence says that she has to 'manage 24–26 prima donnas'. This phrase is usually employed pejoratively but for Florence it is an indication that she values their diversity and their ability, 'they all have different personalities. We have chosen to become a more specialised chambers and to stay relatively small. People here like each other, and one of my jobs is to ensure that it stays that way and that there are no cliques'. She rejects any notion that they are a substitute family, 'I am not at all maternal and I have chosen not to have children, but I admit that sometimes I do say to them, "I am speaking to you as your mother," when I want to give them advice that they might not like'.

Since she became head of chambers, 'I have changed a few things, because I wanted to ensure that we are a functioning, modern set which is going forward'. This concern covers all aspects of chambers' life. She refuses to adopt an autocratic style and has set up numerous committees to involve all her colleagues in decision making, 'especially the youngsters because they are the future. When I started the younger members certainly did not have a voice, but I believe we should have a much more open approach. My door is always open although I will sometimes have to say, please come back later because I am busy right now. In order to improve our training, which I still feel maintains the standard that I received, we ask for a report from all our pupils at the end of their pupillage and we ask them specifically whether there are any areas we could improve, so that we can make it even better for the next year's intake. And we ask our junior tenants the same thing'.

Delegation means that she can also have time to consider the work environment and the first impression given when a client arrives at her chambers at the end of two flights of the traditional communal stairs. Like her office the reception is light and airy, with many open doors, flowers and the current copies of upmarket magazines. 'I insisted on that. I thought that our clients were worth more than the sort of old dog-eared copies that you get in dentists' waiting rooms. And I did not want our clients to be shut away in a waiting room.' Clearly she wants them to feel part of the efficient buzz of barristers and clerks going about their business at a time when they are most probably feeling bruised and unsure.

Women at the Bar

'Go for it!' said without hesitation is the advice that she would give anyone considering a career at the Bar. But it is not a soft option. 'You must recognise that it is a really hard job, but that because you work for yourself you can make it what you want to make it. If you want to reach the highest echelons you need to be able to work really hard. You need to know your papers thoroughly because you cannot go into court to do a cross-examination and not have strategically thought out your questions. It requires lots of dedication.' On the other hand 'it can be financially very rewarding and you can help people. On occasion I have been out shopping when someone has come up to me and said that you really helped me, I got over my divorce and now I am doing well. That is a fantastic accolade'.

There is of course the big question of attempting to combine work at the Bar with family life. Florence's initial reaction was that it was not possible to do both well, then it became clear that her response was postulated from a single-minded career focus. There are in fact four members of her chambers who are mothers and who work. 'They accept that their practices may suffer for a period of time, and that, when their children are very small, they may be just ticking over but not progressing, but we do try to help them by being as flexible as possible.'

What this means is that they will do fewer cases per year, but they are still practising and no one has suggested that they vacate their tenancies. Florence's own views are obviously informed by her personal drive to perfection and her fascination with the law. 'From observation I think that if you try to combine both motherhood and practising at the Bar they will both suffer a little and that you may end up feeling guilty for much of the time. But it is a personal decision that everyone has to make for themselves. If I had been a mother I would have wanted to be the sort of fantastic mother that my mother was, and I could not have done that and worked at the Bar. I do think though that as a society we still undervalue the contribution that mothers make. Many still tend to believe that a pound earned is a pound but that a baby born has no equivalent value. Bringing up the next generation is more valuable and is still being generally undervalued.'

This is clearly a heartfelt and extremely well informed comment coming as it does from one of the foremost family law practitioners in the country.

Susannah Bates

Susannah Bates is the author of *Charmed Lives* and *All About Laura* two successful novels in each of which the central character is a young overworked solicitor who happens to be a woman.

Getting started

Like many writers before her Susannah began by keeping a diary during adolescence, originally as a silent and ubiquitous friend rather than because of any real interest in writing, but as the years passed she found that she took great pleasure from the moments when she expressed something well, and that words themselves could be rhythmically pleasing. It is not surprising to discover that she is also a talented musician.

Her first forays into 'serious' writing came at Durham University where she had gone to read History, but then 'I realised that if I was going to have to stay up all night reading books I would rather that it was Scott Fitzgerald than E. H. Carr.' Combined with the transfer to English Literature came her first attempt at a novel, a 'parlour game' exercise written with a fellow student, where they wrote alternate chapters. This was no more intended for publication than her diaries but by the time that she graduated she knew that she wanted to be a writer.

Enter Susannah's parents

Do a shipping lawyer father and an artist mother provide the right genetic background for a budding author? Or is it simply that they provide the right balance of mental discipline and a creative way of looking at the world? It might be an interesting nature versus nurture debate but it is certainly true that facets of both of her parents' skills have been influential in shaping Susannah's progress from solicitor to established writer.

Although her mother sympathised with her daughter's need for self-expression, both parents took the practical position that if she were going to write she must take it seriously and make money from it; it was not to be a dilettante occupation supported by them. Not unsurprisingly Susannah found this prospect 'quite frightening' and she made a conscious decision to follow her father's profession, which she felt that she might know something about, and to put the writing project on hold for the next four years – two at the College of Law and a subsequent two years of articles at Herbert Smith. As it happened she also worked at Herbert Smith for a further year upon qualification.

'Law was quite a good follow-on for someone who had come out of the long process of being in institutions like school and university and who had been trained to jump through exam hoops.' She found that the process of becoming a lawyer gave her a sense of safety and security and provided the sense of financial independence and 'being responsible about my future. It was a very adult thing to do'.

She soon discovered that her concept of legal life was very different from the reality. 'It was not nearly as glamorous as I had imagined it to be, it was hard work rather than wafting around in a Dynasty-style suit with wide shoulder pads.' But she made it very clear with a shy smile that her descriptions of the long working hours and practices of her two heroines, Mel and Kate were not totally autobiographical. She was aware of, rather than a frequent participant in, the long hours' culture. She did not, as Kate did, 'spend most of my life in a room with no daylight, reading contracts between banks and companies'. At the end of her first year as a qualified lawyer she knew that the law was not for her, and she had saved enough money to survive 'in a very straitened way' for the two years she considered necessary to give her a chance to try out her fledging writer's wings.

At this point it should be made clear that five years had passed since graduation and she had written nothing creative while at Herbert Smith. But this time her parents' attitude was different. Her father was content that she had at least given law a chance and that she would have something to fall back on if the writing did not work out. Her mother, 'who is as much a friend as a traditional mother', took the pragmatic line that if she were going to write she should 'do it now, while you have no responsibilities. There is no one else who will suffer if you fail'.

Café society

On the first day of her new life Susannah sat down in her local café with a clean exercise pad and a pen. She had no idea what would be the subject of her first novel, only that she would do it. The idea of writing a complete novel was daunting, but she set out a list of ground rules. It must involve no research because 'I could not bear the thought of spending a year doing research only for people to tell me that I could not write anyway'. The themes must come from her own experience, even if only secondhand. For example the theme of domestic violence in *All About Laura* comes from the pro bono courses that she was sent on as part of Herbert Smith's commitment to Refuge. She had also decided that she was not aiming for greatness but rather the sense of writing a good story, and that her style should be pared down and not diffuse.

On the first day in the café she wrote a short story in longhand, on the second day she wrote a sequel and on the third the sequel to that, typing up her words at home in the evening. That all sounds very straightforward but Susannah admits to it being 'pretty scary' at first. Then gradually she found that she was putting together a novel based on the themes of infidelity and trust. 'I've always been fascinated by how little one might know about other people. And I thought if you work long hours like my heroines Kate and Mel you will not necessarily know what the person closest to you is doing during the hours that you are not together, especially if that person does not need to work as hard as you do.'

Keats spoke about the 'cameleon (sic) poet' who observes closely and takes as much pleasure from creating 'an Iago as an Imogen' and it is clear that although Susannah uses the backgrounds that fate has dealt her – parents living on the borders of Scotland and England, legal training, chance acquaintances with models, her mother's artistic background – it is the stresses and motivations of those careers and situations that she builds on rather than the biographical detail of the people that she meets. 'I wonder what it would be like to be. . .' is a concept that started off her first two novels, and is behind the next two that she will be writing.

One of her narrative strengths as a writer is a very pacey use of dialogue to move the plot along and that is indeed how many scenes start for her, rather in the same way as 'when someone says something rude to you and you later think about all the wonderful phrases and points that you should have made'.

Susannah makes it sound as though the progress from young solicitor to published author was amazingly smooth, but she had the tenacity to send the first draft of *Charmed Lives* round to eight agents before finding her present agent who immediately told her that it needed 'cranking up' which process involved doubling its length, expanding some of the characters and changing the ending completely. But then Susannah considers that writing has one great advantage over painting, 'you can just have a go and then if it doesn't work, you can just tear it up and do it again'.

How has the law helped her?

The obvious question is whether Susannah could have written two novels without her experience of the law, a question that goes wider than the mere provision of a background environment and plot focus. Does she actually feel that studying and practising law has given her a set of transferable skills that she would not otherwise have acquired? 'I think that I would have been "less fussy" about my writing if I had not gone into the law.' The main benefit was the discipline and high standards that were instilled in her by her three years at Herbert Smith. This is a discipline which now pins her down almost every morning to five hours' work or 2,000 words, whichever comes first, although 'if it is going well, I'll just carry on all day'. While at Herbert Smith she felt herself constrained when writing letters to clients by the need to be legal rather than creative. 'I was always more creative than legal in my letters to clients, and having to accept that I had to use the same legal word over and over again rather than looking for synonyms because that was what imparted precise meaning and would be readily understood by other lawyers.' Now she feels that her legal experience has to some extent dictated her writing style, which needs to be ameliorated by her editor: 'I have a need to be overly clear and am unhappy with ambiguity'.

But there is also a secondary benefit. Her legal background has given her much more confidence in dealing with people in the non-legal world, and she feels that publishers have taken her more seriously because of this. 'It has also taught me about time constraints and about putting myself on the line. When I knew I was giving up practice I spent a lot of time telling people what I intended to do as I wanted to raise the stakes a bit, I wanted them to ask me when I saw them two months later how the book was going. That way I had to get on with it.'

So successful have been Susannah's first two novels, that she has been commissioned by her publishers, Random House, to produce another two books but unlike John Grisham, who mined the American legal system over many novels, Susannah now plans to turn from central solicitor characters to focus on other professions. It would have been relatively straightforward to find another legally oriented plot as many of her friends are still in the profession, but her motivation is clearly not just about making money but about satisfying personal curiosity about what it might be like to be somebody else in a difficult situation, exactly the sort of qualities required when advertisements ask for someone who has good communication and client skills.

She hastens to point out that Kate and Mel are not Susannah, although they would not have been so rounded without her own experience of a legal office. 'It was really important to me that Kate was not me. I wanted to create someone who was a committed lawyer, and that a major part of the plot depended on her career being rock-solid. So Kate and Mel worked much longer hours than I ever did!' When she left 'I did not rate myself highly enough to think that I would be such a loss to the firm'.

Afterthoughts?

Susannah has had no difficulty in shedding the outward appearance of the lawyer, swapping the office suit for the rollneck sweater and jeans. The real loss has been the people that she worked with, and when she still occasionally misses 'that office life' it is because of the people rather than the law. In common with so many young lawyers 'I never felt completely confident about what I was doing, and I had an overwhelming urge to confess what I did not know'. However it is more than likely that her workplace colleagues will have missed a diminutive young lawyer with a ready smile and a shy sense of humour.

Was there anything that would have kept her in the law? It's probably unlikely given that writing was the thing that she really wanted to do, and that she was prepared to live on very little for two years to try out her ambition, but she says thoughtfully that if there had been obvious female role models who managed to combine work and family that might have been a persuasive influence. The senior women that she saw in the law were very dedicated to their work rather than displaying a sense of balance between work and home. She would like to have felt convinced not only that the job could be combined with family but could provide 'a sense of peace'.

Although Susannah is successful in applying the office structure that she learned in the law to her creative work, she has an unexpected comment on the difference between working in a clearly formatted workplace and working at home. 'It seems very selfish. When I was in the office I could easily tell people that I could not see them because leaving work to visit a friend in hospital in the middle of the day would mean that I was letting down someone else, my clients, but when I am writing at home I feel really selfish if I tell friends that I cannot do something because I am writing.' But she agrees that perhaps this is not so very surprising, and is perhaps just part and parcel of being a woman sensitive to the feelings and needs of others.

Margaret Bennett

Margaret Bennett is the senior partner of the family law practice of Margaret Bennett Solicitors which she set up in 1990. She has also sat as a Deputy District Judge in the Principal Registry of the Family Division.

Theatrical lessons

Although much has been said of the similarity between the stage and the Bar, probably not too many solicitors have received an early schooling intended to fit them for a career in acting. Margaret Bennett's education began at the Corona Academy, a theatre school in West London, whose alumni include Dennis Waterman and Francesca Annis. After appearances in *Sunday Night at the Palladium* on television and as one of the precocious young schoolgirls in *Blue Murder at St Trinians* she seemed destined for an entertainment career, but by the time that she left school at 15 in 1961 the British film industry was in a state of collapse.

She then realised that 'I had to study, so I did my O Levels by correspondence course followed by a swift nine months at the City and Westminster College to obtain three A Levels in law, British constitution and economics before reading law at the London School of Economics (LSE)'. But it would be wrong to assume that dance, theatre and film were no longer part of her life. One of her regular relaxations is the cinema and her personal office is sited at the top of a four storey building in Bloomsbury, not one suspects from a sense of grandeur, but so that she can maintain muscle tone by running up and down four flights of stairs several times a day.

In her first year at LSE she studied history and economics as well as law. 'Although I knew fairly early on that I wanted to do law, I think studying other subjects gave me a better perspective on life, because I had come from a completely non-legal, non-academic background.' At the LSE in 1965 she found that 'law was very male-dominated, only 10 per cent of the students were women. And when I started practising we were still very much in the minority, and to be truthful we were still not taken very much notice of'.

Margaret does not see this early experience of being the recipient of chauvinistic attitudes as entirely negative. 'Later when I became a partner and the only woman at partners' meetings, I had ample opportunity to observe how men behave. I would propose something, would be ignored and would then find that three meetings later one of the men would propose the same thing and be applauded. I also noticed that they would talk and talk and talk, whether or not it was to the point because they all felt that they had to say something.' Margaret herself has the potentially disconcerting habit of saying exactly what she wants to say in as many or as few words as she considers necessary and then stopping. Abruptly. Mastery of the pregnant pause in a discussion is just one of the well-learned lessons of her theatrical background.

Legal growth

Margaret spent 22 years with the same firm, Malkin Cullis and Sumption, going from articled clerk to head of department. 'It did not take me long to get salaried partnership and I was made an equity partner soon afterwards. The firm and I grew together; there were five partners when I joined and 29 when I left to set up my own practice in 1990. The firm had a very good reputation for general litigation, one of the partners was a Master in the Costs Division and as an assistant I had a very varied experience, much more varied than you would get today. I did individual tribunal applications, general litigation, entertainment law, and some family law and because it was the early 1970s and VAT had just been introduced I also negotiated with Customs and Excise to settle claims on behalf of our clients. It was a very unusual spread of work.' Quizzed on the subject of the defamation cases with which she was involved she demurs firmly and it is clear that even up to 30 years later her concept of professionalism will not allow her to indulge in legal gossip.

The two decades spent at Malkin Cullis and Sumption were important not only in terms of professional development but also because her husband was a partner there and her two sons were born during that time. Indeed when they asked her what it was like to be a lawyer she came up with a succinct explanation suitable for a child which is also a fairly accurate reflection of much legal work. 'It's like jigsaws, chess and poker. You collect all the evidence, which is the jigsaw part, you formulate your strategy which is the chess part, and then you consider your strategy and tactics and negotiate for your client and that is the poker bit.'

Management and image

As Malkin Cullis and Sumption grew she became more and more involved with the firm's management. Many lawyers might consider that setting up the firm's billing and book-keeping system to accommodate the imposition of VAT in 1973 was a considerable achievement but this is not what Margaret regards as her special contribution to the firm. That related back to her early theatrical experience where 'I had learned the importance of image and presentation'. And she resolutely set about creating a 20th century image for the firm. First she set up a dining-room for the entertainment of clients, a highly unusual move for a small City firm at that time, and then she embarked on changing the 'paper image' of the firm. In both projects she was intimately involved. In the case of the dining room by designing the décor and hiring the chef, and in the wider project by redesigning the firm's notepaper and bills and even persuading her partners to abandon 'the old-fashioned brief paper which was larger even than A3 and required a special typewriter with an especially long carriage. It was this wide', she gestures much like a fisherman describing a catch.

What she wanted was 'integrated graphics. I knew from my theatre background how important design was, and I wanted the whole design and image of the firm to be standardised to give clients some idea of the kind of lawyers that we considered ourselves to be'. It is a concept that she has thought through very carefully in the design of the materials for her present firm, Margaret Bennett Solicitors. Although to some extent she would argue that the location of a firm does not matter because it is the service provided that is important, this is belied in the impression that is gained from the entrance with its upwardly sweeping staircase and its boardrooms with highly polished tables and pictures of old London. This appearance of solidity and comfort is clearly what a stressed client with a marital problem would find comforting.

Family law

By the early 1980s Margaret had realised that setting up a separate family law department would make sound commercial sense in the context of the firm's business. Through her involvement with the International Bar Association (IBA) and other international organisations she had recognised that 'the expansion of air traffic and people's increased mobility had produced new challenges and situations in private client and family work, because people were moving to other countries because of their jobs, buying property and having children there which would have all sorts of consequences for financial and custody disputes. It raised all sorts of issues about which jurisdiction should be used'.

The international dimension of family law clearly fascinates her, and led to her becoming the Chairman of the Family Law Committee of the IBA. 'In the last 20 years family law has become much more standardised in jurisdictions around the world, and the grounds for divorce in the countries of the "old" European Union have become very similar. When Ireland was reforming its divorce legislation I went to Ireland to advise as a consultant to the Law Society of Ireland because it was felt useful to have someone there who had actual practical experience of what happened in practice in England, not just rehearsing what the law says. In Ireland at the time many families did split up and parents who had other children with new partners were not able to divorce and re-marry to legitimise their second families.' For Margaret this sort of international work is 'so worthwhile as people are willing to learn and to introduce similar legislation that has worked in other countries'.

Family law she considers is as much to do with public policy as personal relationships, about the way that the state views its responsibilities to its citizens and their responsibilities towards each other. In the last few decades this has been a rapidly developing area of the law as society's views on the place of women in society and parental rights in respect of their children have changed. 'Social sciences are very much a 20th century invention and if a relevant article is published in one jurisdiction it is very quickly read and commented on in other countries. In my view the pen is very much mightier than the sword.'

But Margaret's practice is of course firmly based in the UK, where most of her clients consult her. Although they are usually what is described as 'high net worth individuals', she was very pleased to have been one of the first four honorary legal advisers to the City of London Citizens' Advice Bureau, and the first woman to chair the London Legal Aid Appeal Committee, her brief being to assist the Legal Aid Board with policy and the introduction of professional and management standards to ensure a nationwide consistency of structure and practice.

Margaret Bennett Solicitors

In 1989 Malkin Cullis and Sumption merged with Janners to form the new and short-lived partnership of Malkin Janners. Two years later the merged firm dissolved and Margaret took this event as her opportunity to establish her own firm, Margaret Bennett Solicitors, devoted solely to family law. Margaret considers that 'we were very fortunate to be very successful right from the start, because there was no direct competition from our former colleagues, and clients remained with us and were happy to recommend us to other people'. Initially they had no relocation problems either as they simply took over part of the old Malkin Janners offices, and by the time that rapid expansion dictated a move to their firm's present premises in Bloomsbury Square its client base and systems were firmly established.

Starting out on her own was simply a new and different challenge. 'I settle down easily wherever I am and I welcomed the chance to start something from scratch.' After some thought she agrees with the suggestion that she is in effect senior partner, managing partner, marketing partner and finance director to her firm of six fee earners. 'Yes, I suppose I am. What is important is to set up the correct systems. At the beginning the bank manager and I were telephoning each other every five minutes until I learned that a system of trigger points was required whereby the bank just did things automatically when certain levels of financing were required. However I did find the management side relatively straightforward as I had been involved in setting up reporting, accounts and appraisal systems in my previous firm, and it was fun creating my own brand.' She is skilled at presenting something difficult as happening with relative ease, and this may well be how she genuinely feels. What is clear is that she took every opportunity while at her previous firm to learn about all aspects of running a legal firm.

Running a small firm may however require a different type or scale of thought. 'I tend to think laterally, and about the outcome that I want and not just the process', to produce sometimes unexpected results. The firm is unable to take on trainees because it would be impossible to offer sufficient choice to satisfy Law Society requirements without a complicated system of reciprocal arrangements; instead it offers paid placements and opportunities to young people and sometimes foreign lawyers at different stages in their careers. Every summer vacation Margaret Bennett Solicitors takes pupils from an associated school for a two week placement, every six months they take a law student from an associated university, and every year a student from an American university with a London base works with them for six weeks.

'And we have a written programme for each person who comes. There are benefits to the firm in terms of the work done by the university students, but I suppose that much of what we do is purely altruistic, because it's about demonstrating to young people what it's like to be a lawyer in a firm with a friendly culture, so that they can see that by working in the law they can help people in a truly professional way and at a high standard.'

'Personally I find helping young people a very satisfying thing to do, and I am very gratified if I go to the law courts and someone comes up to tell me that because of being in our firm they have made their career in the law.' And certainly there is a Margaret Bennett way of doing things. Family law practitioners who join the firm will find that they are expected to 'adopt a problem-solving approach with lateral thinking. They must identify the goals, consider the options available and then get there as soon as possible by the best route, whether that is by litigation or by negotiation. And we also try to ensure that people learn to co-operate even when they are under pressure, because we will all be under pressure at some time or other'.

Perhaps she is helped in this latter aim by being a trained mediator. She does not mediate often because for her the purpose of the training was to enable her 'to use mediation skills to approach cases in the ways that will best help my clients. Mediation itself is just a facilitating process, it's not a way of imparting substantive knowledge'. However she has pioneered family law arbitration training in this country by arranging arbitration seminars to be given here by experienced American arbitration trainers. This she considers is particularly useful when the two high profile parties desire privacy in divorce proceedings or when there are problems about choice of jurisdiction. In either case arbitration may enable the parties to come more easily to a satisfactory agreement.

Financial matters

Margaret has always had what she calls a 'can do' attitude to law, and this has informed much of her practice. By the mid 1980s she had become concerned that, particularly in big money financial settlements, the courts were applying what was known as the 'reasonable requirements' test to the amount that would be allocated to the economically weaker party in a divorce. Courts had found it increasingly useful to have a table prepared by a firm of accountants setting out what the wife (for the weaker party usually, but not always, was the wife) had spent during the previous year; this amount together with a figure representing the remaining years of her life actuarially computed was then used as a basis for a calculation to arrive at the capital sum that would be awarded to her as a clean break settlement. The capital sum was intended to provide for her income requirements for life so that when she died there would be no capital left to leave to any children.

In Margaret's view this was manifestly unfair as the settlement sums were arrived at without recognising the contribution that a wife might have made by looking after the family and thus freeing up her husband's time to build up a business or pursue his career for the benefit of the whole family. In some cases husband and wife might have started a family business together but the wife's involvement might have diminished as her responsibility for the children and the home increased, only to find on divorce that her very real contribution to the family's success was ignored and that she was awarded only her 'reasonable requirements', even though that might represent only a small percentage of the couple's joint wealth.

In Margaret's view this was not what had been contemplated when the Matrimonial Proceedings and Property Act 1970, subsequently consolidated in the Matrimonial Causes Act 1973, was enacted. 'This was not a sexist or gender thing as far as I was concerned although in reality it was usually the husband who had most of the assets by the time that the marriage had ended. It was simply a question of fairness.'

For a number of years she had been trying to persuade leading counsel to 'step out of the box' and to take a more enlightened stance by challenging the approach of the courts, but she had no success in persuading any to 'break through the barrier because the traditional arrangements were so well-established and comfortable,' until in 1995 she represented the wife in a case where the sums involved were sufficiently large to make it worthwhile attacking the reasonable requirements principle, first in the High Court and then in the Court of Appeal.

The Court of Appeal in *Dart* v. *Dart* [1996] 2 FLR 286 not only upheld the reasonable requirements approach but also refused leave to appeal to the House of Lords. However this challenge and the resulting publicity 'pushed the door open' and led to another case, *White* v. *White* [2000] 2 FLR 981 which eventually went to the House of Lords, 'and then made legal history'. The House of Lords decided that equality should be adopted as the new yardstick. The court should ask themselves what would be the result if they divided the family assets equally between husband and wife and whether that would be fair.

This was a significant departure from the previous method of deciding on financial provision, and although she was not professionally involved in the *White* case, Margaret was particularly pleased at this outcome, because she felt that by pursuing the *Dart* case she had gone a long way to ensuring a change in the law and greater justice for the weaker party in a divorce.

Judging

In a relatively small partnership being senior partner is a fairly complex affair, for as well as all the management issues she still needs to bring in, and enjoys, client work. It might be easy for such a position to become obsessive and claustrophobic. So as with the mediation training she is always looking for something else which will give her more 'perspective', something else which she feels might give her an added insight into how to develop her own service to her clients. For ten years she sat as a Deputy District judge in the Principal Registry of the Family Division. In the 20 days a year that she sat she learned much about the need to be meticulous about detail and also about the judge's perspective 'sitting in the middle between two opposing parties'. It has, she feels, enabled her to understand the pressures of judicial responsibility and therefore to give her clients better advice as to how a judge might look on their case.

'Managing a court list is a bit of an art, as if you are not careful you can let things slip and find that at the end of the day there are cases which have not been heard. Of course sometimes this can't be helped where, for example, barristers turn up who were not expected, or when you find that you have two litigants in person. What I did find was that I was quite successful at getting financial dispute resolution cases settled. You have to look at both parties and learn to recognise when someone is being less reasonable than the other person and then let that party know what I expect to happen and what they are going to have to do if it does not. For example, if two parties are in dispute about the allocation of the proceeds of sale of a property it might be possible to get them to agree without going through all the paraphernalia of setting up a formal trust for sale, that the sale of the house will be postponed for a year, which may be enough to give both parties much of what they want.'

Being a woman lawyer

Margaret's early theatrical training shows itself in many aspects of how she approaches her personal and professional life. 'As an actor you learn to stand back from the character that you are playing and then to go into and come out of role at will. You learn to observe people and how they interact and what the dynamics are of particular groups. I actually find that being a woman has often been helpful in professional situations; often I am negotiating on behalf of my client and the male solicitor on the other side has no idea of what I am thinking but I know what he is thinking because I have had so much opportunity to observe how men behave towards each other.'

But she recognises that some young women do have difficulties with male behaviour in 'professional' situations because they have had insufficient experience of being in a male dominated world. 'I've been in so many situations where I have been the only woman present and if I am at a dinner where one of my male neighbours ignores me, I sometimes quietly ask other people at the table "Is he always like this?" It's all that needs to be said.'

Physically slight, she has obviously found that the apparently reasonable but acid phrase reasonably uttered is more telling than a shrill tirade. 'You see, it's only very recently that women have invaded the City in any big way, especially in terms of banking and accountancy, and even more recently in terms of construction and surveying. But, women are good at law.' These five words sum up and are her answer to the question as to whether women should consider the law as a profession. To her it is as clear-cut and succinct as that.

Then she pauses and rephrases the question. 'Why shouldn't a woman become a lawyer?' It's now a lateral question. 'It is a lot easier now than it was when I was an articled clerk, but the people that I really admire are the women who were the generation before mine because they were the ones who really had to fight for their place in the legal sun. Personally I didn't find it difficult, but then I worked right through bringing up a family and that is hard work if very rewarding at the same time. It is very challenging and hard work.'

Working mothers

She is very honest in her appraisal of herself as a working mother, but she also recognises that women do set themselves standards of parenthood that men do not often aspire to, or at least admit to aspiring to. 'Yes, I did lose out and my family lost out. I could have spent more time with them and I didn't because I was pursuing my career.' But there was a sound reason for this. Margaret's father died when she was very young, and 'I decided very early on in my career before I even had children that if I put my career first I could deal with whatever happened in life to myself and to any children that I might have'. She then states with some pride that her two sons are both very independent and very good cooks. Before she even had children she had already decided what qualities she wanted to inculcate in them – independence, a sense of morality, pride in themselves, respect both for themselves and for others and a sense of the value of money.

Tucked away in this list, which would not go amiss as part of a Hippocratic oath for lawyers, is that comment about cooking.

'My children are good cooks, because I don't cook. I can cook but I choose not to.' She refused to accept the role of working wife and mother who does everything, not by arguing, shouting about or even discussing it. She simply observed that the results of certain household chores were more important to her husband than herself. 'He was more concerned if there was some dust left in the corner of the room than I was and it didn't bother me if we were having fish fingers again because that's what the children wanted.' So she carried on performing household tasks to her own 'inadequate' standards until her husband got the message and learned to cook. But to someone who is constantly emphasising standards that must have been hard!

The future

In common with many people of her age and achievement she has recently questioned what should be the next stage in her life, but the possibility of increased leisure has been considered and rejected. 'I want to carry on building up the practice. I'm very proud of it, and I would like to develop it as a place of excellence, because you can never say by definition that you have come to that excellence, because there would be nothing left to aim for. But I do intend to work at this for myself as well as for everyone else in the firm so that we maintain a level of expertise and standards of excellence in all respects. With the help of my partners we have already introduced standards of quality controls and other priorities and systems to help us give the best possible service.'

Margaret Brazier

Margaret Brazier is Professor of Law at Manchester University. A former chairman of the committee which produced the Report of the Review of Current Arrangements for Payments and Regulation of Surrogacy, she currently chairs the Retained Organs Commission.

Background

A woman who creates order out of chaos might be a suitable way to think of Margaret Brazier. Her long office at Manchester University's Williamson Building is awash with papers and books which makes the legal term 'fishing expedition' very apt. But she knows where everything is. It is the same ability to see through the apparent moral chaos to what really matters to people and how the law can help them, which has made her work on the Retained Organs Commission so valuable.

Just to clarify, 'as there are lots of Margarets in my family, they have always called me Margot. In the past I've taken the pedantic view that I should use my official Christian name for publications and official functions but as I've got older I use Margot more and more'. Margot, therefore, had decided to become a lawyer by the age of 11 or 12. 'I had a very glamorous view of lawyers as being people who campaigned to correct injustice. My mother was very interested in politics and new developments in the law, which we would discuss round the dinner table. I remember discussing with my parents both the Abortion Law Reform Act 1967 and the controversial debates which led up to the reform of the law relating to homosexuality in the Sexual Offences Act 1967.'

Margot felt that her father, a local government officer in Preston, if given different financial circumstances, would have enjoyed being part of the legal profession. 'My father did not try to influence me in any way towards the law, but he was always interested in discussing my future career with me.' In any event her parents were very supportive of her choice, and were not deterred by the usual arguments of many during the 1960s (Margot was born in 1950), that spending on the higher education of daughters, who would only get married, was a waste of time and money.

Margot's 'holiday jobs' had some bearing on the direction of her later career. Time spent in a local solicitor's office convinced her that general High Street practice was not for her, and working as a care assistant in the local civic hospital looking after elderly people, 'it was essentially a converted workhouse and it was a very sad experience', made her aware that individuals can often be at a disadvantage in their relationships with the medical profession and those in authority.

Obviously a bright girl she spent the years between 11 and 15 at boarding school, which she hated so much that it influenced her later decision not to apply for Oxford or Cambridge because of the perception that living in an all women college would be more of the same thing. She was much happier at Queen Mary's School at Lytham which although it too was a single sex school was just across the road from the boys' school. 'We had a shared debating society, and somehow there was found to be a need for lots of joint committee meetings.'

University

At 17 Margot became a student at Manchester University School of Law. 'I did not want to live at home but I did not want to be very far away either. In retrospect 17 at that time was not an age to begin a university course. It is not difficult to cope intellectually, but the difference between the social maturity of a 17-year-old and someone who is 18-and-a-half is vast, and I have been confirmed in this opinion many times by talking to the younger students who have come here to read law.'

Academically it was an incredible place to be. Harry Street, the author of *Street on Torts*, was 'a scary but inspirational teacher', as was Peter Bromley, who was committed to very high standards of pastoral care. 'He and Mrs Bromley would invite his students to dinner at his home several times a year, but that could also be a slightly alarming experience for us young students as they frowned on the very short skirts fashionable in the sixties and our dinner table etiquette had to be impeccable.' She was also taught by Brenda Hoggett, now Court of Appeal judge, Dame Brenda Hale (also interviewed in this book), whom she remembers as being 'a smashing teacher', and it was encouraging to find that there were another 10 female students and three female members of staff in the School of Law, including Gillian White, one of the first ever female law professors.

Margot's firm ambition had always been to go the Bar. She knew that she did not wish to be a solicitor, partly because of her High Street experience and partly because she had no interest in the corporate and commercial aspects of the law. 'I have never been particularly interested in money, and am far more fascinated by people.' Consequently she focused as far as possible on tort, criminal law and civil liberties, with some interest in administrative law. 'Now I think that if I had had the opportunity I should have found working in the field of medical negligence as a solicitor fascinating, although that was not a developed branch of the law at that time. But I was definitely more interested in the effect of the law on people rather than in legal structures per se.'

She also concluded that the pleasure that she derived from debating, and she was very active in the Manchester University Debating Society as were many of the other law students, would translate into enjoyment of advocacy. 'It was definitely that way round. I did not participate in debating because I thought that I was equipping myself with a transferable skill. However I must confess that I did not plan my career in the way that we now advise our students to do. Career planning was very much a later phenomenon. Now we suggest that students look critically at as broad a range of options as possible, rather than taking the blinkered view that a prestigious major City firm should be their only objective. We suggest that they think carefully about what they are going to enjoy, and not just about the money that they might earn.'

Career planning for young women has an additional aspect, because 'most will still have or wish to have families, and it is far too easy to find yourself in a trap of not having achieved enough before you have children. I was fortunate in that I did quite a lot in my twenties before I had my daughter. Even so there were people around who said that I would not return to work, and that if I did it would prove that I was not a very good mother!'. In the event she was given a great deal of support by Harry Street, had the assistance of a marvellous day nanny, was fortunate that she also had colleagues with young children and, even more fundamentally, a husband who was prepared to adjust his hours so that childcare was not her sole responsibility.

Her husband is Rodney Brazier, Professor of Constitutional Law at Manchester University. Margot does not believe that having such a husband, who for most of her professional life has lectured in the same faculty in the same university has created any special set of difficulties. 'We have been very fortunate because our careers have more or less kept pace with each other, although I was appointed to my Chair slightly before Rodney was, and we also focus on different areas of the law.'

Some of the time Margot was able to bring her daughter Vicky into the department, 'and when she was older she and her friend would come in and do photocopying for me, which was actually very helpful'. Her daughter has an interesting comment on Margot's success in combining both her personal and professional life. 'What would you have done if you had not worked? You managed to get the award for fusspot mum of the millennium as it is. I couldn't have coped if you hadn't been working.'

Academia

Margot's academic career came about almost by accident. Her postgraduation career strategy had been to work at something else for a few years before applying to the Bar. Margot is slim, neat and tiny. 'At 20 I really did look about 12, and I thought that in a few years I might succeed in looking as though I had a bit more gravitas. I also wanted to have saved some money in the Post Office so that I could get through the early lean years at the Bar without asking anyone for help.'

Consequently the temporary lectureship offered by Harry Street was accepted with alacrity. 'I studied for the Bar exams while I was lecturing and was called in 1973. But my long term plan of switching to the Bar when I was about 30 was completely changed by the arrival of my daughter when I was 28. As a professional mother I wanted to have my cake and to eat it as well, I wanted the career and I wanted to be a hands-on mother. I also knew that if I went to the Bar I would want to be successful which would mean that the time that I could spend with my daughter would be very limited.'

This is not a suggestion that the life of an academic is inherently easy, but a statement that it has a flexibility which may enable a mother to dovetail work and family more easily than the Bar might permit. Margot found that her day could be structured into regular components of teaching and research, time with her daughter and then the inevitable additional period of study when her daughter had gone to bed. 'Now it is probably harder for academics who are mothers than it was in the 1970s and 1980s because of the emphasis on quantification and assessment that began in the nineties after the first Research Assessment Exercise of 1988. In fact that has made it harder for academics generally.' She has very strong feelings about this.

The requirement that academics should publish at least four articles in any one assessment period of four years is, she believes, formulaic and does not take account of those who are not prolific but who after long periods of gestation produce works of great insight and scholarship. There is insufficient recognition that scholarship is creative and that like any other creative endeavour is subject to 'periods of famine, when the academic is occupied with other necessary aspects of the teaching and administrative part of the job while waiting for ideas derived from research to mature almost in the subconscious. There needs to be a recognition that all sorts of things are not subject to assessment in any scientific way. Our administrative burden has increased and the number of students for whose pastoral care we are responsible as individual members of staff has almost doubled. All of this takes time away from teaching and research'.

What needs to be emphasised is that Margot herself places a great deal of emphasis on pastoral care and is as willing to empathise with a student's problems over an unflattering dress that her sister had asked her to wear as a bridesmaid, as with another student's difficulties with the syllabus. 'If you have the time to see students as people it makes the whole business of being an academic and teacher so much more enjoyable. When they keep in touch and even sometimes invite you to their weddings, that is so rewarding.'

Using the law

'The spectrum of legal academics is very wide. Some of my colleagues who are legal theorists produce publications which are in many ways indistinguishable from those of philosophers or sociologists.' Margot on the other hand considers herself to have a more practical attitude. 'I am very much a practical academic, I enjoy research and I enjoy reading, but I like to see how academic law can influence public policy. I am fascinated by how the law can be made better for the people who use it.'

Margot's extensive and very useful grasp of many branches of law derives from her time as a young lecturer when she was required to teach many different subject areas often at short notice. 'I've taught just about everything except tax. Yes, it was hard work, but I enjoyed it. After many years of teaching tort it is easy for me now to make all sorts of assumptions about what students already know, and to take things for granted. It brings you back down to earth when you have to teach something that is not your specialism and you have to learn it very quickly. It gives you a much better idea of what your students are thinking and feeling.'

In her work with the Retained Organs Commission her flexible and practical attitude as well as her inherent sympathy for the human predicament has been clearly shown. After the public enquiry into the practice at Liverpool's Alder Hey Hospital of removing and retaining the organs of dead people with no or limited consent from their near relatives, Margot was asked to chair the Retained Organs Commission. This appointment was the recognition of her many years' work at the intersection of medicine, philosophy and the law which started when in the 1980s she met three colleagues at Manchester who were also fascinated by medical ethics; John Harris, now Sir David Alliance Professor of Bioethics in the law school, the late Tony Dyson, Professor of Sociology and a member of the Warnock Committee and Mary Lobjoit, Deputy Director of the Student Health Centre.

'This was about the time when Victoria Gillick unsuccessfully went to court demanding to be informed if any of her daughters under the age of consent sought contraceptive treatment and so many of our discussions were all about reproductive medicine and informed consent.' The collaborative work of these four academics resulted in Manchester University setting up a course leading to a Master's degree in Healthcare, Medicine and the Law. 'Gradually I found that I was doing more and more work on the relationship between law and medicine. I have a passion for law and I wanted to see how it could help with the difficult issues facing patients and the medical profession.'

Surrogacy

Invited to chair the Home Office Animal Procedures Committee in 1990, which was set up under the Animals (Scientific Procedures) Act 1986 to advise the Home Secretary on the use of animals in scientific procedures and his duties under the Act, she eventually became its chair in 1994/5. This was her first immersion in highly controversial public policy and in 1996 she was asked to chair the committee which produced the *Report of the Review of Current Arrangements for Payments and Regulation of Surrogacy*, examining public policy on payment for surrogate mothers and whether there should be official regulation of this practice. She recognises that 'the role that the law can play in promoting good and ethical medicine is limited but inescapable. There needs to be understanding of the correct regime of legal regulation and its limits, and we as lawyers need to accept what the law can and can't do'.

The recommendations of this committee were undoubtedly an example of appreciating these limitations. Margot felt it would be wrong and impracticable to require or even allow those contemplating surrogacy arrangements to enter into legally binding contracts which could be potentially enforceable through the courts. Her consideration of the evidence presented to the committee led her to the conclusion that there should instead be what the committee termed a 'Memorandum of Understanding'.

'It was clear that each party to such an arrangement might have very different expectations from the other. The woman who was going to carry the baby, who was often very young and sometimes in need of mothering herself, could often have expectations that there would be continuing contact between herself and the recipient parents which was the last thing that they intended. On the other hand the parents would have expectations of how the surrogate mother would behave during pregnancy in terms of personal hygiene and health-care, which would be far in excess of the standards which they would have applied to themselves. It is near impossible to put stip-ulations about antenatal visits, exercise and diet into a legally bind-ing contract, because non-compliance could theoretically result in court proceedings which would not be expeditious enough to give an appropriate remedy. And if for example the foetus was found to have abnormalities, what could you stipulate in a contract, that you would go to the court to ask for specific performance of a termina-tion? It is very difficult when you enter into areas of commodifica-tion of bodily services.'

'But,' she pointed out, 'if everyone sits down and works out a set of desirable outcomes then at least they know what their expectations are, and in some cases they will realise that these are so far apart that it is better to abandon the plan completely.'

The Retained Organs Commission

It was tussling with problems like these and using the law to come up with practical recommendations rather than theoretical solutions that made her a good choice for the Retained Organs Commission. She begins by explaining the problem in legal terms. 'It is an old, if possi-bly apocryphal, maxim that there can be no property in the human body, and yes, it is sufficiently clear that if a husband dies his wife cannot put his body up for auction so that there cannot be "property" in a body in that sense. However, there must be limited property rights in the sense that one class of persons may have a greater right to give permissions as to how a body is disposed of and when and how organs may be removed and retained. We need to deal very sen-sitively with these issues because there are some religions in which it is disastrous if the body is not interred or cremated in a complete state. Orthodox Jews require internment of the whole body and within a short period of time after death, and Hindus believe that the spirit will not be capable of moving on to its next incarnation if the body is not entirely consumed by fire at cremation.'

When she agreed to take it on, 'I thought that we were being asked to do four things, first that there should be guidance and oversight of how the matter should be dealt with, second that the commission should act as a support and a voice for families who were in agonising positions, third that there should be advice to ministers on the regulatory framework as to how the donation and retention of human tissue should be considered in the future, and fourth that there would be advice on the new legislation and what it should involve.'

'I had thought that the commission would be very much involved in the third and fourth areas and would have very little involvement in the first two which would be primarily operational and the province of civil servants who would deal with the practical issues. I was wrong. I found that law reform requires that you are inevitably involved in operational matters because you have to give guidance to hospital and health trusts which have to deal with upset, questioning and sometimes distraught relatives.' There are nuances to the relationship of hospitals and relatives which makes the whole process even more sensitive and difficult. Parents may separately make enquiries about the fate of the organs of their dead child and may have very different views on how matters should proceed. For those dealing with the enquiries there is a minefield of tension and unhappiness to navigate because so often the death of a much-loved child has made it impossible for the parents to carry on living together.

'In about two weeks we had to come up with the first draft of something which was in effect derived from family law in order to consider what was the extent of parental responsibility in respect of a dead child and who should exercise it. Naturally so much of the media attention has focused on grieving parents whose children's organs have been retained, but people forget that about 40 per cent of enquiries are about adults, which leads to another set of difficulties about defining who is the "nearest relative" for the purposes of making decisions about the organs of a dead adult.'

The most important thing for Margot is to ensure that the NHS and the law operate together to respect the great diversity of individuals and their religious and philosophical beliefs while remembering that there might be a public interest which is also of extreme importance. 'The reality is that if doctors ask to be able to take samples, or to explain that whole organs are required and explain why, most people will give the requisite permission.' But it is a very difficult thing to propose to families at a time of great stress, and the temptation has been for doctors to consider that where there is a rare or unusual condition which the taking of tissue samples might assist, the potential benefit of further investigation to the population at large can override the wishes of the individual parent or relative.

This of course is where philosophy, also one of Margot's interests, and the law diverge. Philosophy can content itself at times with posing questions; the law has to come up with some sort of answer to the question posed.

Methods of study, modes of thought

Margot has found that her early experience of teaching multiple legal subjects has been invaluable in helping her understand the complex issues raised in the commissions and committees which she has chaired. 'When we were considering surrogacy I found that I was using smatterings of law that have nothing to do with tort or medical negligence,' again because of the need to examine the property and consent issues. Now she says that young lecturers are reluctant to take on the teaching of subjects other than those which are core to their own personal spheres of interest, perhaps as a consequence of the research publication requirement. 'There is a strong analogy here to the position of medicine. A friend of mine who is a neurologist says that younger colleagues in the field undoubtedly have a much greater understanding of that specialism than he did at a comparable age, but they are much less capable of recognising that a symptom points to a problem in a medical area other than their own specialism.'

Here Margot risks a comment that she considers 'might not be politically correct, but I think from observation that there is a difference in the attitudes of women and men to specialism or diversity, which may have something to do with our women's supposed propensity for multi-tasking. It's a vast generalisation, but I think that more of my female colleagues are more interested in getting something in context whereas more of my male colleagues are more likely to be focused in depth on one single topic'.

She is very happy to admit that she is one of those who positively enjoy a smörgåsbord of legal research, 'I prefer to do my research in the library with books rather than on a computer and that means that quite often I am looking through a journal and find that the article beside the one that I am supposed to be reading is just as, if not more interesting!'.

Summing up

Margot is in no doubt that the profession that she chose is the right one for her. 'Of course like everyone else I get tired and I whine and I moan, but this job has been incredibly rewarding.' Her decision to reject the Bar and to opt for academia was clearly a good decision, but she retains great admiration for those who practise at the Bar and for what 'judges can do incredibly well, and that is to be good at interpreting a lot of information very quickly. My students ask me how to cope with judgments that are over 100 pages long and I tell them that they must learn to skim read and to pick out all the salient points. Very fast. Most of the time it is not necessary to read everything in detail, but of course it takes time to develop confidence in this skill'.

She would have no hesitation in recommending the law, and academic law in particular, as a career for women. 'It's a profession in which all the evidence shows that women can do very well indeed, because they bring a number of skills that are more commonly found in women than in men.' She advises women to be clear about setting the boundaries of what they will and will not do, as it is so easy for them to be taken for granted. 'In academic life if women offer to do a people-oriented job they will be expected to do it and to go on doing it as well as undertaking a heavy academic workload.'

It is still however important to be quite tough, and still more important to ensure that you have command of the area of the law that you are working in, 'because there is still always a risk that if you perform inadequately on a particular occasion you will be dismissed as the little girl who is not quite up to it, whereas a chap in the same situation will be excused because he has had a bad night'. The need to be tough and visibly ultra competent can however result in something she finds less attractive. 'Unfortunately I have noticed that some successful women of my generation have taken the view that they want to be as much like a man as anyone with two X chromosomes can be, and that's a great pity because they are denying the qualities that they can bring as women to academic life and legal practice.'

'Women are good communicators and can communicate in lots of different ways, whereas often men are superb lecturers but are not so good at dealing with small groups. And women have a greater understanding of what the limits of legal regulation are, and appreciate that rationality alone cannot always be decisive.' As an example she holds up Brenda Hale's judgment in *Parkhouse* v. *St James and Seagrove University NHS Hospital Trust* where Hale LJ questions the classification of the birth of an unplanned child as economic loss. 'The judge's reflection on the nature of pregnancy and childbirth and their impact on a woman could not have been written by a male member of the Court of Appeal.'

Fiona Bruce

Fiona Bruce is the founding principal of Fiona Bruce & Co in Warrington. She is also the 2003 National Winner of the Women into Business Awards.

Starting out

There is a street in Manchester called Peter Street, near the site of the Peterloo Massacre in 1819. Walking along this street in the late 1980s, Fiona Bruce, then almost 30, a successful partner in a central Manchester practice, with a new BMW, a city flat and a country cottage, stopped and said to herself, 'There's *got* to be more to life than this!'.

Born in Wick, Fiona was brought up in Scotland, England and Wales, which she left in 1975 after a very traditional education at Llandaff Girl's School in Cardiff to go to Manchester University. She decided to be a lawyer at the age of seven, despite having no legal connections in her family and no real idea of what it meant, so influenced had she been by watching *The Main Chance* on television. 'I wanted a smart office and two secretaries just like the actor John Stride, because he seemed to be providing a service which was working.' Although her school was supportive, 'their idea of career guidance was to tell you to apply to university to read your best subject. So I applied to read German. A few weeks after submitting my application I realised that this was ridiculous, because I had always wanted to be a lawyer. So I had to write to all the universities to whom I had applied, informing them that law was really my preferred option!'.

After Manchester University, where, despite working hard, she obtained a Lower Second ('my sister is the brilliant one; she got a First from Oxford') and the mandatory Law Society finals at Chester College of Law, she was faced with the challenge of finding a job. 'I had no contacts, and at the time (1979) there was little help from within the profession about obtaining articles. As I knew that I wanted to work in Manchester, I picked up the telephone directory

and literally worked my way through all the solicitors' firms starting at A. Seventy-six applications later and feeling a mite desperate, I finally managed to get articles with a firm whose name began
with W!'.

Fiona points out that articles in the 1970s were a very different
proposition from today. 'At our firm our trainees have individual
training plans to ensure that they cover a variety of fields of law
and gain genuine expertise in practical skills such as interviewing, time management and advocacy. We conduct regular workplace
reviews with trainees, and actively work with them to find the post-
qualification position which suits them, whether with our firm or
elsewhere. When I trained we were often just directed to do what
our firms required. I spent almost my entire articles doing residen-
tial conveyancing! Also, because there was little dialogue, I didn't
know until the very day I qualified, in 1981, whether I would have
a job with that firm at the end of my training period, and I didn't
have the courage to ask!'

Sudden elevation

The call to the room of the senior partner on the day she qualified
brought Fiona not just a job but huge additional responsibility.
Offered a partnership on the spot, she was 'too astonished to ask any
questions or for a written partnership agreement. I was so relieved
that I had a job! Looking back, I think it was because I was hardworking. I believe that most people who make a successful fist of what they
do, do so not because they are naturally brilliant but because they
work hard'.

Now Fiona would 'never advise anyone to go into partnership like I
did. You should always take plenty of time to reflect and consider if
that is really what you want to do. Your relationship with your partners is a profound one – not to be entered into without considerable
thought and discussion about your respective objectives, values and
priorities. But all too often we don't stand back and consider how we
can use our professional expertise to contribute to society, whether
on the bench, as a commercial City lawyer or at a community law
centre. We should encourage young lawyers not to allow "busy-
ness" to preclude reflection on how they can best use their skills and
gifts, only to find that 20 years later that they have been climbing a
ladder which has been leaning against the wrong wall!'. (For further
reading she recommends Rob Parsons (2002) *The Heart of Success*,
Hodder and Stoughton.)

When she qualified Fiona admits that her initial instinct was simply to survive! All seemed well for several years until, with much

disposable income and many long hours of work behind her, she was walking up Peter Street. Her thoughts led her to the radical idea of setting up a firm with a completely different culture. This was not a chance passing thought, but one which had gradually been growing as a result of her commitment to the Christian faith. She felt that there had to be a more meaningful purpose to her life than merely making money and enjoying what society traditionally regards as success. Her commitment to Christianity in her late twenties 'fundamentally changed the way I looked at life, and the way that I regarded the traditional law firm's structure. Too many firms were driven by the personal ambitions of the senior partner which produced fear in the staff, resentment from other partners, poor working relationships, little joy or genuine fulfilment in life, and a success defined merely materially'.

'So I decided to set up on my own! At the very least I would have a story to tell my grandchildren, should I ever have any!' Her vision was of a different kind of law firm, where staff would be genuinely appreciated and feel valued, where a real endeavour would be made to understand the stress felt by clients by 'standing in their shoes' and which would make a positive difference to the local community and where possible to society at a broader level.

As she had by then been several years in partnership, Fiona was advised to give her former firm six months' notice, in order to effect an orderly and amicable withdrawal. So one Friday evening in 1988 she explained to the senior partner that it was time for her to move on. The following Monday morning she returned to the office to find her partnership mandates with the bank had been cancelled and her desk had been totally cleared. This was when she realised that the absence of a written partnership agreement meant a total lack of business security. She was truly on her own.

New practice – new challenges

Fortunately, Fiona had two things in her favour; a good relationship with her bank and a loyal group of friends who had become personal clients over the years. At first her business was conducted from the front room of her flat whilst she trawled the streets of Manchester in what little spare time she had, looking for 'offices to let' signs.

In quick succession she got the smart *Main Chance* offices in Manchester, met her husband Richard, a chartered surveyor (whom she married in 1990), and was hit by a severe recession in the property market, on which the bulk of her legal work was based. 'The only way I could keep the law firm going was by working literally all hours – often from five in the morning until eleven at night'. With holidays rarely an option and profitability non-existent, Fiona and Richard even got married at Christmas so that their honeymoon could coincide with the office Christmas break.

At the same time, Fiona found herself fighting a series of prolonged and enormously stressful legal battles with her erstwhile firm resulting from the absence of a written partnership agreement. Determined to defend her professional reputation she finally won her case after over 10 years!

Over those years in the struggle to keep going she lost her Manchester office and her home, acquired a huge overdraft and faced the very real possibility of going bankrupt. 'I lay in bed one night really quite frightened. But as I lay there, I felt a presence in the room with me and that it was the presence of Jesus Christ, telling me that He had been with me when I started; He was with me now; and that He would be with me in the future. A tremendous peace came over me, and I have never worried about the financial side of my practice since.'

Just surviving meant moving her files from one makeshift arrangement to another, even at one point because of a BT muddle over telephone lines, conducting her business from a phone box at the end of the road, juggling her files and a pile of coins, as she tried to calculate just how long she could speak to her clients before the money ran out!

She deals cheerfully with the narration of what must have been substantial difficulties in her life during the early and mid-nineties. Following a major abdominal operation during her first pregnancy she gave birth to her son Samuel in 1993, 'conveniently at teatime on Maundy Thursday. I'm not proud of taking just one working day off! It's not what I want for any of our female staff in the future, but it was a matter of survival because I was the only net-contributing fee earner. I even found myself negotiating the wording of various clauses in a lease with another solicitor from Manchester on the other end of the phone while I was in the labour ward, because otherwise the deal would have been off'.

Samuel, who was born with a congenital club foot, needed several hospital visits a week for the first year of his life, a splint as a baby, night callipers until he was three and then had to spend time in a wheelchair after a corrective operation. 'His grandparents helped with those visits and were wonderful.' Fiona herself is a notorious coper; she minimises traumas such as these, and the difficulty of running her firm from her bed in the flat above the office, after being cut from the mangled wreckage of a high speed head-on collision where she had been a passenger. She plays down the suggestion of others that this period of incapacity changed the way she ran the firm; 'It was a little blip, and it would be wrong to make too much of it, because it was really what I learned from the principals of the Christian faith which informed the way I envisaged the firm.'

Investing in people

Fiona quickly realised that there is a big difference between being a good lawyer and running a business. 'When I set up in 1988 the Law Society did not provide the help it now does to assist solicitors to think through the practicalities of setting up alone. As business pressure mounted I realised that I needed external help, and I applied to the Enterprise Initiative Scheme, who sent a business adviser to help me draw up a proper business plan and to look at my business systems and procedures strategically. The adviser said quite bluntly, "You'll have to grow or die". Well, death didn't seem an attractive option to me at the time!'

To develop her management expertise Fiona signed up for the Investors in People scheme, but when she first saw their literature, speaking of 'cascading, empowerment, and induction', she thought 'What *is* all this about? And they say that lawyers speak in jargon!'. In a letter to someone she knew at the local Training and Enterprise Council (TEC) she said simply 'Dear Sue, re: Investors in People, Help! Fiona Bruce'. She will always be grateful to the TEC for the assistance which they gave her to develop her management skills, and in 1993 Fiona Bruce & Co became the first sole practitioner firm in the country to obtain the Investors in People Award.

Fiona Bruce & Co was also the first sole practitioner firm to be awarded the Lexcel Standard from the Law Society in 1998. 'I think we are all very good at criticising the Law Society, but Lexcel is actually a highly effective basis for good law firm management. Both the Lexcel and law management sections of the Law Society are immensely helpful, in very practical ways, to solicitors wanting to develop management skills'.

1993 was a turning point for the business, when her father gave her the deposit for a large former doctors' surgery and her husband Richard gave up his job to join the firm as its practice development manager. The renamed 'Justice House' was split into offices downstairs and a flat upstairs for Fiona and Richard, except that 'the staff tea and coffee-making area was our kitchen'.

From this base she was able to develop her vision of what a legal firm should be, concentrating on client care and staff care and drawing its business from, and being part of, the local community. By the mid-nineties the extreme financial pressures had receded, and Fiona could begin to 'spread the load' amongst her colleagues. Today in 2003, Fiona Bruce & Co is one of the foremost Warrington law firms with some 30 staff including over 10 solicitors, all specialising in their own chosen fields.

Fiona says that it makes good business sense to make clients feel that you value them and empathise with the stresses they are under. Richard endeavours to speak to or see every new client, and 'makes them feel special and welcome. He tries to find the right lawyer to deal with their problems, even if it means recommending someone to a firm other than ours'. He has, according to Fiona, a number of aphorisms, which although they are truisms, make for sound business practice, such as 'it's nice to be important, but its important to be nice', 'it's not what you say, but how you say it', and 'clients don't care how much you know until they know how much you care'.

Women solicitors and flexible working

Her firm is not an all female one; indeed the majority of its qualified solicitors are men, 'although that is just how it has worked out'. She is a firm believer in trying to make it possible for women to continue their careers whilst giving the right amount of time to their families, particularly as children grow up, and operates flexitime for over half her staff. 'Your career goes on for a long time' she says, 'but you only have a few precious years to spend with your children.' One of her staff is a returner who having not office-worked for a decade before joining her, worked only school hours for the first three months, and another is a young female solicitor gradually working up from two days a week to five at her own pace after extended maternity leave. Fiona says thoughtfully that if one of her male staff made a sound case for similar treatment she would be sympathetic; indeed the firm's consultant solicitor works half the week from home and half from the office as a prelude to retirement.

Perhaps her concern for family friendly policies is informed by her own experiences which were in stark contrast to the more amiable arrangements she describes above. Given the way that her career has developed it is not surprising that she feels that she has never encountered any discrimination because she is a woman; one feels that it would be a brave man who would take on this smiling dynamo, but what she wants to change even further is the profession's general attitude to flexible working. She feels there are still too many firms, in the City in particular, 'who have focused too much on an excessive bottom line and do not understand how much human capital they are devaluing'.

Despite this last comment women should consider their responsibilities in their relationships with employers before asserting their rights. 'We are so quick in society nowadays to claim our rights, without considering that we have responsibilities too. Flexible arrangements must work for the firm as well as the staff member – otherwise firms will go out of business. But employers who listen to their staff, who take their views into account when making decisions will ultimately have a better run firm, because staff can see things from a perspective that partners cannot. Everyone should be treated with equal courtesy from the cleaner to the consultant solicitor. You should be kind to your staff and support them when they have problems.'

She strongly advises young women not to sacrifice their marriages and family life to their careers. 'There are hundreds of clients out there who can and will find another solicitor if you are not available, but a child has only one mother and no one can take your place as that child's mother.' Fiona has deliberately tried not to sacrifice her children to the business; she picks up her two sons, Samuel, now ten, and Daniel, seven, from school most days, helps with their music lessons at their countryside home and insists (unless in dire emergency) that her weekends with them are sacrosanct.

Setting up a law firm today – can it be done?

'Everyone says that starting your own practice now can't be done, but my view is that if you really have an intense desire to do it, if there is a way you want to work, a particular service you want to give, or a niche you can fill – then go for it! But don't just do it to make money – there are far easier ways to make a living. It is vital to import business expertise early and to write a professional business plan. You should also ensure that your family is behind you, because it's going to take up a lot of your time and energy, and probably theirs too. And when you start up, cut your coat according to your cloth – it's far better to survive then to go under driving a Porsche Carerra!'

Recruitment must be done 'with intense care, because you simply can't afford to make mistakes. Recruit to fill gaps in your own expertise, and don't be afraid to take on lawyers more experienced or brilliant than yourself. Involve your staff in your business, because poor communication quickly disengages and disenfranchises staff and reduces their effectiveness. You need to constantly encourage, continuously retrain, and facilitate sharing professional know-how. It surprises me how many solicitors within firms still operate as isolated units, when working together improves productivity and

reduces stress. We have a framed sign on the wall in our firm –
"TEAM stands for Together Everyone Achieves More!" Whatever
you do for clients, do it well. Listen to them rather than talk at them
all the time. Delegate as much as you can – including management
– and don't take on too much work. Although I'm only just beginning to get hold of that latter concept myself!'.

What makes a good lawyer?

Fiona's response to this question is unusual but consistent with her
own core values. 'Obviously professional expertise and competence
are prerequisites. But more than that you need to ask yourself "What
is life all about for me?" Without working that out and without a
cohesive set of values, you will tend to make erratic decisions and
may well regret them in the long run.' Students, she thinks, often
acquire a very one dimensional image of life in the law, that it is
about money and status and city success, whereas what we should
be esteeming is the effectiveness of our service to society. With so
much legal talent appearing to be channelled towards highly paid
commercial firms, many lawyers are getting to about 40 (Fiona is 46)
only to feel burned out. 'We are in danger of creating a profession
that is reliant on the vigour of youth and has cast aside the wisdom
of age. The tragedy is that going down that route results in a lot of
damaged relationships with partners and children, impaired health,
and the realisation of wasted time.'

Good lawyers not only ask 'What positive difference could I make?'
but find ways to make their careers last so that they are continuously, and indeed increasingly, effective to the end of it. Working
long hours was for Fiona an initial business necessity, but as soon as
possible she chose to change her working patterns. Although solicitors often feel trapped in the long-hours culture, Fiona feels many
could choose to change if they set their minds to it, perhaps the first
step to changing working patterns and priorities across the profession and even altering the public image of the profession itself.

To that end enlightened law firm management has a positive responsibility to ensure that older solicitors feel valued and encouraged to
use their hard-won experience for the benefit of the profession as a
whole – perhaps by scaling down their client contact/fee earning
time, and instead devoting a proportion of their week to mentoring
younger lawyers, a policy she has instituted in her own firm.

'Fundamental qualities such as integrity, honesty, commitment and
a willingness to apologise if we get things wrong, should all be part
of a lawyer's make up, as well as trying to see the other person's

point of view. We must try to communicate fully with clients, in plain English, and not leave them in the dark about procedure when they are under stress. Some of us would be better solicitors if we were a little less pompous and put ourselves in the shoes of our clients.' These latter remarks indicate how much she has absorbed from herself being a client at the sharp end of litigation, once leaving a solicitor's letter to her unopened for two days because she could not face the contents.

Wider responsibilities

Fiona wants her firm now to be an example of an efficiently functioning law firm, 'where staff and clients are valued, service is good and the profession's reputation is enhanced as a result'. To make an impact on the community in its widest sense she gives all her staff, not just the qualified solicitors, opportunities to make a difference. Solicitors from her firm working on a rota basis, have provided a free legal advice clinic in a church hall in an area of Warrington with no CAB every Monday morning for the past 10 years. Many firms engage in such pro bono work, but how many would also give three weeks' paid leave to a solicitor to help build a school in Ecuador, or organise shipments of toys, shoes and food to Romania?

'I want my staff to be well remunerated, to have time for their families, and to fulfil their individual potential in life. I also feel that lawyers have a tremendous, often untapped, potential for good, partly because we can see what legislative changes are likely to happen and can consider the impact on society before they are enacted.' She has written recently in her local newspaper column about proposed changes in the law classifying cannabis. Because she considers that this is sending out the wrong message to a younger generation as cannabis use fractures family life and damages the health of children, she has with others made representations to Parliament, as 'It's not just about practising the law but influencing it too. Hopefully, for good'.

Lawyers can also see where injustices need rectifying. One of her clients, who had six children, was left a widow by her husband who had died without making a will. The statutory provisions on intestacy meant that she was entitled to only £125,000 plus a life interest in half of the remainder of his estate. Unfortunately in this case, much of the value of the estate was tied up in the family home and a voluntary variation from these provisions proved difficult to achieve. Fiona took up the issue through her local law society and prepared an early day motion for her MP which was presented to Parliament. As a result this regulation is being reviewed.

The Women into Business Award

Fiona was nominated for the Women into Business Award by her bank, the Royal Bank of Scotland. The judges of the national competition were equally impressed by her firm's businesslike professionalism, its ethical outlook and its commitment to making a difference to their local community and beyond. However Fiona is the first to acknowledge that no working environment is perfect; 'There is no such thing as the ideal law firm. We are all on a continuous learning curve.'

Every staff member at her firm has an individual annual action plan, incorporating their aspirations, personal development and training needs and agreed objectives. Fiona now sees her role as primarily to serve and facilitate others so that they in turn can do a really good job for clients. 'I'm endeavouring to follow what is really a biblical model of leadership, and I try to remember that everyone flourishes best on a ratio of about 95 per cent encouragement to 5 per cent constructive criticism.'

If by chance someone is in the wrong role, 'we need to make adjustments. We talk. We listen. We review roles. We retrain, because every member of the team needs to understand the importance of their role in our vision for the business and should have a real opportunity to help to make that vision a reality'. Much of her firm's success is attributable to 'making sure that the right-shaped pegs are in the right-shaped holes'.

During the interview Fiona's hands have been constantly at work, 'I am always doodling'. Constantly drawing diagrams to clarify her words. Most of them involve directional arrows rather than bounded circles. She has also made copious notes prior to the interview 'to make the best use of our time and to stop me waffling'. What is clear is that she has a very laterally thinking mind, constantly analysing and working towards solutions, exactly the sort of mind, although she does not claim this for herself, which would make her an invaluable resource for clients.

Dame Elizabeth Butler-Sloss

Dame Elizabeth Butler-Sloss was the first woman to become a Court of Appeal judge. As President of the Family Division she was appointed to the highest office ever attained by a woman in the English legal system.

Background

Elizabeth Butler-Sloss should in theory be exactly the sort of judge that people consider out of touch with the general population, and yet ensconced in the Gothic splendour of the Royal Courts of Justice in the Strand, behind the necessary gates and security of the modern courts system, she is the humane rather than the aloof face of the law.

Her family appears to be either legal or thespian. Her grandfather was a Norwich solicitor, who became Under Sheriff of Norwich, and her father, Sir Cecil Havers, after a spell as a solicitor in Norfolk 'took the very brave step of leaving Norfolk for London to become the pupil of the great Pat Hastings', and a career at the Bar which led to his eventual appointment as a High Court judge. Her elder brother Michael became a QC, Attorney General and briefly the Lord Chancellor, her husband is a retired judge, her nephew is a QC, while her daughter, formerly a partner in a City firm, is now a human rights consultant to the House of Commons.

On the other hand her mother was a talented amateur painter who would have been 'a professional artist had she not married my father at such a young age', her nephew Nigel is a well-known actor, her younger son writes for the theatre and the other is a producer in Los Angeles. Truly the close linkage that is often made between the Bar and the stage is very clear in the Havers family. 'Barristers are more likely to want to be out there in the limelight than solicitors. Both professions need a lot of self-confidence and a bit of brashness.'

But what of Dame Elizabeth herself? She was the youngest of four children; of her three elder brothers, only one of them, Michael, also went into the law. She considers that her parents, although both born in the 19th century, were 'very enlightened. Their view was that women should have exactly the same rights as men, so that when I said that I wanted to go to boarding school after the war at the age of 12 just like my brothers, that was fine, and when I said that I wanted to go to the Bar just like my brother Michael, that was fine as well. My father said that it would be difficult for me because I was a woman, but that he would support me'.

Becoming a barrister

Dame Elizabeth had decided fairly early on that she wanted to be a lawyer and from that ambition 'I never wavered'. She visited court with her father, by whom she felt influenced but never directed, but she was probably influenced just as much by her brother's tales of studying law at Cambridge. Dame Elizabeth is very unusual in reaching such high judicial office without having attended university. Having attained the Higher School Certificate at the age of 16 (the equivalent of today's A Levels), she 'tried for Cambridge, but I was not very interested, and so I did not get in. I was much more interested in going to Switzerland to study in Lausanne'.

Unfortunately when she came home after her first year in Switzerland it was to find that her mother was very seriously ill, and that she was expected to take charge of the household. 'I couldn't cook, but I had to decide the meals with my old nanny who had taken on the role of housekeeper to the family, and generally be in charge.' At the same time she embarked on a nine month secretarial course. 'I was so bad at it that the nice man who employed me very briefly was completely relieved to learn that I was going to the Bar as he said that I would never be able to earn my living as a secretary.'

So with no university background and indifferent typing skills she was called to the Bar at the age of 21 to find herself one of only 60 women among 2,000 barristers. 'None of us had any work, and none of us had any money.' Being a judge's daughter had helped in securing chambers, 'everyone knew who I was, and everyone knew my brother, but initially I did not get any work because solicitors were unwilling to brief a woman'. One Cambridge solicitor seeking a barrister to represent his client in an undefended divorce case and told that Miss Havers was available, asked her clerk, 'Haven't you got anyone who is a man? Even a pupil?'.

Parliament and the law

Following in the footsteps of her father who had been a founder member of the Inns of Court Conservative and Unionist Party, Dame Elizabeth had a brief flirtation with another profession where declamatory skills are useful, standing as the Conservative candidate for Vauxhall. As a keen Young Conservative she had previously been 'sent out to rally the troops in South London before the London County Council elections', then as the Chairman of the Vauxhall Young Conservatives, she stood unsuccessfully as the Conservative candidate for the LCC elections. In 1959 the year after she married another barrister, Joseph Butler-Sloss, she was asked to stand as parliamentary candidate for that seat. She was well aware that this was a hopeless challenge for the seat was a Labour stronghold held by George Strauss. Heavily pregnant she lost the election, gained a daughter a week later and gave up all future ideas of standing for Parliament. She noted that one of the most persistent questions during her campaign was what she would do in Parliament if she had a young baby.

'After the election I decided that my marriage, my baby and the Bar were more important to me than politics.' This bald statement needs to be construed carefully, for what she is saying is not that she had thought of substituting the House of Commons for the Bar, but whether she could take it on in addition to the Bar, just as her brother had done. Although she has never regretted her decision, she has felt at times when walking across corridors in the Houses of Parliament that this is to be in the centre of power, a concept which is clearly attractive to her. But then she reflects that even those who reach high governmental office will find that that this power is 'ephemeral' and subject to withdrawal in a way that judicial office is not.

While the independence of the judiciary needs to be maintained strong lines of communication between the Government and the judiciary are essential. She is visited frequently by Harriet Harman, the Solicitor General, to discuss the 'workability' of government legislative proposals relating to family law, because the implications of a particular policy might not always be immediately obvious.

Life as a young barrister

Success at the Bar did not come immediately, and she has sensible advice for young women starting out now, although she frequently states that any advice that she has to give might equally be considered by young men. To the young barrister she has two astute injunctions. 'Don't give up. And make yourself useful.'

The first injunction she considers more relevant to the past, when women could be bypassed by solicitors and clerks, but the second is certainly still sound advice. Although her particular chambers specialised in divorce work, they also had 'an extensive sub-interest in buses and lorries, which in those days all needed licences'. Her chambers acted mostly for businesses whose applications for more extensive licences had gone to enquiry. Initially she was given those enquiries which were too awkward for the more senior people in chambers to attend, gradually she built up her own reputation and client base, but writing a book on the topic together with a Bristol solicitor 'with my name on the cover gave me a tremendous marketing tool, as it meant that all the tribunal chairmen knew who I was'.

On one occasion she travelled to Falmouth to represent a client who was very dubious about her ability to win his case; he was normally represented by a Bristol solicitor who thought that the distance was too far to travel. Accompanied by the client and his even more dubious friends, who were opposing his application 'because it was all a big game you see', Dame Elizabeth entered the court to be greeted by the Chairman, 'Ah good morning, Miss Havers, what a great pleasure to see you again'. The case was won, much to the surprise of the client and his friends who averred that they 'did not think that a bloody woman would get the licence for you'.

Leaving the Bar

Her fortunate elevation to the judiciary coincided with a change in the law of lorry licensing which would have rendered her particular expertise almost useless. Dame Elizabeth speaks of 'leaving the Bar' as though a great episode of her life had come to an end, almost as though she were speaking of leaving one country for another, and she describes the decision-making process in detail because it illustrates her analysis of what was important to her. 'And even when you think that you are giving some future possibility up for altruistic reasons that possibility may not be completely dead.'

At the age of 21 she had been called to the Bar and went straight into practice. 'In those days you could be in court on day one and I was in fact in court on day two. I learned on the job and I learned on the clients.' At the age of 24 she had married another barrister, six years her senior who 'fortunately had more money than I had', and at the age of 25 she had her first child, a daughter. By 1967 her family totalled three children (two boys and a girl) and she had 'quite a good practice. It's my view and it's the view of most women barristers with whom I have discussed this that having children will undoubtedly change the nature of your practice but you will go forward'.

But three years later she was beginning to find that the demands of her family and the travelling required by her 'lorry practice' were taking their toll, even with a full-time nanny for the children and a husband whose chambers were conveniently next door to their flat in King's Bench Walk. 'My father who was about to retire was getting worried and my husband was getting worried about the amount of time that I was spending away from home and the amount of energy that was not being devoted to the children.'

The potential diminution of her practice and her physical exhaustion coincided with a growing concern about the number of women in the judiciary. Just about the time when Elizabeth Lane had been appointed as a High Court judge, Dame Elizabeth was summoned by the President of the Family Division, and 'in this very room' was asked to become a Registrar in the Divorce Registry. 'They felt that it was time to appoint a married woman with children to the position if at all possible. I said that I was very flattered, but thought that I was a bit young at 36 for this position. The President then told me that he had already told the Lord Chancellor that I was 46.' Fortunately the Lord Chancellor was not deterred by this additional information!

Still uncertain she consulted her whole family. Her father, who had always been her best mentor told her that 'I think that you must take it, because you will have certainty of income, continuity in your life and your children will know where you are, but you will have to give up all thought of one day becoming a High Court judge. You have a duty to your husband and family to do it'. Her husband was equally positive. 'I'm not going to stop you having our own private practice at the Bar, but I'd love you to take it for the sake of the children.'

She took up the appointment in 1970 having replied affirmatively to her 10-year-old daughter's question, 'Does that mean we shall know where you are, Mummy?'. Nine years later, when she was promoted to the ranks of High Court judges, the position that she thought that she would never attain, her daughter, now 19 asked her, 'Does that mean we shall not know where you are now, Mummy?' because it meant that she would once again be travelling the country dispensing justice.

To the High Court

Her promotion out of what she terms 'a very nice little backwater job' in the late 1970s caused quite a stir. It was unheard of for registrars to become High Court judges; despite the high regard in which she was held by family lawyers because of her courtesy and sound judgment, her appointment was regarded by some as 'simply amazing', and there was much press comment. 'There was,' she explains, 'a serious shortage of women with the requisite experience and age available to become High Court judges. I am convinced that I got the position because I was female. This is not to say that I wasn't very good at the registry, but there was a serious shortage of women and the new government of Mrs Thatcher with Lord Hailsham as Lord Chancellor was very keen to appoint women. So they did a bit of lateral thinking and plucked me out from the registry. They wouldn't have had to do any lateral thinking if they had been looking for a man to fill the post.'

There is an interesting dichotomy in her analysis of the position of women at the Bar and the position of professional women who are mothers. She considers that in many ways it is more difficult now to be at the Bar because of the hours required and the intensity of the profession. On the other hand it is much more acceptable now to be a working mother; the workability of the position now depends entirely on the mother's relationship with her partner and has very little to do with the general expectation of the rest of society. However, even with the best possible and most helpful partner many women feel an almost proprietorial relationship towards their children and find it very difficult to pursue a career when the children are young.

She observes, and obviously finds it sad, that so many young women feel that they must give up their legal careers just when they have begun to become interesting and profitable. In her early days the majority of women did not have huge practices. Now 'if you make the grade you are very busy early on', with pressure from clerks to maximise profits.

'This is not strictly a mother problem. It is a parental problem.' As a judge who has had to deliver many difficult decisions in family law cases she is acutely aware of the difficulties. 'There is a distinct lack of parenting by the middle classes where both parents have good jobs. It's not their fault. It's the fault of the system, and we need to change the culture so that being a parent is seen as being as important as having a good job.' At the Bar 'if you want to become a silk, etc. you have to go down a well-trodden road of over-work and long hours. This should not be seen as a female problem. It should be seen as a parent problem. We are too concerned about work, and should be more concerned about the needs of the family. The City is particularly bad for this.'

She herself was extremely fortunate in her physical circumstances. She and her husband still live in the Temple apartment in which they brought up their children; once she had eschewed the barrister's life on the road, she was able to settle down to a comfortable routine which enabled her to rise from court to go home for tea and the *Magic Roundabout* with the children before settling down again to her papers for the rest of the evening. It was a time which obviously brought her close to her daughter who she considers has 'influenced me more than I have her'.

This may seem a strange statement for one of the most important judges in the land to make, but her daughter, having given up a West End partnership is now a human rights consultant to the House of Commons. 'She has influenced me just as much in my thinking about human rights as I have influenced her,' she says proudly. Clearly her family lives the law.

The attractions of the Bar

Despite these apparent criticisms Dame Elizabeth would still recommend young women to go into the law and into the Bar if they have the qualities required, because the Bar gives what the solicitors' profession cannot give, and that is self-employment. 'Even as a partner, you are still really "employed". I admit that as a barrister you are at the beck and call of the clerk or practice manager, but you are really only answerable to yourself, and your practice and your future are not owned by anyone. You will be helped along the road, but you will stand or fall by your own abilities.'

What clearly fascinates her is advocacy. Very early on in her career she decided that to make an impact she would have to change the timbre of her voice which was 'very high pitched. I worked on that as much as I have worked on anything in order to get it deeper. I also spoke far too fast and I have had to learn to speak much more slowly to make myself understood'. Perhaps there was a latent acting ability but the voice that now delivers judgments and talks with interest in chambers is a deep and well modulated testament to an unexpressed assumption in her life that many things are possible if you try hard enough. 'But advocacy is important in so many aspects of life. It is just as important in the boardroom and in meetings, in government and at conferences to be able to marshall your facts, to order them and to put your point of view in a reasoned way.'

She is clear about the other attributes required in a good barrister. 'First of all you must have stamina. And you must have resilience to get over the knocks and disappointments especially when you are younger and just starting out.' She was clearly not fazed by the solicitor who asked for a pupil rather than a qualified woman, or by the client who did not think that 'a bloody woman' could get the licence that he wanted. 'And you must be quick. Except at the Chancery Bar it's almost more important to be able to think on your feet than to be a good lawyer, especially for knockabout criminal, family and straightforward litigation work. And you must be able to put together an argument that will convince the judge and the jury.'

Being a judge

The attributes required in a good judge move on from there. Speed reading is a sine qua non. 'I read very fast but I read everything, but then if I am giving the lead judgment particularly I go back and read with a great deal more care.' The utmost concentration that she gives to this aspect of her work means that she does not read anything 'at all difficult during term-time. P D James perhaps and Patrick O'Brien, but certainly not that chap who wrote about things past, Marcel Proust, which I read as a student and I promise myself that I shall read again when I retire'.

'And there are a lot of qualities that I don't have. Such as patience. Patience is very important. An enormous amount of common sense and good sound judgment of people. That's not so important in the criminal side, that's rather different, because your view of people is subject to the over-riding decision making powers of the jury, although you do have the opportunity to direct them, your role comes later when you have to decide on the appropriate punish-ment. It's different in the civil and family courts when you are assessing credibility and whom you should believe.'

Being an Appeal Court judge is again different. 'Once a judge has made a decision based on character judgment and assessment of the facts it is very difficult for the Court of Appeal to intervene except of course on points of law.' In this connection she remembers one of her own early decisions as a High Court judge. The father in custody proceedings was a complex and manipulative man and the mother was an inadequate young woman who was devoted to the child. 'I agonised about my decision as it seemed that whatever conclusion I came to could not be the right one. In the end I set out all the pros and cons in my judgment, and noted that although I had to come to a decision, whatever I decided would in some respects be wrong. I granted custody to the mother as I felt that that would be the least detrimental alternative, but of course I had given the father clear grounds to appeal, which he duly did. The Court of Appeal upheld my decision, but told me firmly that I must never again say that my decision was wrong.'

Obviously a really good knowledge of the law is required, but that 'is not the first requisite. You don't have to be an erudite lawyer to be a trial judge, unless of course you are sitting in Chancery. But you do need a reasonably quick mind and sufficient diligence to be able to pick out the important points and to research them if necessary'. As far as custody cases are concerned, and she has had many, 'you have to have a grasp of basic legal principle and an ability to assess the bona fides and character of the mother and father, to receive information from them and to assess it. And finally in any case you have to have a fairly tidy mind, because at the end of the day you have to give a coherent judgment. And you have to be able to make decisions'.

Decision making

Decision making is not easy. Lawyers are notorious for their 'on the one hand this, on the other hand that' stance. She points out that some people may be excellent lawyers, but may still find taking decisions desperately difficult. When writing a judgment she often finds that 95 per cent of the judgment is clear before she writes it, but that the final five per cent will only emerge when the 95 per cent has been written. And that five per cent is the decision itself, the few words that will decide the immediate and future consequences for those who have come to court for judgment.

It is an onerous challenge and one which she has learned to deal with in the same way that women have learned to cope with the process of childbirth; at the time it is all-absorbing, but once over it must be forgotten. It is another skill that judges must learn, especially in the family courts because 'what you are dealing with is human misery'. On the other hand as well as acquiring a certain degree of self-protective detachment, 'you must feel for people in order to work out what is best for their lives. If you are dealing with the misery of others, you must try to understand where they are coming from and what makes them tick'.

Many of the cases that come before her are inevitably the subject of much media comment and speculation because they deal with life and death situations concerning the desirability or otherwise of the giving or withholding of medical treatment. With experience 'understanding the medical part becomes easier, although every case will deal with an aspect of medical care that I will not have encountered before. It is terribly interesting and at times I feel that I know more about certain treatments than 90 per cent of the medical profession'.

It is one of these cases, the case of *Miss B* which displays most poignantly the difficult and sometimes agonising position in which the President of the Family Division can find herself. *Miss B* was someone who despite a very difficult upbringing had worked hard and by force of character had realised a position as a social worker where she felt that she was making a difference to her community, when because of a blood vessel bursting in her neck she was rendered quadraplegic. She asked that treatment be withheld as she had no quality of life and there was no possibility of rehabilitation.

Dame Elizabeth went to the hospital to take Miss B's evidence on commission in a private room surrounded by lawyers representing all parties. She was moved by Miss B's situation and her courage, 'because what this clearly intelligent woman wanted was to be taken seriously and not to be treated as a child because she had total inability to move'. The hospital authorities on the other hand who were inexperienced in giving the sort of palliative care that hospices provide 'could not bring themselves to the idea that she might want to die. I agreed with her that paraplegics have a right to be taken seriously but although I granted her wish to be permitted to refuse treatment, I unusually put in my judgment that I hoped that she would reconsider the decision that she could now make because I felt that she had so much to give'.

'So much to give' may seem a strange phrase to use in these circumstances, but it illuminates Dame Elizabeth's feelings towards those whose lives she has been authorised to direct. 'I felt that she had a lot to offer to people in her situation by her example, by forcing the hospital and those in authority to take her seriously.' This was a case that has remained with her, which defies the protective mechanism which usually permits her to give a judgment and then move on to the next one.

What is ahead?

And what of the future for the most senior woman in the English judiciary? She could if she wished continue as a judge until she is 75 because she was appointed under 'the old system'. but it is probably unlikely that she would do so. She has five grandchildren and numerous great-nieces and nephews that she would like to see more of, there is travel to do with her husband 'before we get too old, and a great deal of reading that I still want to do. But I haven't done five years as president yet. And then', because there is always a next step with someone of Dame Elizabeth's energy and understanding, 'I have charitable projects I'd like to get involved in, particularly with children'.

Eileen Carroll

Eileen Carroll was a commercial litigation partner in two London law firms before she became the Deputy Chief Executive of the Centre for Effective Dispute Resolution of which she was a co-founder in 1989.

Irish ambition

Eileen Carroll is fond of quoting John Lennon, 'Life is what happens to you when you're busy making other plans', but her career is in fact an example of how a vision can gradually evolve and inform the direction that life can take.

Asked if her father was influential in her choice of career, she replied without hesitation, 'Not as much as my mother was. She was a nurse who did not want to spend her life as a private nurse as her Welsh aunt wanted, so she set up her own business running nursing homes for the elderly. She was filled with the ambition that her children would have the educational opportunities that she and my father had not had'.

Eileen is extraordinarily proud of her mother, who was 'full of immigrant energy. Both my parents came from Irish farming communities where the land went to the eldest son and the other members of the family just had to make their own way. My mother's business was very successful, and I don't mean just financially although it was that as well, because she was able to send us all to private schools, but in the quality of care that she provided for the elderly in her nursing homes. My brother, sister and I wanted for nothing but we were expected to work hard during the holidays reading to the old people and playing cards with them. My mother instilled in me a belief that you must work hard and that you must also respect other people, and that although you could have privileges, there was also a price to pay'.

If the price is an ability to work hard towards a goal that you believe in, then it was perhaps not such a severe one. Eileen refers several times to 'the very strong work ethic that runs through our family'. It was her mother's belief in the virtue of hard work and in what might be termed social progress that influenced Eileen towards the law. 'My mother wanted me to have a profession, either medicine or the law, and I think that like lots of young people I eventually chose the law and rejected medicine because my mother so strongly wanted me to become a doctor.'

Choosing law

At her strict convent school, Eileen had shown an early penchant for taking on authority. Her headmistress had a rigid 'hemlines on the knee policy', and one day Eileen together with some of her peer group were 'called out for having hemlines that were too high. In fact my hem was definitely on the knee and I'm convinced to this day that what she was objecting to was the fashionable Nehru collar and zip up style of the dress. In any event she was quite rude, and I stood up to her and told her that she could be sued for slander. I took her on because I thought that she was being unfair to a whole group of girls. Anyway I carried on wearing the dress, and we still exchange Christmas cards many years on'.

This seems typical. Eileen has that Irish interest in other people combined with a rush of words and a willingness to do battle prob-ably born out of centuries of a sense of oppression by another race – although that is a sentiment that she never voices. She will stand for no nonsense, and then afterwards, battle done, that will be it. It is hard to imagine her dwelling on resentments because that would prevent her getting on with the next great thing.

In fact the final rejection of medicine came quite late, because Eileen had gone as far as to choose scientific A levels with the intention of training as a doctor. By the time that she decided that she might pre-fer law, she thought erroneously that her scientific background would disqualify her from reading law at university. In 1972, after having rejected the idea of medicine and also a place to read bio-chemistry at Kings College London, she went to work for the British Sulphur Group, a small international consultancy in Victoria, where as assistant to a dynamic female geologist she spent a happy and productive two years 'learning about the world of work', before mov-ing to Fontainebleau and Paris to work as an au pair for a year for a model agency proprietor, mixing with models and Formula One rac-ing drivers, 'all heady stuff for a young woman from New Malden'.

By the time that she set off for the University of Kent to read law she was 21 and had learned a great deal about the difference between work and school, and that 'I was not going to pass up the opportunity of going to university'.

Eileen would now recommend a similar experience to young people, and also to her own 10-year-old daughter, 'although I would like her to make her own decisions'. When she arrived at Kent, chosen for its broader curriculum, its collegiate system and a certain leftish political bias, she had 'learned about life, built up my confidence and self-esteem, had improved my French, had a car and a job to go back to (at the British Sulphur Group) every vacation'. She feels that this is now particularly important with the present Government's increasing emphasis on tuition fees for students. 'Young people going to university now have to think carefully about whether they want to make that financial investment in their future, particularly as so many young people go to university and leave without any idea of what they are going to do next.'

University

At Kent Eileen did not find her natural peer group among her fellow English students arriving straight from school but with the American students studying there as the result of a long-established exchange programme with Californian universities. She naturally gravitated towards the American students who were older and not only had 'three wonderful years', at Kent but was able to build up a network of future professional relationships with lawyers in New York, California and Washington, invaluable when much later she had developed an interest in American mediation practices.

Again her willingness to court controversy on the side of what she felt was right came in useful. The students on her constitutional law course were caught in the crossfire between two of their lecturers, both brilliant but with diametrically opposed views on their subject. It was Eileen who put the students' concerns to the more senior of the two, pointing out that 'it's our futures that are at stake', and thus facilitating an examination paper truce. As a result of this she 'gained a lot of respect. But that was not my prime motivation, my personal benefit was not on the agenda, it's just that if something needs to be done, I'm fairly fearless. I believe that you should not sit on the fence and complain. You should put up or shut up'.

At Kent she also had her first taste of practical law at the university's law clinic, where she realised that she was not cut out as she had thought for 'social law'. Eileen had succeeded in obtaining an ouster order against the husband of a battered wife, 'I was rather proud of myself, but when I came back after the Christmas vac it was to find that they had made up and he had moved back in. That was the beginning of my disillusionment with the social side of law, because it seemed to me that we were not able to prevent any future abuse'.

Given the way that Eileen's career subsequently developed that may seem a strange conclusion, but perhaps it is just that she prefers the apparent finality of commercial decisions to the messiness of personal law.

Articles

Obtaining a training contract in the early 1980s recession was not easy. She wrote to firms all over London, hours and hours of hand-written letters before she eventually secured a contract with the help of an old family friend. 'Interestingly I was not informed about the difference between the City and smaller West End firms when I did my articles, because universities other than Oxford and Cambridge were not sophisticated in those days in giving careers advice to their students.'

As it turned out 'my articles were just what I needed'. The firm had not told her in advance that the solicitor with whom she would be sharing a room for her first six months was blind; after recovering from the initial shock she found this the best experience that she could have desired. She was in effect his eyes, reading everything to him, textbooks and long leases, so that far from the silent and distant supervision suffered by many trainees she was involved from minute to minute in all her supervisor's matters. Her only frisson of anxiety came when he went on holiday for three weeks leaving her in charge of his work and his clients.

Although it was a small firm in which she was 'thrown in at the deep end, we had some incredible clients and issues. It was amazing experience for a young articled clerk. We acted for Bob Hoskins in his dispute with the potential purchasers of *The Long Good Friday* who were proposing to dub his voice for the film's American release (he was saved by a takeover by Handmade Films) in the course of which I took affidavits from Sir Alec Guinness and Helen Mirren and went to the opening night in the West End'.

More significantly the firm also had a strong personal injury practice, which was involved in taking cases to the Court of Appeal. Eileen recalls 'seeing stacks and stacks of green files full of acres of correspondence going backwards and forwards over many months and thinking where was it all going to end, and how much was it costing the client. There was all this hot air and then often it went to settlement at the door of the court, where under pressure there was a quick fast approval and a deal was done'. She confesses that she has 'never enjoyed the long drawn out procedural stuff'.

Qualified in 1981 she felt that she 'needed one more overseas trip before settling down'. By this time she had acquired her own home with the help of her parents and taken in a tenant, and had saved enough money to go off for six months to North and South America visiting friends and to the Caribbean 'hanging out in T-shirts and shorts, snorkelling and diving with sharks off Belize. Of course it was a risk because I did not know what I was coming back to. I had to face up to the reality of finding a job, but on my return I was lucky that my old firm wanted someone on a short term contract to handle a case that was going to the Court of Appeal'.

From assistant to partner

Her first real post-qualification job was at Turner Peacock (later Turner Kenneth Brown). Interviewed by them and by Linklaters she was offered the job by Turner Peacock and a second interview by Linklaters. She chose immediate certainty but in retrospect wonders whether that was in the event the correct choice as she much later discovered that the litigation partner with whom she might have worked at Linklaters took the view that the first obligation of his lawyers was to get the claim settled with recourse to the courts being very much an option of last choice. It is the only note of retrospective regret that she evinces in the whole interview but perhaps this has less to do with any loss of perceived benefit to herself than with a possible postponement of a vision that would be helpful to others.

'In any event,' she opines from her office in London's Docklands, 'Turner Peacock was probably the right firm at the time because it was adventurous and forward looking'. She was very much left to her own devices on her first case, a complex matter involving oppression of minority shareholders 'and remember that I had had no corporate experience during articles. Anyway I worked 12 hour days to ensure that I was up to speed, and with the help of Denis Levy QC, a very kind silk, I managed to get the case settled'. Libel work for Koo Stark, Prince Andrew's then girlfriend, work for Granada Television, representing clients in Singapore, she gobbled up everything that came her way in a 'quite small litigation department with all sorts of corporate clients'.

She insisted on travelling to Singapore to see her Singapore clients at their request, something not usually done by assistants. This was a slight shock to the partners but the clients wanted a young woman representing them against Shell in an action that required her to travel to Brunei and Hong Kong as well taking affidavits. She developed an international practice with clients in Brunei, India and

Asia, often taking on the more demanding clients. 'I have a bit of a history of standing up to people, then getting lots of work from difficult clients. I believe in being robust but fair and developing a mutual respect with clients and colleagues.'

She certainly benefited from the aspirations of her firm (Turner Kenneth Brown or TKB, a Top 20 firm by this time) who made her their third female partner when she was only five-and-a-half years qualified. Shortly after making partner she was seconded to San Francisco to see how a US firm operated. She wanted to have a tangible project and came up with an idea.

Dispute resolution

By the end of the 1980s she had seen too many situations where she felt that clients were not getting the best deal because 'not enough effort was being put into negotiation. Where it did occur it was at the door of the court where time pressure was paramount'. She was aware that a culture of mediation was developing in North California particularly in the intellectual property area. Her proposal was that she should investigate how mediation was being used in the American legal context and whether the American experience could be translated into a UK legal environment. She found herself 'very impressed. I was so amazed to find mediation working so well in the context of the American legal system, and how effective the mediation process was, because it is in American lawyers' blood to be so much more adversarial than we are, probably because of the high rewards of litigation'.

In the courts of California and New York she was able to see the mediation process in action. The Americans had dubbed this alternative dispute resolution (ADR) because it was an 'alternative' to litigation, 'and I was amazed to see people going into it unwillingly because forced by order of the courts and coming out satisfied. I began to form the idea that I could write a book called *The Resolution of Legal Disputes* for use in the UK'.

Fate sometimes takes a hand in unexpected ways. 'I have learned that often bad or difficult experiences can be productive if you survive them and learn from them.' Eileen decided that instead of returning directly from San Francisco to London she would combine work and travel by visiting Australia and Singapore. Unfortunately she fell off a racehorse during 'a pretty wild ride with some three day eventers' in the Australian outback and although she pretended to herself that the accident was unimportant, she ended up in traction in a Singapore hospital and in recovery for several months. This gave her ample time to reflect and to reassess her goals.

Merely writing a book would not in itself be sufficient to realise her vision. What was needed she decided was a 'neutral non-TKB product' which would facilitate mediation. She also thought that the term alternative dispute resolution was insufficiently dynamic but decided that for the time they would need to keep it. What she wanted was 'effective' dispute resolution, or EDR. TKB as it turned out were very supportive of the youngest partner on their management committee 'probably because I was a major fee earner', and with the help of the firm's librarian she compiled a database of City lawyers and academics who might be interested. There were a number of raised eyebrows and looks of incredulity from some City lawyers. Today a number play an active part in the mediation community. Her greatest discovery was Dr Karl Mackie who was teaching negotiation to business in Nottingham University. They forged a dynamic working relationship beginning with a shared dinner with the Lord Chancellor, Lord Mackay of Clashfern at an American Bar Conference in Hawaii. Today Eileen works alongside Karl Mackie at the Centre for Effective Dispute Resolution (CEDR) and they married a few years ago.

Eileen was not looking for mere acceptance of an idea which was new to the UK legal world. She felt that the concept could not work unless there was provision for the training of lawyers and others as mediators, and this required funding. Having sought advice from some of the best mediation trainers in America on the presentation of her ideas and the quantum of funding required, she was able to bring the idea of ADR to a wider audience. The small £12,000 initial funding gathered from two firms of accountants, six law firms and four companies just about paid for a dedicated telephone line and stationery, but she had been so persuasive in her personal marketing that CEDR's launch in 1989 at the CBI was attended by 300 people. Being on the platform with John Banham, Sir Alec Jarrett and Karl Mackie, with her father, her sister and partners in the audience was one of her proudest professional moments.

Soon afterwards difficulties at TKB led to the dissolution of the partnership and Eileen found herself with a young baby and no legal base from which to operate just at the time when her ideas were coming to fruition. This was not an easy period in her life, but Eileen would not wish to make too much of the difficulty. She moved to Howard Kennedy to run their international group before she was 'enticed to join CEDR on a permanent basis. I had only wanted to set up CEDR, I had not intended to become a mediator myself, that was not on my personal agenda'. But she realised that it was with CEDR that her future undoubtedly lay and with her parents' help in looking after her daughter, she survived, and flourished with her new organisation.

CEDR itself

CEDR itself is a charity with a money-earning arm, CEDR Solve, which facilitates the mediation process. The role of a good mediator is to 'get the best interaction out of two groups of people with a lot at stake, and to facilitate dialogue between them to get the best outcome. This means that you need to control the information flow between the parties, you need to know when to keep them apart and when to bring them together. They need to know that you are acting for everyone and not just for one party, because you want to find with them a resolution that everyone finds acceptable'.

This clearly requires a great deal of skill, and two key elements in the equation are the commitment of the mediator and also the mediator's credibility with the parties in dispute. 'If the mediator was not there it's very unlikely that the parties would stay in the same building working things out for six to 10 hours. They need to feel committed to being there and they constantly need the reassurance of the mediator that even if things are going very slowly the process is moving forward. The process in itself creates a discipline for people to stick at what is extremely difficult. It may be the first time that the commercial people in the opposing parties find themselves together, able to put their cards on the table and to say what they really want rather than communicating through their lawyers. So it is essential that there should be people present from both sides who are able to take decisions.'

The process is structured to 'get clarity of communication between the parties, and as the mediator travels backwards and forwards from room to room she can get the sense of what additional information is required and see where bridges might be built. But what she must not do is to divulge information from one party to the other without getting permission to do so'. As Eileen speaks some of the qualities of a good mediator begin to become apparent, an attention to detail, an ability to assess the mood and the personality of both parties and a cheerful representation that of course it is possible, 'that difficulties are meant to be solved'.

CEDR is housed on an open plan sixth floor of a tall building in Docklands and designed with mediation in mind. Staff specialists, who come from many different backgrounds, architecture, accountancy, academia as well as the Health Service, work desk to desk with the caseworkers who organise training and assess matters presented to CEDR. Meeting rooms are placed on the periphery of the floor strategically not adjacent to each other. The offices of the Chief Executive and the Deputy Chief Executive are small privacy pods for managing the firm, not grandiose power statements, and reflect

Eileen's description of a good mediator, who needs to be 'patient, but intelligently, not annoyingly, persistent. Because sometimes the mediation does not effect a settlement on the day, the mediator needs to be able to enable the parties to continue their communication. Sometimes this is done on the phone and sometimes they need to come back into the building. If the mediation is not going to be final on that day people need to leave in a good frame of mind, sufficiently positive and optimistic that they think that a resolution will come'.

She finds her work 'immensely rewarding'. The Woolf reforms and the introduction of the Civil Procedure Rules (SI 1998/3132) put 'mediation squarely on the agenda as far as the civil justice system is concerned. And proportionality became important in terms of the law courts system. We need to realise that now clients and lawyers have obligations to ensure that their use of the courts is proportional to the dispute involved'.

'But I'm fundamentally still a lawyer at heart. I'm not into lawyer bashing. What I enjoy as a mediator is assisting people to get to a solution from the legal and commercial perspective working with good lawyers.' On the other hand she 'has no regrets about giving up the law'. Although it is clearly exciting for her to see where she 'has arrived in life having been involved in pioneering work for mediation in England and Wales, taking on responsibility for a large number of people and helping to produce a new environment' she is much more interested in looking forward, to where CEDR can go next.

Adding value

As to her own personal future, what she wants is to 'continue to contribute to the public good, not necessarily in this environment. I'm always open to suggestions as to how I can add value. All of us like diversity after all, and I am particularly interested in the whole area of education'.

'I believe that life is a journey and that you learn from adversity. And I also believe that no one can make something happen on their own. All my achievements come down to a very large group of people. And mediators must have enough humility not to expect to have a high profile for what they have achieved. It is the people who have resolved their difficulties who get and should get the publicity.' The mediator must take satisfaction from a job well done, and with any luck future recommendations from those whom they have assisted. We speculate that the same might be said of mothers.

Eileen values the time that she spends with her daughter, and her attitude to motherhood and its responsibilities have clearly developed from her mother's counsel. 'Being a parent is a highly undervalued occupation. People should ensure that they take proper maternity leave and make space for their families. We have potentially a long life and many years to achieve what we want but only a short time when our children need us.'

'Women have challenges that men don't have. And we can easily set ourselves up to fail by setting impossible goals. We should try not to be too hard on ourselves and congratulate ourselves on our successes, see ourselves in the round and recognise our achievements in all environments. Even if we don't make it to partnership we can still take satisfaction from being damn good lawyers. The trick is working out what is going to work for you.'

And she has one final word of advice for young people, 'If you want to achieve something, write it down'.

Eva Crawley

Eva Crawley was awarded an OBE in 1999 for services to women solicitors. She is a former President of North Middlesex Law Society, a past President of the Solicitors Benevolent Association, and was responsible for founding the Association of Women Solicitors' Returners Course.

It is possible that without Eva Crawley and her friend Rosalind Bax, the first woman to be made a full equity partner in a major City law firm, there would today be no Association of Women Solicitors (AWS) and a great many women would have found it more difficult to return to the legal profession after having a career break.

In 1969 the membership of the 1919 Club, as the AWS was then called, was languishing. Membership stood at 100 members, most of whom lived in the London area and the benefits of membership were very slight. In return for their 10/6 (ten shillings and six pence) per annum membership subscription members were offered the opportunity to attend their AGM and perhaps one or two theatre outings a year. Not surprisingly Eva's involvement was restricted to paying her subscription. She had two young children and was more involved with the Young Solicitors Group, of which she had been a co-founder. However a letter from the committee proposing to wind up the 1919 Club because of lack of interest and to dispose of its funds in one final celebratory dinner for members galvanised her into attending the EGM where this was to be decided.

Eva pointed out that there was still a need for the club but that it should be more proactive in organising inter-professional conferences and then found herself appointed as the club's new Secretary; Rosalind whom she knew slightly at the time was appointed Treasurer. The first inter-professional conference organised by the AWS was opened in 1974 by the then President of the Law Society.

This may seem a minimal beginning to a career of thirty years' service to women in the profession, but Eva applied her undoubted energy – 'I went back to work as soon as my younger daughter went to school because I was terribly bored with children's tea-parties' – to ensure that there would be future events of some substance at the 1919 club which would be of particular value to young female solicitors.

Beginnings

Eva wanted to follow in the footsteps of her father and grandfather who were doctors, but her ambition was thwarted because 'I wasn't any good at science'. On her father's insistence that she must have 'a profession' she opted for law because 'law was easy to get into provided that you had the money'. Her father paid £400 as a premium to a Lincoln's Inn Fields firm where as the firm's first female articled clerk, 'I enjoyed myself enormously but did not learn very much'. This latter comment is unduly modest as she gained Second Class Honours in her Finals. She did all the 'outdoor' work of going to court and standing around in the 'bearpit' at the Royal Courts of Justice in the Strand with other articled clerks. Although she clearly did not feel that this required much intellectual ability she was told very firmly by the senior partner that she should maintain the difference in status from the other young women in the office when one day endeavouring to be helpful she made the tea. 'This is not what you are paid to do,' he declared firmly.

Eva together with Geoffrey Heggs and Madeleine Calderan was one of the founding members of the Solicitors Articled Clerks Society, now the Trainee Solicitors Group of which she eventually became vice chairman, and she says wryly, 'You'll think this very strange coming from me, but when it came to my turn to be chairman I turned it down because I thought that there were very few women in the profession, and I just thought that it was not suitable for a woman to do it'.

A job for young women

Eva qualified in 1954 when the social mores of the time had a confusing influence on even the most independent women. There were very much two schools of thought on whether women should receive equal pay for equal work. One view held that common justice required that women should be paid the same amount as men if they performed the same work, and 'there was the view that a married man should earn more even for the same job because he would have a wife and children to support, and it was difficult not to have some sympathy for that view'. Seen in the social climate of the times it seemed reasonable that a very bright young woman like Eva should accept a job which had been advertised as 'being suitable for a woman', for the sole reason that there were no prospects of partnership and accept a salary of £520 per annum, 10 per cent less than was being paid by another local firm to a young man in her law class whom she considered, 'much less intelligent'.

'But you see it was what we all wanted at that time. A job for a few years and then to have children. And we accepted that we would then stop working.'

Eva's working life did indeed come to a full stop after she married Freddie Crawley, and had her first child. Until one evening she was asked by a friend at a dinner party if she would do the conveyancing on his property purchase. Initially she demurred but was persuaded by her husband because 'we need the money'. This was the beginning of a 'kitchen table property and probate practice' which grew into 'quite a good practice' mostly as the result of recommendations of friends and her husband's colleagues.

Running a small practice in this way was logistically difficult without answering machines, faxes or e-mail and with only a part time typist, and building societies were reluctant to put part time sole practitioners on their panels. In 1963 she opted for the 'convenient' if not very well paid solution of working for a local firm who advertised in the *Gazette* for a full time assistant. Typically Eva persuaded them to employ her part time and remained there for 10 years, until her request for an increase in salary was met with the response that 'your husband is doing so well. Why do you need any more?'. This was of course exactly the sort of attitude which had necessitated the passing of the Equal Pay Act 1970.

Public appointments

Eva's next move to sit on a Social Security Tribunal was instigated partly by a friend's recommendation, but for a woman who had originally intended to be a doctor wishing to give assistance rather than to deny it, this was 'deadly. It was footling law not interesting law, dealing with all those rules and regulations and cross-referring all the time'.

When people speak of the inherent exclusion of the Old Boys' Network, Eva can point ironically to the 'Old Girls' Network' at work. Her name was put forward to the Home Secretary by a fellow member of the Old Girls' Committee at North London Collegiate School. 'Ordinary people' were required to serve on the Police Complaints Authority (PCA), recently set up as the result of the Police and Criminal Evidence Act 1984. She was bemused by the letter from a firm of headhunters which began 'We understand that you are interested in joining the PCA . . .' but her husband, always an enthusiastic supporter of his wife, insisted that she went for interview at which she recalls 'I was so relaxed you wouldn't believe it, so relaxed that the interviewer said to me "You interrupt all the time and you speak too much and I'm sure your husband thinks so as well!" I could not possibly comment!'

For three years Eva served as a lay member on the PCA, not as a solicitor. It was her first experience of dealing with civil servants and the standard practice of being given files by them with a draft letter of response attached to the cover was an irritant to a woman of independent mind. She admits that she did not relish taking direction, and also decided very quickly that the PCA simply did not have sufficient powers. Its members were not permitted to interview complainants or the members of the police who had been the subject of complaint, 'and if the police did not agree there was not a lot that you could do'. On one occasion she arrived at Bramshill, the police training college, to give a lecture and was met with such coldness and discourtesy that the double disability of being a member of the PCA and a woman was forcefully brought home to her.

It is difficult to keep in focus the age at which Eva embarked on the various voyages of her career as she sits trim, grey-haired, upright and attentive telling you about her past. 'I was 59 when I came off the PCA, and I wrote to the Law Society pointing out how suitable I was for a post on the Office for the Supervision of Solicitors (OSS) because I had already been on a committee at the Law Society dealing with complaints. I did however think that I should tell them how old I was when they offered me the job, and when they hesitated I pointed out that although they indicated that women should retire at 60, they said in all their literature that they were an Equal Opportunity Employer, and that they did not expect men to retire until they were 65. We compromised. They employed me on the basis that they would not pay pension contributions for me for the five years between 60 and 65.'

In this role she had 'five years of intense interest' during the last six months of which her office relocated to Leamington Spa. 'My husband was very busy at the time,' she says of this period quite matter of factly, but for those six months she spent two nights a week in Leamington Spa, managed her home in London and also sat on the Parole Board, to which she had also been appointed.

It would probably be fair to say that she found the Solicitors' Complaints Bureau (SCB) and the Parole Board interesting, fascinating and full of frustration for very different reasons. She found, and still finds (because now in her seventies she still works for the OSS) that the unwillingness of solicitors to apologise for mistakes that they have made is not only incredible but also intensely silly. 'So often a simple sorry, perhaps combined with a really small amount of compensation is all that the client wants.' She feels that it is not only a waste of time for individual solicitors to 'mess around when clearly they have done something inadequate like not sending a form to a client', but that it is also bad marketing both for themselves and for the rest of the profession.

The Parole Board on which she served for four years brought her into contact with 'all sorts of eminent people such as the Bishop of Shrewsbury, the Headmaster of St Paul's and many forensic scientists'. She attended the Parole Board for half a day every fortnight and Eva's commitment to its work was shown by her allocating some of her holidays to it in addition to the eight days a year that the SCB gave her so that she could combine both roles.

By visiting prisons she gained an insight into the punishment regime in this country and the lives of people with 'whom I would never otherwise have come into contact.' Incarceration she concluded was for the most part 'a waste of time, money and effort' because lack of funds precluded the provision of any worthwhile training or rehabilitation for anyone other than the 'lifers'. It seems to Eva that it would be much better if non-violent offenders were kept in the community and punished in other ways, for example being taken into prison at the weekends or prohibited from football matches, so as to disrupt the 'fun' in their lives.

'I was struck by one chap who was not very bright and had no educational qualifications and whose main wish was "to go to another prison 'when I come back next time'". He clearly expected that it was a fact of life, like a parking fine, that he would spend more time in prison, and when I asked him why, he told me that if I could find him a job that paid as well as his present one, he would give this one up.'

The AWS

There have been very much two strands to Eva's professional life. There is what she has done for very little money and what she has done for absolutely no money at all. In the latter category comes over 30 years of encouraging and working for the benefit of other women solicitors.

Most of Eva's work for other women has been carried out through the umbrella of the AWS. This is time spent encouraging and inspiring other women to aim high, to put themselves forward, to network and to help others. As can be seen from her comments on the peccadilloes of solicitors generally she is intolerant of what she sees as inefficiency or slackness because she has so much energy and commitment herself, and is clearly so used to juggling balls of many different colours simultaneously. She feels that women can and should help each other because they are the ones who understand the difficulties that other women have in combining the roles of wife and mother, and in her case grandmother. A call to her about Returners' Course finances or asking for information about one of her innumerable contacts is quite likely to be met with the answer that 'I'll ring you back. I'm just seeing the grandchildren off'.

The AWS now prides itself on the variety of its commitment to pastoral care, and Eva has been involved at the beginning of most of it. As well as encouraging Judith Willis, a young law lecturer to set up a maternity helpline, she also ran the AWS mentoring scheme on a purely voluntary basis from her sitting-room desk, 'ringing up people I knew and persuading them that they could help someone who had rung up with a problem'. This is an extension of the informal counselling that she believes that women can give each other as a result of chance meetings at social events. The mentoring scheme, which now has a paid administrator and is financed by the Law Society, matches women who need guidance on how to manage the next stage of their careers with other women who may be able to help them.

Eva is perhaps best known for being the guiding spirit behind the AWS Returners' Course held annually at Lucy Cavendish College, Cambridge, a college for mature women part of whose ethos is to help professional women returning to work after a career break. This began when Eva, ever the opportunist, arranged to sit next to the Bursar of Lucy Cavendish at a dinner and somehow was invited to dine at the college, where she met Jillinda Tiley, Lucy Cavendish's law tutor, and the plan to hold an annual week-long conference was born.

Despite the initial refusal of the Law Society to fund the course because remarkably it felt that 'there was no demand for it', lecturers were persuaded to give their time at reduced rates and AWS committee members volunteered to provide administrative assistance, after dinner talks and encouragement. From her own experience Eva is acutely aware that the rewards of staying at home bringing up children can come at a high price in diminished professional confidence, so she sees part of the purpose of the week's intensive tuition as being to get women to see that they still have a place in a rapidly changing legal world. Even now, 25 years later, Eva can still be found for most of that week giving practical words of advice, which have come out of a long, varied, and continuing career.

Despite being well over the age inherent in anyone's definition of retirement Eva is still involved with helping those whom she considers less fortunate than herself. A past chairman of the Solicitors' Benevolent Association, she takes an active role in interviewing and assessing those who apply to them for help, whether the children of deceased members of the profession or elderly retired solicitors living in nursing homes. Her compassion is very much laced with practicality. 'We have limited funds and people have to be realistic. If we agree to fund someone on the Returners' Course and for three years running there is some last minute reason why they say they can't go on it, then there isn't much point in offering it a fourth time because their ability to hold down a job would be very much in question.'

Reflections

After this long and full life would Eva looking back have done anything differently? Probably in an ideal world she would have gone back to work more quickly, but she recognises that to do so would have been swimming against the social tide of the time, when it was still a matter for debate as to whether women should go back to work at all. Her two daughters consider that it was 'a good thing' to have had a working mother, because she understood more of their world as they grew up and was a sound role model for them. 'Interestingly,' she says, 'one of them works full time with a husband who looks after the children while my other daughter stays at home with her children.' She then adds, 'her husband's a solicitor and she helps as his office manager.' Not exactly the usual definition of the stay-at-home wife; Eva was definitely a role model!

In a very good situation to consider the position of women in the profession over the years, Eva's thoughtful comment that it 'is now a very different world, and not one that I think I should enjoy as a private practitioner any more', is not an assessment that can be dismissed as a comment from crabbed age to youth. What she is concerned about is the refocusing of the ambitions of young solicitors away from the sense of serving and being part of a local community to specialisation and making large amounts of money. She sees the dichotomy between City commercial practices and provincial and suburban practices as detrimental to the profession as a whole, and considers that it makes it very difficult for young women to maintain a fulfilled family and legal life at a high level.

On the other hand she feels that young women must realise that unless the social context of the world changes or young women are fortunate enough to have a partner who will take an equal or even disproportionately large share of domestic responsibilities, it is unrealistic of them to expect that their firms must change to accommodate them in every respect. As she tells her Returners, 'if you really want work you will find it. If you want part-time work it is out there, but you will have to go out and get it. And you will have to be prepared to be paid less than what you think you are worth to start with'.

This is probably an accurate summary of how she has pursued a life which she has undoubtedly enjoyed, and it seems appropriate that when the AWS instituted an award to be given every two years to a woman who has made an outstanding, but possibly relatively unremunerated, contribution to the progress of women in the law, it should be called the Eva Crawley Award. Eva, the first recipient, was presented with the award by Cherie Booth QC at the AWS 75th Anniversary Dinner held at the Banqueting House in 1998.

Alison Eddy

Alison Eddy leads the clinical negligence team in the London office of Irwin Mitchell. As well as being a member of the Law Society Clinical Negligence and Personal Injury Panels, she is also a director of three charities relating to brain injuries and children's disabilities and is a mother of five children aged 10–18.

The words, 'stamina', 'determination' and 'energy' occur often in conversation with Alison and fairly readily sum up important aspects of her character. The other word that she does not use but would be equally applicable would be 'realism'. Born into a Welsh family Alison was encouraged by her mother to become the first member of that family to go to university. Her initial ambition was not to become a lawyer; in fact she read American Studies at Manchester University between 1973 and 1976, but a vague idea of going into social work to help people was refocused in a legal direction when she formed the idea that if she worked in a law centre she would more ambitiously be able to help 'whole groups of people'. It was from one of these law centres that the suggestion came that she would be better able to fulfil this ambition if she qualified as a solicitor first. So after academic training at the College of Law she was articled with Brian Thompson & Partners in Cardiff.

Early legal experience

On qualification Alison remained at Thompsons, where her practice developed into 50 per cent clinical negligence and 50 per cent employment law. Thompsons' involvement in trade union work meant that its employment law practice was focused on acting for the applicants in sex discrimination and equal pay cases. 'Given that one has to work it was a fantastic thing to do.'

One of the male partners at Thompsons (there were few female partners in the firm at this time) 'opened doors for me' and presented opportunities; it was he who suggested quite early on in her legal career that she should attend the women's TUC. This she found strengthening, inspirational and, as the partner had intended, a very good source of future work! This was, Alison feels, the only positive instance of guidance or mentoring that she has ever received, but it is perhaps this lack in her own career which has made her such a good guide and mentor to the young women in her team. Most interviewers give a pen portrait of the physical appearance and the surroundings of their subject. Alison is all energy – her red hair, her smile and her way of dress are all energetic and she treated the occasion as an opportunity for interesting conversation rather than self-promotion. Her commitment to training and the development of her staff was shown in that this was the only interview that I have ever conducted where someone else (a newly qualified member of her team) was using it as an opportunity to learn how to interview.

Employment law and clinical negligence

Because of her area of work Alison often found herself working in an all female team including female counsel. In *Meade-Hill* v. *British Council,* a 1995 case concerning mobility clauses in employment contracts, she and Cherie Booth successfully argued against the British Council that such contracts operated against women indirectly as women were traditionally less mobile than men.

Alison considers herself to be a 'dreamer' who wants everything 'to be perfect', although this is undoubtedly modified by a strong streak of realism. She had to jettison the employment side of her practice when she joined Irwin Mitchell. This she opined somewhat ruefully was the inevitable consequence of increased specialisation within the law, but it is also the result of her need to give her clients the best possible advice and attention. What she wants is for those who are the victims of clinical negligence, and their families, to be able to enjoy as normal a life as possible. Law she feels would be a very difficult profession to pursue 'just for the money' because of the long hours and the responsibility required, and she personally gets a 'tremendous buzz' from making a real difference to people's lives. The settlements which she succeeds in negotiating can provide rehabilitation for the victims and take pressure off their families so that they are not ground down into self-destruction. Not only does she feel that her team makes a substantial input into the quality of life of individual clients, but the existence of the court system and the ability of victims to pursue litigation can operate advantageously to change practices within hospitals. For example, she now considers midwives to be much better and more consistently trained because of some of the successful actions which she and her team have pursued.

This is why she is not an advocate of 'no fault' compensation because there would then be in the end no real accountability, and without accountability there is no impetus for changes in practice. And even if 'no fault' compensation were accepted, 'causation will still also require to be proved because the law does not recognise the right of an individual to substantial compensation for a natural genetic defect'. Where it would help in Alison's view is if the NHS would 'admit liability and pay up' more expeditiously. She also considers that present changes mooted in the procedure for pursuing small negligence claims would be of considerable advantage. 'There must be a means of resolving these cases quickly as the court costs are disproportionate to the damages received.' Her team has been involved in a pilot study where both sides operate on the basis that only one agreed expert will be instructed.

Alison's practice has become more specialised so that now about a third of her work is acting for head injury victims. This was perhaps a natural progression from acting for children who were brain damaged at birth or clients who had suffered as the result of negligent neurosurgery. Now she acts more generally for the victims of traumatic brain injury mostly derived from road traffic accidents. It is an interest which spills over into her charitable work as she is also a trustee of the charity Headcase which exists to help those who have suffered brain injury.

Family life

Alison laughingly describes herself as 'driven'; she left Thompsons together with two other partners to set up Irwin Mitchell's London office when her youngest child, the youngest of five, was three. She says that she is the product of a decade (the 1970s) where 'feminism was the order of the day' and whose credo was 'not to be financially dependent on any man', which was 'terribly important to me'. Like so many young women of her time she was convinced that she could 'have it all', which in her case meant having a successful legal career and also having a large family, 'where everyone talks very loudly and eats very fast'.

Belief in this philosophy has led to a 'tendency to taking on too much'. But it can work if you have stamina, healthy children, do not wish for frivolous pursuits and have very good support. Support in Alison's case means a husband who is willing to take on the cooking, and having succeeded in solving the childcare issue by getting good nannies to stay for long periods of time during her children's childhood (six years and five years) and employing very reliable au pairs subsequently. That obviously does not happen by chance; it takes people management skills.

She is extremely aware that her energy and the apparent ease with which she combines life at the office with life at home could seduce young women into believing that it is all very easy. 'I do not think anyone should underestimate the difficulty of juggling being a parent with a career in the law. If you think you are going to be the perfect mother as well as have a top career then forget it. What you will need more than anything else is stamina,' which she attempts, not always successfully to reinforce by going to a gym 'once or twice in a good week.' It is possible that Alison's definition of the 'perfect' mother is sharper and higher than that of the majority of the population. She recognises that she will never 'get to bake that cake' and regrets not being able to help her children with homework. She tells some amusing anecdotes which demonstrate her efforts to juggle the dual roles, like the time she heard her youngest child practise cello over her mobile phone while sitting on a train on her way back from a meeting. And she is honest enough to admit that 'sometimes it feels as if I am on the edge. Arriving home at 10 p.m. to be told that I need to get a costume ready for *Comedy of Errors* the following day is the kind of thing which can tip me over'. What she does do is to try to use her financial success not to buy her children expensive goodies but to enrich their lives and to cement her relationship with them. 'I keep the weekends free for the children, and Saturday nights are often spent with whichever children happen to be at home. I try to spend time with the children individually and I might take one of the older ones away for the weekend.' Most teenagers would probably be happy to trade homework supervision and home made cakes for being regularly taken to the theatre or out to eat with some adult conversation, but it's the old concept of the 'perfect' mother at work again!

The net position for the children is that they need to 'be pretty well motivated to succeed' as their mother will not be available for nagging duty, and Alison is aware that this may suit some children more than others. There is also the influence of her work on family life in other less pragmatic ways. She suspects that she could be overprotective because 'the nature of the work means that I see danger everywhere. Every time I see a child bounce a tennis ball on the pavement I see the potential accident played out in front of me'. On the other hand she could take comfort that 'I must have been doing something right' when her daughter came home from school to tell her that she had written about her mother for an exam essay whose subject was 'The person I most admire'.

Managing a department

It is clear that managing her department combines both aspects of her personality, the maternal and the professional. Her staff confirm that her goal of being accessible and operating an open-door policy is more than successful. 'It is rewarding to impart knowledge to lawyers of the future and I hope also that engenders the same sort of enthusiasm in others that I have myself.' (One of her staff chuckles, 'her enthusiasm is very infectious'.) Alison considers that it is 'a pressure but hugely rewarding to manage other people', and it is clear that the combination of legal practice, people management and running a family while all providing inter-related pressures all also provide this huge personal reward for the head of the clinical negligence department at Irwin Mitchell.

Work-life balance

So the big question to be asked is whether having children has hindered Alison's career, although I suspect given the way that her mind operates the real issue for her is whether her having a career has hindered her children. In her view women certainly are not represented in partnerships proportionate to the number who enter the profession. 'My experience is that this is not so much the result of discrimination as the difficulty of combining a demanding career with family life. The hours are a major issue. I am rarely home before 7.30 p.m. and at least one or two nights a week will probably be home much later.'

'I suspect that it is harder for women in the City. You have to be really driven to succeed in a number of these practices and you have to buy into the profit culture. The reason so many women leave City firms after the early years is because of the over-challenging billing and chargeable hours' targets. To achieve a more balanced lifestyle the entire culture would have to change.' Even in her own specialism, where clinical negligence solicitors are predominantly female, they 'are still under-represented at partnership level'. She notes, however, that medical experts are predominantly male, as perhaps the medical profession has not progressed quite as quickly as the law when it comes to promoting women.

She considers that the intrinsic nature of the work in City firms means that there is little choice about long hours, and that 'it would certainly be easier for women if there was more opportunity for home working and flexitime'. Irwin Mitchell is presently making a substantial investment in IT which will enable its case management system to be accessed from home and fee earners working at home to dictate to a centralised typing facility which will work overnight to produce copy on fee earners' screens the next morning. It is this sort of innovatory approach which could make it easier for working mothers to spend regular hours with their children even when there are crisis demands to complete transactions.

Janet Gaymer

Janet Gaymer, the senior partner of Simmons & Simmons, was the first woman to be appointed senior partner of a Top 10 City firm with an international practice.

On first encounter with her warm welcome it might be easy to pigeonhole Janet Gaymer as motherly – but how wide of the mark that would be! She encourages confidences, listens to her clients with obvious interest and smiles frequently but her attentive eyes reveal the workings of a very shrewd brain. Hardly surprising in a woman with two law degrees, several books on employment law and numerous accolades including *The Times' Woman of Achievement in the Law* award to her credit.

Why have her (mainly male) partners now entrusted her with the task of leading their firm, which she joined as an articled clerk 30 years ago, into the 21st century? The answer probably lies in the pragmatism with which she deploys her undoubted intelligence, and the sense that there is a very firm hand within the velvet glove.

From trainee to partner

The first born girl in her family with parents who both worked in the family grocery business, she spent much of her holidays on her own 'reading and reading, fortunately I was a very studious child'. This is probably why she mentions, without displaying obvious guilt, that she was not able to spend much time with her two daughters supervising their homework. Janet has certainly not conformed to recent research findings which have suggested that children of working mothers thrive less well academically. Her two daughters, one at university and one now training as a solicitor, feel that they have benefited from having to learn self-motivation.

When looking for articles she was refused an interview with a major and unnamed City firm in a letter that read, 'We are prejudiced against female articled clerks because of an unfortunate experience we have had in the past.' Janet did not have 'an adverse reaction' to this blatant discrimination but noted it as an indicator of the environment in which she would be operating; it was something that she could learn from. Even at Simmons, a firm recommended to her by her tutor and mentor Lord Hoffman, the tenor of the working environment was indicated, as it so often is, by the 'Loo Question'. The door signs that read 'Men', 'Women', 'Partners' and 'Partners' Secretaries' had to be changed in 1977 when she became Simmons' first female UK partner.

In her 30 years at Simmons Janet has only once considered leaving, when her salary increase was neither to her liking nor at market rate. When she announced that she was leaving for the Treasury Solicitor's Department negotiations were swiftly instigated by her head of department and Janet remained.

The injunction to 'do what you enjoy' is almost a refrain in her conversation and her own obvious interest and enjoyment in what she does is probably another reason for her partners' choice. 'I am a firm believer that when you are doing what you really want to be doing it shows in your face and your demeanour, and that makes you more convincing.'

Janet has worked out a way to progress through the ranks of her firm to her present prominent position but she has always consulted those who mean most to her before taking the final decision. When offered partnership she asked her husband, a commercial property lawyer, whether he would mind that she would be a partner before him, to which his answer was, 'We need the money. Take it.' Her partners were equally encouraging when she became pregnant in her first year of partnership when as the only employment solicitor in the firm she had to write her own maternity policy.

Senior partner

When she says that becoming senior partner was 'rather like taking over the running of the family' this does not sound trite because after 30 years she was literally the senior partner, the partner who had been with the firm for the longest period. And she does sound like an understanding parent when she says that she thinks that what she has learned as a mother has been of assistance. Just as with her family her colleagues at Simmons are obviously a group of people for whom she cares very much.

Again and again she says things which indicate that her style of management goes beyond rules just as her understanding of the employment relationship goes beyond legislation and its interpretation. She feels that in the wider world of employment the employer/employee relationship can sometimes be hindered by legal advisers offering too great an analysis of the letter of legislation and too little empathy and common sense. In her view the role of the employment lawyer is also to encourage a meaningful exchange between employer and employee, an attitude recognised in 1998 by her appointment for a second term to the Council of the Advisory Conciliation and Arbitration Service.

Stress and change

She is greatly concerned about the increase in legal workplace stress since the 1970s. 'There is no doubt that practice now is much more potentially health-damaging than when I started.' This, she says, is not a problem confined to women, although women may experience it more acutely as they attempt to juggle family and work. One of the major contributors she feels is technological advance, which enables documents to be transmitted and responses demanded without a proper allowance of thinking time. Solicitors are employed to provide reasoned advice, but very often they can no longer find that quiet corner to think through the problem astutely for the benefit of the client.

Although she does not consider that in her field the volume of legislation has increased, improved technology has made it possible to access more case law. And so the pressure builds. The more senior the solicitor the easier it is for her to say that she requires time to think out a response, but younger solicitors have no such luxury. They lack control over their working lives and this produces more stress. Pressure on partners reduces the time for supervision and training, which increases the pressure of uncertainty in their assistants. Janet feels that it is important that individuals learn what they can and cannot do themselves, and that the giving of assistance by senior members in a department to its junior members is a way of enhancing the collegiate feeling within that department.

So how does she herself relax? She and her husband both enjoy opera, and she hopes that foreign trips might include visits to foreign opera houses. She has always loved drawing and took the opportunity during her sabbatical two years ago to spend a week learning how to paint in Cornwall. 'I was shocked at how much I enjoyed it, and how good I was at it,' and then she retreated slightly 'well I could do it quite well.' This is an indication of how she is more centred on her concern to make work in a legal firm more satisfying, less stressful and more 'what you want to do' for other people, than with a CV list of formal achievements. Being reviewed by

Janet Gaymer might feel quite pleasant but would leave one with a lot of food for thought.

Women in the law

The word 'negotiation' is one that is key to her vocabulary. Difficulties should be 'worked out' or 'worked through'. Her firm does not operate a formal flexible working policy, but many people there work flexibly. 'I am in two minds about formal policies,' she explained, 'formal policies can stifle the very practices that they are meant to implement by being too rigorous. Of course we should be flexible because we don't want good staff to leave. They are expensive to train and we have a business to run.' On the other hand it must be recognised that different practice areas have different requirements and different attitudes to how they can be flexible. She considers it is probably easier for her own department, employment, to be flexible than, say, corporate finance.

Was this a reason for women to choose areas of law which might offer more apparent choice if they were to have children? An emphatic no. 'You should always do what you enjoy. Where you then choose to practise and how you want to run your life is then a matter for you to work out.'

'Learning is very invigorating.' Accustomed to discipline and a schedule developed over 30 years at the firm she has had to adapt to a different sequencing of her working day. The previous possibility of scheduling two hours most days to chew over a problem has disappeared because the problems facing a senior partner are very often immediate. Now time to think means booking a slot in a very busy diary. She has discovered that this is a common problem for other senior partners and other business figures, and that many of them have come to value plane travel because it offers the uninterrupted time for thought.

For a practising partner lines of delegation are much more clear-cut, as research can be delegated to trainees and problem solving and dealing with clients to assistants. Now she regards her job as 'pressing the buttons of management'; any one situation might involve more than one person and might require a consensual rather than an individual solution, resulting in a much more collaborative method of solving a problem.

She has been very much confirmed in her initial view that being in charge of a partnership might be rather like managing a family. A senior partner must be fair, transparent, firm at times and have the ability to give out 'sweeties' when she feels able to do so, provided that everyone has access to the 'sweetie jar'. Just as a parent has she sometimes has to deal with 'troubled children', but there is the same sense as in a family that they are all in it together. The main attribute of a senior partner in her view is to be able to 'listen and to listen and to listen, and to listen not only to the things that are said but to the things that are not being said'.

After so many years building up client relationships she finds that she has to 'try very hard not to continue practising, because that could get in the way of my real role in the firm'. Instead she has chosen to take on some one-off projects which are strategic or very specific in nature. 'I have come to the conclusion that this is a very good thing to do, because it puts my own thoughts in a wider arena and enables me to see my tasks from a very different vantage point. Previously I was only an adviser but now I am both adviser and implementer, and being as it were on both sides of the fence has enabled me to be a better lawyer and a better senior partner.'

At the beginning of her tenure she underwent psychological testing as part of a senior management training programme organised by the Cabinet Office. In the view of the evaluative psychiatrist her profile was so unusual that he had only seen one similar to hers before, before listing the very substantial achievements of the other person. 'He told me that by 18 months into the job I would have changed but that I would be able to do the job and would enjoy it. Although many of the things that he said were particularly insightful, the most important thing for me was that he told me I could do it. The act of that being said was hugely helpful. And particularly for women this is terribly, terribly important.'

A compulsive list maker, at the beginning of her year Janet wrote out a 'little list' which is 'still there but with the items re-ordered'. She has recognised as the result of her experience that some things which she had ear-marked for the future now need to be brought forward.

In her first six months of being a senior partner two things happened which made her aware of her wider responsibilities and that the 'scenery had changed'. In the second week of her new role, on 11 September 2001, the Twin Towers were attacked. 'The news was breaking and being updated from our New York office, which thankfully was some way away from the Twin Towers, but at the same time there was a bomb scare in the office and everyone had to be evacuated. It was at this point that I knew that I had to be efficient and that I had no time for personal emotion.' Standing back afterwards and evaluating her performance she was surprised at how coolly she had been able to stand outside herself and to do all the things that needed to be done in the crisis.

Then only a month later, in October 2001, the DTI asked her to chair a government task force involving employment tribunal reform. The timetable for this was very challenging and after agonising about it for seven days and with the total agreement of her husband she took it on, resolving that it must not interfere with her senior partner role. For eight months she worked Monday to Friday on her firm's business and on Saturdays and Sundays on the task force. 'But,' she says proudly 'I did it and I learned a lot.' What was particularly satisfying and which she obviously feels has benefits for her role in Simmons was her success in bringing together people with different views to fashion a general agreement.

One of the things that she has learned is that she must take her own health very seriously because she cannot afford for the firm's sake to break down. She 'runs around a lot – but not on a treadmill' and she is 'vicious' about taking holidays. 'Some people try to go on and on and on without taking holidays but this is not possible.'

Advice for young lawyers

With 30 years' experience behind her she has clear ideas of the qualities needed by young lawyers to survive and to succeed. Curiosity, a sense of fun and adaptability.

First the curiosity. 'If you are curious about an area of law that interests you, you are likely to continue to be curious for a good part of or even all of your working life.' This is certainly how she feels about employment law, for she is as fascinated by it now as she was when she began as a trainee. At conferences she is as likely to be speaking on employment law as about management.

Second, a sense of humour is vital. Good lawyers have got to be able to laugh at themself and the situation they find themselves in. 'It's the work that must be taken seriously but not the self.' Research should be done meticulously, problems should be analysed and solutions proposed imaginatively and again meticulously but the lawyer must always remember that the person on the other side of the desk is a client who wants practical advice not a smug demonstration of how clever the lawyer is.

And the third quality, adaptability, is necessary because of the changing demands of legal practice. 'What a lawyer starts dealing with now at the outset of a career may be very different in 10 or 15 years' time. Many lawyers have either through choice or force of circumstances, made radical changes in the type of law that they practise, and new lawyers should be prepared for this.'

Partnership

Janet has no hesitation in saying that a good partner is 'someone who instils trust in her colleagues'. Other partners are reliant on their partners to safeguard their own livelihood. It is not just about being a good lawyer but it is about confidence that your partners will take the rough as well as the smooth. Technical excellence in partners is nowadays taken as read and it is these qualities of trust that are looked for. Not everyone is necessarily a born manager and in larger partnerships with access to a larger range of skills it is important to identify those who have natural managerial skills and to help them to develop them for specific roles within the firm. 'Once upon a time partners would look round the table and ask, "Who fancies doing that?". Now we are a lot more sophisticated.'

One of Janet's roles is to keep a watching brief on the psychological wellbeing of the firm. This means that she must be concerned not only with the problems brought to her by her partners but with the working atmosphere and efficiency of particular departments and teams. She hopes that she will be able to pick up warning signs before matters become too serious but she has to accept that sometimes it might be too late and that the remedial action which should have been taken is no longer possible so that she is then into damage limitation mode. What she therefore wants to feel is that she has an open door and that people will speak to her as she listens and listens and listens.

Advice for trainees

To those young people who are considering the law she has one very important piece of advice, 'Go and do it.' Young people should try out work experience in as many different legal environments as possible, whether in legal offices, legal aid centres or barristers' chambers for there is no substitute for 'doing it and feeling it. When our new trainees arrive I have a well-rehearsed speech, which I have delivered many times but which I still feel is good advice'.

First, 'Have an open mind and as few preconceptions as possible.' Trainees should be prepared to find that their natural talent and skills are perhaps more suited to commercial property negotiation than to the corporate finance transactions where they envisaged their futures.

Second, 'Have fun, because the law is enjoyable.'

And finally, 'Don't be shy about asking questions.' It is much cheaper to ask questions as a trainee than after qualification. This goes partly with the next injunction which is to be honest and to be truthful. 'If someone confesses a mistake as soon as it becomes apparent the damage to the client and to the firm's reputation will be that much less.'

She is very well aware that many of the trainees who come to Simmons have had glittering academic careers and they may never have experienced any serious failure in their lives before. The first time someone experiences failure is 'very bruising' so that in her opinion it is far better for failure to be experienced as a trainee than later on in a solicitor's career. She does not expect unnatural perfection but rather a real attempt to achieve it.

Dame Brenda Hale

Dame Brenda Hale pursued two slightly intertwined careers as academic and advocate and is now one of only three Lady Justices of Appeal in the Court of Appeal.

Dame Brenda operates behind a large desk in a large room which is orderly, neat, tidy but not oppressive. A large clock on the wall ticks, she sits behind an elaborate inkstand containing a small basalt statue of a kneeling woman and there are cheerful cards on her window sill. Everything is orderly; orderly texts, orderly papers and orderly staff. It is a comfortable room arranged so that research can be done, thinking can take place and decisions can be made. It is probably everyone's idea of the quintessential judge's room but with a feminine face.

School and university

There were no lawyers in Dame Brenda's family, who were mainly teachers or clergymen, 'that sort of poor professional'. Both her parents were head teachers, her father the headmaster of a small independent boys' boarding school and her mother headmistress of a primary school. Dame Brenda herself attended a small girls' grammar school where only two girls had previously progressed to Oxbridge. 'It was in fact a very good school for academics.' History was her favourite subject but discussions with her headmistress elicited the career advice that although she was 'Oxbridge material, she was not a natural historian'. Dame Brenda rejected her headmistress's suggestion that she study economics because she did not think that economic theory was 'very congenial. I came up with the idea of law myself possibly because I was interested in constitutional history, but I don't really know where I got the idea from'.

Her scores at the Cambridge entrance exams were high enough for the Director of Studies to say later that she would have been 'thrilled to have her do history', but by that time the die had been cast. She had no practical reason behind reading law, it was simply that she thought that it might be a subject in which she could be 'really interested'. She had a default assumption, if she thought forward at all to a postgraduation future, that she might become a solicitor. The idea of going to the Bar 'would not seriously have crossed the mind of someone like me' who came from North Yorkshire and whose mother by this time was a widow. She knew the solicitors in her local market town but had never met a barrister, and the possibility of teaching law was 'beyond imagination' because of the class of degree she considered would be required. 'At that early point I did not have either the arrogance or the confidence in my own abilities to contemplate the Bar or academia.'

When she went up to Cambridge in 1963 there were only three women's colleges, and only two had law students, so that in effect a quota system operated for women in the law faculty. Out of an overall tally of 100–120 law students in her year at Cambridge, Girton supplied five and Newnham only one. Despite the disparity in numbers she was not conscious of any prejudicial difference between male and female students because 'I was young and having a whale of a time although I was expected to work hard and did work hard'.

Merely thrilled to be at university female students in the 1960s were not 'sensitised to discrimination', although looking back now Dame Brenda considers that it was a gross injustice that there were so few places for women, and that most of the law students came from public and direct grant schools. 'For some quaint reason supervisions were conducted mainly in single-sex groups, presumably so that the girls would not distract the boys or vice versa.' Whatever the tuition methods she obtained 'a very good degree, a starred First, and was top of my class'. She says this without boastfulness, but matter-of-factly describing an academic record, a part of a disembodied curriculum vitae with a separate existence of its own. She had successfully combined 'the whale of a time' with working in a very disciplined way. Every day she worked for only five hours but during those hours with supreme concentration, a skill which must aid her now in assessing the legal bundles so carefully prepared by others for her consideration.

What to do next?

On leaving Cambridge Dame Brenda became a lecturer at Manchester University but not before flirting theoretically at least with both branches of the legal profession. During her first year she had applied to one of the Inns of Court for a scholarship. The interview took place before her first year exams so that she had no real concept of her legal abilities; it was not a success, the Inns of Court felt alien and over-privileged to the young Yorkshire woman and she put all thoughts of the Bar out of her mind. She was confirmed in her view of the Bar's élitism when a scholarship was given to the son of a High Court judge, and another candidate described to her in detail the 'very good breakfast' he had had on the train from Cambridge to London. This costly indulgence to which she could not possibly aspire at the time, seemed to illustrate to her the difference that there was between the Bar and the world she knew.

Two long vacations spent working in the offices of a three-partner firm in the town where she had gone to school and one long vacation on the student placement scheme at Linklaters produced the thought that she might become a solicitor. Perhaps selflessly, the Yorkshire firm advised her that it would be 'a terrible waste' if she were to come back to work for them, and so she applied for and was offered articles at Linklaters. Dame Brenda is someone whose intellectual abilities are not only obvious, but whose character invites others to offer very positive advice and assistance to advance her talents.

Despite Linklaters no longer asking for premiums and being prepared to pay her 'a reasonable amount of money' during articles, which was very much a consideration to a young woman with a widowed mother, she decided in her final year that she could not face studying for yet more examinations in the shape of Solicitors' Finals straight after graduation. Advised by her Director of Studies that 'you could walk into an assistant lectureship tomorrow', she applied to two universities; both Manchester and Bristol made offers, she accepted Manchester and thus set out on her academic career.

Manchester

Manchester was very practitioner-dominated in the 1960s and several part-time members of staff were local practitioners, so the Dean's suggestion that she qualify as a barrister was not too unusual. In her first long vacation she studied by correspondence course, thus finding herself almost in the very examination situation she wished to avoid after her time at Cambridge, passed the Bar Finals in 1967 but was not called until July 1969 when she had 'eaten her two years' worth of dinners'. From 1969 to 1972 she divided her time between the lecture theatre and the court.

Her pupillage was conducted in a set of Manchester chambers which was used to academics and Dame Brenda considers that she owes a great deal to Sir Rhys Davies QC, later the Recorder of Manchester, who persuaded her pupilmaster to take her on. Half way through her pupillage this same pupilmaster confessed that he thoroughly disapproved of women at the Bar not because he was a misogynist but because the Bar was a 'fighting profession'. Women he considered did not know how to fight but veered from being too yielding to being too obstinate. Far from being upset by this comment, Dame Brenda thought about it carefully as guidance as to how she should conduct herself at the Bar. Now she believes that getting the right balance between being tough and being sensible is the key to anything in law and life in general. Taking offence would not have been helpful; instead she asked herself why this man whom she respected had come to this particular conclusion, and she decided that he was uncomfortable with women as adversaries because he did not know how to 'read the clues' to interpret what they were thinking. It is a masculine trait which she considers is at the heart of much behaviour that is interpreted as sexual discrimination.

Two legal pathways

It was possible for her to combine academic life and chambers' life at this point because her particular chambers was used to having part-timers and organised the allocation of expenses on a percentage of fees basis. Sympathetic organisation of work was also possible because of the general practice nature of the chambers. However at the end of two-and-a-half years both her chambers and her university department 'put me to my election' requiring her to make a choice between the two strands of legal life she was pursuing, and she realised that her attempt to combine both academic and court life was in fact militating against success in either of them. The commitment to academic life prevented her from taking on jury trials and High Court work, and the time spent at court meant that she would also hamper her progress up the academic hierarchy because it reduced the time available for research and publication.

Possibly accelerated by the departure of some members of her chambers to set up a new set of chambers, the reasons for her decision to opt for the academic life 'were threefold and in no particular order'. First, although she enjoyed both the Bar and the academic world she would describe the academic and teaching side as being 'thoroughly enjoyable' whereas the Bar life was merely 'enjoyable'. Secondly, both she and her husband were in practice at the Manchester Bar and on three occasions had narrowly avoided being on opposite sides of the same case, 'a potentially uncomfortable situation to be in. My husband was clearly more entranced by and committed to the Bar than I was', so, as at that time university salaries were 'not as abysmal as they later became', it seemed more than sensible for them as an economic unit to opt for at least one regular salary. A third consideration was that it would be very much easier to combine teaching with having a family. She had as her examplar, Diana Kloss, another lecturer in the law faculty, who a few years ahead of Dame Brenda had shown that it was possible to combine an academic career with raising a family. 'She had already fought all the battles for maternity leave.' The desire to have children made life at the Bar very much less attractive for, as she put it, 'when you're at the Bar, you're completely on your own as a cottage industry, a one-woman band. Chambers being composed of a group of sole practitioners not in partnership, did not have maternity policies and the best that you could expect was not to have to pay, or not have to pay very much of chambers' expenses while you were away and somehow your historic debt would keep coming in to support you'.

Dame Brenda clearly revelled in the variety of her teaching and academic experience, which was in effect an unintended preparation for her later life on the bench. She taught constitutional law, contract, tort, family law, Roman law and law for social workers, 'almost everything apart from criminal law, although I had argued criminal cases while at the Bar',

Not a typical career path

Dame Brenda describes her progress to the senior ranks of the judiciary as 'very unusual. I am not a typical role model'. And indeed that is true, although that does not make admiration of her achievements any less valid. Much of that progress was unsought and was suggested to her by others because she was a highly competent lawyer and the person most suitable for the job. She herself would describe her progress as being 'very fortunate, very fortunate indeed'. After having been a legal member of Mental Health Review Tribunals, mainly as a result of the chairman of the North West Tribunal having read her book on mental health law, she was appointed to the Council on Tribunals in 1980.

In 1982 she was the beneficiary of a new policy at the Lord Chancellor's Department to appoint 'a few practically-minded academics' as assistant recorders; she accepted but initially found this a 'terrifying experience' because she had not been a serious criminal practitioner. Fairly quickly she was appointed a law commissioner and moved to London, where she says, self-deprecatingly, she was 'a very attractive proposition because the Lord Chancellor's department effectively got a law commissioner with an assistant recorder thrown in'. However the more sensible assessment of her appointment was that it was helpful for a commissioner promoting law reform to have practical court experience.

In 1989, under a practice which no longer appertains, there was a category of employed silk, and it was suggested to Dame Brenda that she might be 'sufficiently meritorious' to apply. She did so and was appointed and almost simultaneously became a professor at King's College London (though still on secondment to the Law Commission).

Motherhood

Although when her daughter was born in 1973 she took only three months' maternity leave, she had come to appreciate the wisdom in her case of opting for the academic life, 'because I had quite a lot of time off in hospital beforehand because of pre-eclampsia and was given a considerable amount of consideration by the university for the rest of that academic year'. Regularity of childcare and competent childcare was obviously essential, and her daughter was brought up with the help of a weekly nanny, and later a nanny who could drive when her daughter went to school so that she could be collected from school by someone responsible other than her mother.

Her daughter is not a lawyer but a merchant banker who 'probably works harder in terms of hours than I do myself', possibly because she used to 'go to sleep to the sound of my typewriter'. Now she regards her mother as a role model who encouraged her to think that working hard and combining a career and family life was not only possible but was in fact 'the normal thing to do'. Dame Brenda is not totally convinced by this because she feels that there might be a genetic component in her daughter's determination and focus on work, and that her daughter's attitudes were as much influenced by her father as by her mother's example, but it is a nice point to debate, and probably there would be insufficient evidence either way to persuade Dame Brenda's judicial mind.

Working mothers

Dame Brenda herself obviously has a slightly ambivalent attitude to the 'have it all' view of professional women. She recognises that she would have found it extraordinarily hard to remain at home without the stimulus of external work but she also recognises, and mentions this several times, that 'I could work only because another woman would be paid comparatively peanuts to look after my child'. She was also supported by a husband who, himself fascinated by the law, understood that it would be inconceivable for her to give up work. However she is also very clear that 'the last thing that I would do would be to criticise or patronise women who want to stay at home to bring up their children, although', she adds sadly, 'this is very frequently a choice that is made by the husband rather than the woman herself'.

Her wide experience of the family in legal situations has led her to the conclusion that although family relationships are all very individual, 'many people still have a great desire to keep personal privacy and confidentiality even within a close relationship and it is perhaps an illusion that sharing assets within the marriage or even the knowledge of the value of those assets is very common'. This can make the whole assessment of what is fair on marriage breakdowns extremely difficult, especially when children are involved. Dame Brenda has been targeted by several fathers' organisations, for in their view not respecting their equal rights to custody of, or access to, their children. She feels this is somewhat undeserved. 'Most of these organisations criticise judges for not respecting the spirit of the Children Act [1989] for which I was, ironically, partly responsible.' Far from being against shared parenting as some organisations are, she is very firmly in support of it, 'if it is genuine shared parenting because that it what is best for the child'. While she considers that she did not 'become a judge in order to be liked', she feels that criticisms of her for undermining the role of the father are particularly unjust. We have a natural expectation as citizens that judges should be impartial, but when we do not get what we want as individuals we perhaps equally as naturally single out judges rather than the disembodied law for our opprobrium.

Coming from a generation where it would not be likely that women would have other women as mentors, she can point to very few women who were influential in shaping her life. Her headmistress was one because of the encouragement she gave her, but her real mentor was probably her present husband, Julian Farrand, who was the Dean of the Faculty of Law at Manchester University who had been responsible for requiring her to choose between the academic and chambers life. He was, she said, very good at encouraging all the junior lecturers in his department and instituting all sorts of good employment practices. And, as well as showing how to combine work and family life, Diana Kloss was 'a shining example of intelligence and getting to the heart of the issue'.

On being a judge

Many women who were educated in the 1960s have found that they acquire the soubriquet of 'the first woman who' and Dame Brenda was no exception. She was the first woman on the Law Commission and sat there for nearly 10 years without being joined by another.

'What one notices,' she says, 'is that because so many colleagues of my age or above and even some of the younger ones are not very used to having women as equal colleagues in the legal environment, there is a lack of familiarity with how women think and operate. This must obviously be prejudicial to the appointment of judges and in fact the experiences of women judges when they are once appointed.'

She cites the formal domestic traditions of the past which are still a feature of life in judges' lodgings. The expectation at the end of a formal dinner is that all women will retire to another room while the men will remain for port and conversation. Dame Brenda has been not unnaturally 'deeply affronted' by the assumption in some places that she too, despite being one of the judges, will also retire. On one occasion she insisted that neither she nor the female barrister, who was 'junior of the circuit' and had been invited as a guest, would withdraw in order to leave the men to their masculine conversations, because she felt that this would have been 'quite insulting' to her younger colleague.

As far as the judiciary is concerned there needs to be 'a reassessment of who gets appointed'. The old assumptions about how merit is assessed must be revisited, 'because the requirement is not just for a more gender-balanced bench, but for a more varied bench. We need to look very carefully at the criteria for a particular appointment and how the process is carried out'. She is however wary of any assessment process resulting in a set of rigid selection criteria, as that will exclude many people who would otherwise be productive and strong members of the judiciary – including perhaps Dame Brenda herself.

She is indeed very concerned about the public face of the law. To the obvious question as to whether there should be women law lords, a somewhat naïve question I realise after I have put it, she replies that it is wrong that the ultimate court in the land should be composed of judges from such a narrow section of the community and 'I am not just talking about women' because that narrow section of the community has had a very particular set of experiences. Although the Scottish and Irish law lords, she feels, have had more general experience, the experience of the English law lords has been mainly confined to the Commercial or Chancery Bar. They have had little experience at the sharp end in the magistrates' and county courts of cases on which they will be required to be the ultimate arbiters in the Lords. Although they are very acute and able and probably could make the leap of imagination required into that mind set, the general public may not be capable of making the further leap of imagination to accept that the law lords so constituted could understand the situations of women and, more importantly, other groups.

The legal profession now

The character of the profession is generally changing because young women are not willing to put up with discrimination. She does not feel that there is intentional discrimination, but rather that it is 'institutional discrimination' where people behave as they always have done and cling to old traditions because that makes life much easier. She counsels against complacency. 'Young women should not delude themselves that just because some things have changed, the struggle for equality is all over.' There are still many issues which need to be addressed and discussed. 'Young women need to recognise that everything changes when you have children, and that whatever views you had when you started you have to change them to accommodate the changes in family life.' And again she points out that all successful women are dependent on other women to make it happen, 'and it is other women usually and not other men on whom they depend'. It is unrealistic for women to consider that merely relying on 'just giving it time' will be any more effective than it has been in other professions because of the continuing necessity to juggle career and the more varied life that most women want to have or have forced upon them.

Her choice of the law as a career she considers to have been 'very, very fortunate', but she would not encourage anyone to go to the Bar for either 'unduly romantic or unduly mercenary reasons. Romance and the opportunity to make money are there, but the romance of the Bar is grossly exaggerated and most is hard mind-numbing work requiring many different personal skills'. Young lawyers should recognise too that there is no certainty of substantial or indeed very much remuneration in Bar work, and undue mistiness about romance or money could be the recipe for an unhappy life. However, 'if young people go into the law because it is interesting, challenging and worthwhile work, and recognising that there might be a chance of making a respectable amount of money, then they are less likely to be disappointed'. She herself loves the law and everything about it. She finds it 'all fascinating'.

What is clear is that a judge's mind needs to operate on several levels at once. In many cases she must find the compassion and the compassionate words to deal with very hard situations particularly involving families while at the same time shuffling the precise legal possibilities and outcomes of the facts of the case and her decision. It is possible to detect a change of gear when she speaks, as a sharp internal interrogator works out whether she should comment on something, what she should say about it, whether it will affect other people, whether she should mention them by name or whether she should simply refuse to say anything about it at all. And all this is accompanied by a genuine friendliness which does not wish to erect barriers but is aware constantly of the difference between the private persona and the public face of the law.

Melissa Hardee

Melissa Hardee is one of the few non-fee earning partners in the City of London. She is training partner, corporate knowledge management partner and quality partner at CMS Cameron McKenna, a member of the Law Society Training Committee, the chairman of the City of London Training Sub-Committee, and a member of the Lord Chancellor's Standing Conference on Legal Education.

Knowledge management

The word 'quality' occurs frequently in conversation with Melissa Hardee, quality of training, quality of professional support and how both of these can provide quality of service to clients. Knowledge management is 'all about quality in the practice. The reality of what we are doing is providing knowledge and experience to our clients and it would be crazy not to be more efficient in utilizing that'.

Knowledge management is simply harnessing the intellectual capital ('a much over-used but very accurate phrase') of a firm so that the clients who instruct that firm can benefit from the fact that it is an organisation of professionals with a common purpose rather than an agglomeration of sole practitioners. Melissa considers that for the firm itself it has four main benefits. 'Sharing knowledge rather than re-inventing the wheel every time is more economical, it helps with the training of young lawyers, it ensures quality control, and, most importantly for the partners, it provides an element of a sound risk management strategy.' Her firm is not now purely UK based and she has noticed that although there has been a sea change in the perception of the value of professional support lawyers and systems in the last 15 years, 'our continental colleagues are also now discovering that sharing knowledge is a good thing'.

Unfortunately when people perceive knowledge as conferring power they can often find it difficult to share with anyone other than those who are far too junior to be a threat to their own power base. A firm's lawyers really need to see themselves as part of an organisation where 'everyone is contributing for and to the common good'.

It might be quite hard to find someone with a better basic background to be in charge of such important issues.

Australia

Melissa was born in Australia and lived there until 1989. Her parents, both head teachers, somewhat disillusioned with the state education at that time, were insistent that their daughter did not follow them into the profession. After 'an excellent education' at Sydney Girls' High School, following two years at a school for gifted children, Melissa's first ambition was to train in medicine, but she found herself at the tender age of 17 enrolled in law at Sydney University. When she examined the first year curriculum, though, she had what she describes as a, 'Torts, what on earth are torts?' moment, and transferred to arts majoring in German as well as studying several other languages.

'When I graduated with my shiny new BA (Hons) I came up against the difficulties of having a non-vocational qualification. After various deadends, in desperation I went for a job as a debt collector at a law firm. However the HR manager, who seemed to select people on their zodiac sign, offered me a position as a secretary to one of the partners (whose sign I apparently matched) when she learned that I could type, a skill that I had taught myself one Easter vacation.' Melissa firmly believes that no skill or knowledge that you acquire is ever useless. Her accomplishment on the piano probably aided her typing which got her into a law firm after university. QED!

She was also fortunate to find herself working for a partner who was 'a broadly-educated as opposed to well-educated lawyer, a linguist and an aesthete', who came to believe that having a BA should be a minimum requirement for a secretary. Given a great deal of responsibility Melissa became increasingly involved in his trademark practice and increasingly keen to do more than just type – particularly as her consumption of correcting tape was above the national average. After a year as a trademark paralegal in another firm (her first firm did not employ paralegals) she decided that 'I could be more than a paralegal, in fact I was sure that I could be a lawyer too. So, I decided to go back to where I had originally started and do a law degree'. And back to Sydney University she went and added a very good law degree to her CV.

Melissa considers that she has always been fairly idealistic, and perhaps because of that idealism as well as her linguistic background 'I saw law as a different language, where the role of lawyers was to interpret this language for those who need the law but who do not "speak" it. Unfortunately now this facilitative interpretative role of the lawyer has receded to the extent that being a lawyer has become an end in its own right rather than a role required in response to need'.

Fortunately university education in Australia at that time was totally free so that funding for a second degree was not an issue. Indeed Melissa believes passionately that higher education should be free, and that there is no point in the Law Society or the Government bemoaning access to the profession if financial constraints make it impossible for people from disadvantaged backgrounds to pay for their academic training. The only way to provide unfettered access to the profession is to make it free.

There is no requirement to serve articles in Australia. In Melissa's day qualifying law degrees provided all the academic learning, so that the 'vocational stage' of legal education which provides the bridge between the academic stage and practice was a truly practical type of Legal Practice Course (LPC) with the Professional Skills Course (PSC) thrown in. The students worked in 'virtual' firms for the six-month course, running transactions and cases with each other. Everything was included from conveyances and leases, to sales of businesses, personal injury claims and divorces. Unfortunately, whether that training and development continued following qualification was very much a matter of chance because of the lack of any sort of structured and supervised articles which meant that the first few years of a young solicitor's legal life could be very variable.

On arriving at the doors of their first firms as qualified solicitors they found that there was no requirement for experience in different areas of the law. 'It was all luck of the draw and any learning was based very much on the principle of osmosis. Even as newly qualified solicitors we all had an office each, so we were out of sight and out of mind to a large extent and did not have the benefit of learning by observing.' With no experience of any of the practice areas, Melissa was given the choice whilst still studying of qualifying into banking, property or litigation and chose banking, 'because it sounded as though it could have international possibilities'. Confined as she then was for seeming eternity to banking transactions she is 'not unsurprisingly a big fan of the training contract system over here because of the opportunity it gives trainees to try their hand at all sorts of things before their qualified career really starts'.

To London

After experience in two Sydney law firms it was time for the experience that she had promised herself since 1979 at the age of 21. 'I had always been fairly Eurocentric, but in that year I came to London for a few weeks and I fell in love with it, and I said that one day I would go back there to work for a few years.' This opportunity arose in 1989 when many of Melissa's peers were going to the UK to work for a couple of years, and coincided with a dearth of lawyers in the UK, particularly in the banking sector. Melissa rang a firm of Sydney recruitment consultants to discuss possibilities; they thought that she had rung about the banking position they had just advertised with Barlow Lyde & Gilbert. 'Serendipity,' she thought. She borrowed the money for her air fare, packed her bags and came to London. 'When I arrived and started work though I realised just how small a pool I had been swimming in, and how large a pool I was now drowning in. At the interview I had been asked if I had done a syndicated loan. I had said yes proudly because I had – the only one my firm had ever done. However, over here all loans were syndicated!'

'Also, in Australia our documents were shorter, the banks were very much in charge and did not negotiate.' Grittily she embarked on 'a hell of a learning curve' because Melissa is clearly someone who relishes hard work and a challenge, but then came the early 1990s recession, a steep dive in banking work which, on her assessment, meant little chance of overcoming the learning curve and a decision which redirected the focus of her professional life.

'Academically I love learning, perhaps it is because of being brought up in a teaching family and the very good education that I had been given, but I do believe that knowledge is the key to everything.' Melissa saw an advertisement in the Law Society *Gazette* for a Head of Banking Know-how at Clifford Chance at the same time that she assessed her progress on her learning curve. Serendipity again, although 'at the time I knew that I had to accept that when I moved from fee earning that I had taken myself off the upwardly mobile career path, but I didn't really care as I was actually doing something I was equally good at and found creative and stimulating'. Instead she would concentrate on 'putting into practice my intuitions about how the knowledge that lawyers acquire can be organised and disseminated for the benefit of others'. She assumed that there could never be any prospect of partnership for someone who did not earn fees and 'that would be that'.

Working in Old Royex House with its 'shabby genteel' atmosphere was a very productive and happy period of her professional life when she was indeed able to put many of her ideas into practice. Some firms consider that the installation of sophisticated intranet systems is about all that is required, but Melissa feels that knowledge management goes far beyond this. 'It is really about people and human behaviour. In fact, it is all about self-reflection – thinking about what you have done, what you have learned that could help you or others in the future, how you could do it better next time, what you would need in order to do it better, and so on. All the systems in the world are not going to work if the users themselves are not self-reflective. If they are, then knowledge management happens naturally.'

Moving to McKenna's

However after about two years a management change in the banking department removed the 'fruitful supportive atmosphere that had nurtured me', and Melissa seriously considered returning to fee earning as that appeared to be the only way of being truly valued in the City legal arena. However, when she approached recruitment consultancies, and they realised the depth of her experience in knowledge management, she found herself inundated with offers of know-how roles. In the end McKenna's head of personnel took the initiative, phoned her at home, and persuaded her to accept their offer, 'I was flattered. There is nothing like appealing to one's ego and I fell for it immediately.' Serendipity at work again as things turned out.

As happy as she had been at Clifford Chance she had, 'never experienced the sort of hands-on support from the partners (plural) that I found at McKenna's and anything that I have achieved has been because of that early support. When I am asked by PSLs (professional support lawyers) how to gain fee earners' co-operation and set up the right culture in their firms, my answer is always that you need a champion. You cannot do it on your own'. As this was also the time when she met and married her husband, a successful and talented surgeon, Melissa unexpectedly found the life that she wanted, and in London. She had 'come home'.

Two years later she was made up to partner in charge both of know-how and training at McKenna's, a responsibility which expanded with the firm's merger into CMS Cameron McKenna. From those early beginnings when she was the only professional support lawyer in the firm there are now around 20 professional support lawyers, as well as training personnel and IT staff involved in providing a complete knowledge management strategy.

Melissa has always been prepared to work hard for what she wanted, and realised on joining McKenna's that bridges needed to be built within the firm between herself and the different practice areas, as well as between the practice areas themselves. So, she attended all the team meetings that she could, with 'sandwich lunches almost every day for a year', to get to know the diverse teams that came under the corporate umbrella, and to learn about their know-how needs. 'What I wanted to achieve was a free flow of useful information and knowledge and this would only happen if there was an atmosphere of trust.'

'I don't believe that knowledge sharing can be subject to exceptions, as that is like saying that all people are equal but some are more equal than others. Some people fear that if they make their knowledge available to other people it could be misused, and unfortunately some people do try their hands at things which are not within their field of expertise even when there is an expert available. In my view the solution to this is not to lock up know-how but to look at why such "cottage industries" are happening in the first place. Is it because of ignorance about the existence of people with expertise or is it a lack of confidence in the experts because of a prior unfortunate experience? Whatever the reasons, these are behavioural issues that need to be dealt with in appropriate ways and not by locking up know-how.'

This opinion is informed by Melissa's view that what makes a really good lawyer is 'strong peripheral vision, someone with a breadth of knowledge who is truly broad-minded so that they can recognise where issues may arise even if they do not have the particular specialist expertise – and they know someone who does! I am a great believer in the Renaissance man'.

Professional support lawyers

Increasingly being a professional support lawyer (PSL) is a positive career choice for those who prefer the backroom academic side of law to negotiation and confrontation; indeed Melissa is very heartened that one of the firm's highly-regarded corporate fee earners (male) has recently opted to become a PSL in her corporate team.

'Being a PSL is engaging in highly creative work. It often involves looking for lateral solutions, thinking about how people work and anticipating the systems and the information that they will require, and persuading people to co-operate.'

She is somewhat saddened that, although the profile of PSLs has improved and it is a legitimate career option for good lawyers, there is still no obvious career progression. Melissa herself is still very much a one-off. It is still necessary, she opines, for a PSL to have a partner in the department who will champion activities and initiatives, and to give support for what can be seen as merely cost and not profit-centre activities. From her own perspective she considers herself fortunate that she is part of 'an enlightened firm' and she considers that her own appointment as a partner with no fee earning responsibilities is a good allocation of partnerial time, 'because you need someone at that level looking after things ultimately. If the partner concerned is combining that role with fee earning then the soft stuff will always end up at the bottom of the pile. And although know-how and training might be "soft"; they are still important. In fact, I would say essential for today's law firms'.

The real prejudice which exists for someone in a PSL role has nothing to do with one's gender, but comes from 'the fee earning machismo, the perception of fee earners that if you are not fee earning you can't be any good, and this can be translated into the way management may only recognise those contributions which are easily measurable in short-term financial gain. Fortunately for me my profile both within and without the firm is such that even if I have been made to feel like Cinderella at times, I am a Cinderella who gets to go to a lot of balls'.

The future?

As to the future? 'Well if I wanted to be provocative, I could say that I see a time when there were fewer lawyers actually dealing with clients, their roles being more on the client marketing side and actual work being done behind the scenes particularly with improved technology. Of course there will always be a need for negotiation, but more automated support and automated document management systems might reduce the number of transactional lawyer hours required on a transaction.' These comments hint at innovations which Melissa has instigated in her firm over the last nine years in a constant drive to respond to the needs of practice.

This vision she considers can only help women in the long run. She feels honestly that she has never come across instances of overt prejudice against women in the workplace, but admits that there are people with whom it is just difficult to work and that perhaps women are more ready to try to make those situations work, even beyond the point where such attempts are futile. 'It is so important to find the right environment,' she says several times, 'to find somewhere you can flourish and where you are appreciated, and to do that you need to be aware, to be self-reflective.'

Melissa is 'by nature an optimist. There is no point in looking back with the benefit of hindsight and being more mature and imagining what I might have done differently. I learned a long time ago that life isn't easy, particularly as a non-fee earning partner. As hackneyed as it may be, life is a journey and there will be some things that happen along the way which are simply awful. The skill is to learn and come through it with something that will help you in the future'. The optimism certainly informs the statement that 'even when the worst things happen I believe that it's just before something really positive will happen'.

That having been said she explains matter-of-factly that women do have to face an uncomfortable reality in pursuing a career in law firms. Biology causes the difference, it is women who have the babies, and it is only natural that they should want to. But it means women having to make very difficult choices. Either they or their husbands need to be earning enough for very good childcare, or the husband stays at home to bring up the children, or the woman needs flexibility in the workplace in order to be able to manage both. Until there is greater flexibility there will of necessity be fewer female partners. Whether or not women would, all things being equal, in fact want to be partners is quite another issue. 'But I firmly believe, even though I don't have children myself, that women should be able to have both a career and a family without feeling that they are making the ultimate sacrifice in some way. It is all about flexibility, and to make an outrageous generalisation, it is flexibility that men do not generally understand and therefore do not champion. As long as women have to feel that working less than full time means a lack of commitment to their firms then there is never going to be parity in numbers of female and male partners in the same proportion as enter the profession.'

Her advice to trainees is to get the best, broadest education that they can and not to specialise too soon. 'Remember too that it's an easy option when you are younger to doubt your own intellectual ability. If you feel intuitively that something is wrong, it is too easy to assume that it is you who has it wrong. However, it may be that you are the fresh pair of eyes that can see the wood from the trees. It is important to remember that being junior is a reflection of one's level of knowledge, not one's intellectual capacity.' This is of course where she considers that her PSLs play an invaluable role in informal help given to trainees and young assistants on the proper way to approach problems, and has led to her work in legal education and training, because she wants to 'see beyond the firm' to improve the training of solicitors generally. 'Training is part and parcel of knowledge management, another way of disseminating or sharing knowledge.' On legal education she is particularly passionate and is heavily involved in the Law Society's 'Training Framework Review' of legal education and training. She also sits on various advisory boards and recently took the Chair of the City of London Training Sub-Committee after stepping down from four years as chairman of the UK Legal Education and Training Group. And it was Melissa whom the Law Society asked to chair the current review of management development training for solicitors.

Challenged to consider what qualities have enabled her to succeed other than obvious hard work and intellectual flexibility (as well her linguistic fluency and academic qualification), Melissa considers that she has very good right hand/left hand brain connections and it is this which enables her to analyse problems and come up with creative solutions and then be able to implement them at the detail level.

'I think the way I came to knowledge management was a bit like coming out of the primeval swamp. My early years as a lawyer could best be described as "character building" but out of them came various experiences and influences which provided the necessary elements.' However, it is clear that her personal strengths were present at a very early stage together with a strong dose of passion for carrying out her visions. One of her professors described her very early on as, 'intelligent, imaginative and resourceful, always conspicuous for her capacity for leadership. Her initiatives are shrewd in judgment and win the confidence of others. She handles people with firmness, but with a tact and charm that never fails to gain co-operation.'

'My friends tell me that I work too hard. Maybe it's because we don't have children that I feel the need to be active and involved, and helping young lawyers develop is my way of giving back or leaving something behind or whatever. My Methodist upbringing just will not allow me to put my feet up and make hedonism my goal.'

Harriet Harman

Harriet Harman is the first ever solicitor to become Solicitor-General, and also the first woman who has attained that position.

'Do I regret having qualified as a solicitor, having worked at Brent Community Advice Centre and the National Council for Civil Liberties, as an MP and now as Solicitor-General? No definitely not. That's not to say that I have not gnashed my teeth from time to time, but having something as work that you believe in and makes you feel that it is worthwhile getting up in the morning because what you are doing is challenging and interesting, that is an absolute luxury.'

That is Harriet Harman's conclusion on a career that has got her, so far, to the highest governmental legal position ever reached by a woman. Her waiting room is lined with pictures of centuries of Solicitors-General from Sir James Herbert, 1486 through Sir Francis Bacon to Sir William Murray, 1756 and then on up the stairs to her first floor office overlooking Buckingham Palace Yard to the picture of her predecessor, Ross Cranston. One day she will join them, 'but not for a long time yet, I hope. You only get your picture on the wall when you are no longer Solicitor-General'.

Becoming a solicitor

Harriet does not know why she went to York University after St Paul's Girls School to read law; it is a question that does not really interest her, it is enough that she progressed through it to begin 'her real career'. She may have been influenced by her mother's former career as a barrister, rather than by her father who was a surgeon, but there was obviously some sort of predisposition to the law in the Harman household because all four Harman daughters became solicitors as did their mother who re-qualified as a solicitor in her 50s before going into practice with Harriet's sister, Sarah.

'It's very easy to drift through university with no clear ambition, and going to the College of Law was just the next step. There was nothing vocational about it, no feeling that I was going to love the law, just the knowledge that I needed to qualify in order to earn a living.' What is unusual, and something that many solicitors will find surprising, was that Harriet loved being at the College of Law itself. 'Most people tell me that they loved university but hated the College of Law, learning all those long lists, but as soon as I was asked to consider the elements of an offence I bonded with the law. And it was there that I learned to work, because up until then I had done very little work at all, either at school or at university.'

Her choice of articles was as pragmatically practical as the decision to go to the College of Law, but this time there was no Damascene conversion. What Harriet looked for was a good firm which would provide a good training and look well on her CV, and this was certainly provided by Knapp Fisher. Her expectation that she would not be in sympathy with the firm's clients was also fulfilled when she found herself acting for a brewery engaged in evicting its general managers from their pubs, 'leaving them homeless and with huge debts'. Harriet was never going to be in sympathy with the commercial purpose of a firm which was also involved in obtaining planning permission 'for huge ugly office blocks, and to keep me sane I went along to the Fulham Legal Advice Centre as a volunteer on Tuesday evenings'.

Brent

It was at Fulham Legal Advice Centre that she spent her time listening to and trying to help 'individual people with individual problems'; it was worthwhile and was a counterbalance to the commercial work that she did for the rest of the week, but Harriet felt that there was something lacking. It was a political, larger scale aspect of working for the disadvantaged that she was unconsciously looking for when she went along to a talk given by the Brent Community Advice Centre. Up to this point the avowed role of legal advice centres was to help individuals as discrete individuals, not to empower low income groups, but Brent Community Advice Centre saw its purpose as strengthening the community by helping local people as groups to help themselves through proper access to legal services.

'It was exactly what I believed in and exactly what I wanted to do.' She volunteered to help them on an unpaid basis, and when articles were over and a paid job at the centre appeared she applied and was accepted. The work that she was now doing was more or less the obverse of what she had been doing in articles, acting for tenants in landlord and tenant matters, representing employees in employment cases, and acting for tenants' associations on planning applications. She felt that she was at the cutting edge of the law aimed at improving conditions for women that was enacted in the Equal Pay Act 1970 and the Sex Discrimination Act 1975.

Although she was covering a vast area of new law and taking on companies with substantial resources at their disposal, 'I did not find it at all scary'. In one case where she represented a tenants' association objecting to a planning application because the factory involved would have been in production all night, she found herself up against Michael Howard, later a Conservative Home Secretary, but then 'a very upmarket barrister. I have to say that we won because we were right'.

'I worked night and day. It was my whole life, and', she pauses because she knows that the next statement goes against much of what she has spent her legal and political career fighting for, 'I had no work-life balance at all. We were a young and committed team and we didn't mind working hard, but I did meet my future husband there.'

This terse association of the personal and the public is a feature of Harriet's discourse, the speech of someone who unflamboyantly tries to live her beliefs. In Brent she felt that she had found 'my spiritual home', and was full of the excitement of being able to use her new skills for the benefit of what she believed in and perhaps that intellectual energy of youth that simply thinks that it is unstoppable. So unstoppable that she soon expanded her horizons to the National Council for Civil Liberties (NCCL) (now Liberty) where she joined a very committed group of young women on the NCCL Sub-Committee on Women's Rights; Tess Gill, Anna Coote, Patricia Hewitt and Ann Sedley. Convinced that a society which permits sex discrimination in the education process cannot be truly equal and effective she wrote a pamphlet on the topic for the NCCL. This she regarded as her 'kind of evening work'.

As seems to happen with many women the impetus for career changing decisions came not from herself but from other people recognising her talents. The post of NCCL Legal Officer became vacant and she was asked to apply for it. This time she did have a tremor of doubt. 'In my mind it was one of the most important jobs that you could do, and I felt that I could never do such an important, bold national job.' Nevertheless she applied, was appointed to the post and began a long partnership with Patricia Hewitt who was then the NCCL General Secretary and is now Secretary of State for Trade and Industry and the Minister for Women. 'Having done a degree I was not interested in, and articles I was not interested in, here I was doing what I believed in. I felt incredibly lucky.' And she was still only 25.

By now Harriet had both established connections in the legal advice world and also made somewhat of a name for herself in the aftermath of the sex discrimination legislation by highlighting the need to use that legislation to accelerate change and progress. She felt very strongly that Parliament had passed legislation to enable women to have equal access to the employment market, and yet the place where women were most under-represented was Parliament itself. And she said so. Frequently. The result was that people began to ask her why she did not herself stand for Parliament, 'to put my money where my mouth was sort of thing'.

The opportunity came in an odd way when Fulham Labour Party went through the process of selecting their next parliamentary candidate to succeed the retiring incumbent. At that same time a group of women in the Fulham Labour Party 'were trying to get a women's group going, and they asked me if I would stand as a potential candidate before the Selection Committee'. Harriet agreed, 'really out of a sense of pure altruism, to help them out, because I did not think that I would get the nomination and I did not particularly want to become an MP for Fulham'. However, the Women's Group was sufficiently well organised, she enjoyed the campaigning and the networking across the Fulham wards, and she came runner up, only one vote away from becoming the official Fulham Labour Party candidate.

'I had been going through the process, helping them out, but at this point I thought to myself that I could be doing this and that I should be doing this for real. I realised that because I had been thinking of other people, because the Women's Group did not think that I would have much of a chance either, and I had just been helping them to get started and I was so relaxed about it that I had invested the event with none of my personal ambitions or any fear of failure.'

Parliament

Armed with this new self-knowledge she applied to be and was accepted as the candidate for Peckham. In 2002 she celebrated her 20th anniversary as the MP for that constituency, known as Camberwell and Peckham since 1992 because of the boundary changes.

'We were a long time in opposition,' offers Harriet, but she used that time well. 'If you are on the front bench in opposition you get experience of a lot of things.' In her case it was health, social services, campaigning for the concept of a minimum wage and a low pay commission which was finally constituted in 1998. She was however never prepared to be involved with education policy because her children were still at school. This may seem a strange omission for someone who considers that education in its various forms is the key to so much, but she decided that when she met the teachers of her children, now 20, 18 and 16, she wanted to be regarded simply as her children's mother and not someone who had been making policy statements about education a few hours previously.

She has learned to be a private person as far as her family is concerned, and questions in that direction are politely and monosyllabically answered or lost in an aura of deliberate vagueness. Except when there is something to set straight because almost inevitably given the tenor of the House of Commons at that time, the election of any woman, let alone a young woman, or a young woman with a child produced an adverse reaction. One particular rumour was reported in the press and has since then attained the status of 'fact' by unresearched repetition. This is the story that she 'breast-fed her first child in the Chamber of the House of Commons'. Far from being true Harriet says that she would never have taken her baby anywhere near the Chamber of the House, but that the rumour was born out of the 'atmosphere of near hysteria in the House of Commons at that time when I became the first pregnant MP. In an environment where only three per cent of MPs were women, the thought of a woman MP with a child made the men very uncomfortable indeed'.

This also led to another rumour, that she had gone through the division lobby one night with her baby under her jacket; as only members can go through the division lobby and a baby cannot qualify as a member, this would have been a serious breach of parliamentary protocol. 'However,' says Harriet, 'I had just not lost all the weight that I had put on during pregnancy. Far from having my child under my jacket, as if I would, I was just fat.'

Towards proper representation

Now 30 per cent of MPs are women, which Harriet considers is still woefully short of proper representation, but at that time the general impression of what was right and proper was not in any way in accordance with what was acceptable to the general populace. 'Subsequently babies were breast-fed in the Chamber of the GLC, and why not? But at that time most male MPs thought that a woman's place was addressing the kitchen and not addressing legislation.'

She clearly feels that much still has to be done to make Parliament a more comfortable and possible place for women. 'The hours were absolutely ridiculous. Since January this year there has been some improvement, because the House now starts at 11 a.m. instead of

2.30 p.m., but it is still not easy. I was determined to campaign to change the working hours but it took me a bit longer than I thought it would.' The compensating factor for her is that the recesses are very long, and although MPs will still have work to do, they are more able to tailor the hours they work to their own particular circumstances. But in her own case, working as an MP with young children, it did mean that a full-time nanny who slept in for four nights a week was required to enable her to fulfil her Parliamentary commitments. 'And fortunately my sister lived round the corner.'

Harriet has campaigned long and hard for family friendly hours and working practices and extended maternity leave and pay. More generous provisions have just come into force in April 2003, but the women who campaigned for them through Parliament laboured surprisingly under a lack of proper maternity provision for MPs. 'There were very few Labour MPs in London at that time, women MPs were an oddity and a woman MP with a baby was regarded as a freak.' Despite the Labour Party in opposition being very much a minority party during the period of her children's infancy, and her personal vote being of no crucial importance in the grand scheme of things, the Labour Whips 'gave me very little latitude' and were insistent that she turned up to vote at every possible opportunity.

At that time Harriet felt very isolated among the people who would have seemed her natural peer group, 'but my peer group developed outside the House of Commons with people like Patricia Hewitt who have since become very influential. I did think then and I do think now that there must be more women in Parliament and in senior positions so that we can put issues of fairness and equality on the agenda.'

Fairness, equality and the judiciary

For Harriet fairness and equality extends beyond the position of women in the state. It covers the position of ethnic minority groups and those who are disadvantaged because of lack of educational and economic opportunities. Her definition of providing opportunities is very wide, and in the Crown Prosecution Service (CPS), which is within her bailiwick, it encompasses staff at all levels. In the CPS there are many people in the lower grades 'who have acquired expertise and who are studying for legal qualifications in their spare time and with their own money'. Harriet is very proud that the CPS Law Scholarship Programme can make it easier to increase the diversity of those able to proceed to the higher ranks in the service.

She has also noticed that because the CPS is a civil service department it has the benefit of many of the civil service family friendly policies which have resulted in many women and people from ethnic minorities being able to attain senior positions. 'The pool of available talent for the judiciary requires considerable broadening and the consideration of senior CPS staff for judicial office is one way to do this.' This would result in both an actual broadening of the bench's understanding of the difficulties and concerns of ordinary people and also the general public having a greater faith in the judicial system.

She speaks interestingly about 'judicial confidence'. This is two-pronged. It means not only the confidence of the public in its judiciary, but also the confidence of the judiciary itself that it is dealing with individual cases with understanding and firmness. She says that she is 'very impressed' by women CPS prosecutors who deal with rape victims who say that they do not wish to prosecute. 'Where often a man might accept this, because he perhaps does not understand or does not wish to be seen to harass the victim, female prosecutors often review the evidence and point out that they are going to go ahead with the prosecution anyway because that is the right course of action.'

She has a great belief that the bench should be 'gender neutral', and that if we had a mixed bench that state would be attained. 'The law is still totally unrepresentative of society as a whole. It does matter that there are not enough women on the bench, because in a society where we are trying to encourage women to reach their full potential, and to regard themselves as equal to men, the judiciary looks old-fashioned and prejudiced.' In that regard she feels that 'It is a great step forward that we have our first woman President of the Law Society, but look how long that has taken. After all this time we are still celebrating new examples of the "First Woman Who ..." became something.'

All that criticism of various aspects of the law having been voiced, she is still of the opinion that it is a very suitable career for a woman. 'A legal training is never wasted, because it encourages rigorous thought processes, and teaches discipline. I draw on my legal training all the time in my work as an MP in terms of dealing with court cases, because it is another way of thinking and it is logical.'

As she rises to go to the House, she has 10 minutes to get from Buckingham Gate to the Front Bench, she offers to send me additional material to flesh out what I have scribbled 'did I talk too fast for you?'. There is the question of how much one has learned about the woman rather than the minister from this short session, but then perhaps the minister is the woman and there is no work-life balance for someone who is totally committed to a cause.

Madeleine Heggs

Madeleine Heggs was the first woman and the first practising solicitor to be appointed as a Social Security and Child Support Commissioner.

Family background

Madeleine's father, Emilio Calderan, came from a Venetian family specialising in silk weaving. He had qualified as an engineer before settling in England in 1919. His original intention had been to study the development of dying processes before returning to Turin where his father had now settled and become a well-known textile manufacturer. In the event, he set up in business on his own account by establishing a silk weaving factory in London, supplying silk, velvet and other soft and furnishing fabrics to Liberty and various specialist couturiers and upholsterers. So successful was he that members of the Royal family were included amongst his customers. Her mother, Graziella Grilli, came from Lausanne in Switzerland, where her father was a Calvinist Minister. Madeleine, who was born in London in 1929, was brought up speaking English, French and Italian, a linguistic accomplishment which she later found useful in her legal practice.

Following the outbreak of World War Two, Madeleine and her elder brother, John, were initially evacuated with other school children to Blandford, Dorset but returned to London in 1940 following the entry of Italy into the war and the subsequent death of their father. 'My mother was left to care for John (then aged 12), myself (aged 10) and a newly-born son (Robert) with no financial means other than the house she lived in. The factory was closed because of the death of my father and the premises, machinery and other assets had to be sold to pay the outstanding business indebtedness. My mother had never worked before, but she supported the family by teaching Latin, Greek and French and by taking in paying guests.' Madeleine was a pupil at Notting Hill and Ealing High School, a Public Girls Day School Trust (PGDST) school, and with the assistance of a bursary from the PGDST she was able to continue attending school for the duration of the War. This generosity is 'something for which I have always been grateful'.

Madeleine left school in 1948 at the age of 18, having passed School Certificate and Higher School Certificate, with the ambition of qualifying as a doctor. Medicine at that time, although nominally open to women, was not an easy profession for them to enter. Training places for women were restricted to the Royal Free Hospital, while universities, understandably, gave preference to the admission of ex-service personnel. Madeleine's choice was further constrained when she learned that a financial grant, which she would have required to continue academic education would only be available if she undertook to work as a teacher after graduation.

Articles of clerkship

Fortunately Madeleine's guardian, Antonio de Reya, offered to help. Originally from Trieste, he was a partner in the City firm of Crawley & de Reya, which specialised in work connected with the newly emerging film industry. He took on both Madeleine and her brother John as articled clerks without charging the premium which was then customarily payable. In addition he paid each of them '£1 per week as a contribution towards our travelling expenses, but I also supplemented my income during articles by undertaking maths coaching in my spare time'.

The Law Society's exercise of control over the content of the practical training of articled clerks at that time was 'rudimentary' and Madeleine spent most of her time during articles acting as an outdoor clerk, attending at the Royal Courts of Justice to issue writs and subpoenas and delivering letters and briefs and instructions to counsel's chambers. In the office 'I was not taught how to draft a will, wind up an estate, administer a trust, undertake litigation, prepare a brief or undertake elementary unregistered and registered conveyancing. My knowledge of all branches of current law and practice was gained through private study and attending courses at the Law Society's School of Law at Lancaster Gate.' In the early years most of the students were ex-servicemen and the provision of toilet and other facilities at Lancaster Gate for the handful of women students was 'not at all sophisticated. By way of compensation, we women students were at least noticed and treated tolerantly and courteously by the lecturers and male students'.

While attending courses at Lancaster Gate, Madeleine met Geoffrey Heggs, one of the founder members in 1952 of the Solicitors' Articled Clerks Society (SACS), which later became the Young

Solicitors' Group. This was the first organisation to be recognised by the Law Society as representative of the interests of articled clerks, leading eventually, following amendment of the Society's Royal Charter, to establishment of Associate Membership of the Society. Geoffrey was elected as the first President of SACS while Eva Crawley was elected to membership of the committee, thereby commencing her many years of committee service in the interest of women solicitors.

America

Madeleine had passed both parts of her Intermediate, obtained an external LLB at London University, had completed her articles of clerkship and was about to commence her Finals' course at Lancaster Gate in 1953 when Geoffrey was awarded a postgraduate fellowship tenable at Yale Law School. Deciding that this was their opportunity to embark upon a joint career they married in March 1953. 'It was an exciting time. When we arrived at New Haven, Connecticut in September 1953 the Korean War had just ended and I joined "the Yale wives", the wives of students in the graduate schools who were looking for employment. Most were fortunate if they obtained employment as librarians or shop assistants but because of my English law degree I was engaged as a legal research assistant in the trial law department of Wiggin & Dana, the attorneys for Yale University. In that capacity I not only researched points of law but also drafted submissions for lodgment in court based upon applying the applicable legal principles to the facts in issue. At last I was learning some of the skills which I should have acquired during my service under articles.'

Qualified solicitor

Although Geoffrey could have remained at Yale after having obtained his postgraduate degree, he returned with Madeleine to the UK in the autumn of 1954 to enable her to complete her professional training as a solicitor. After qualification in 1955 she obtained employment as a conveyancing solicitor with Blundell Baker & Co. in Bedford Row at a salary of £500 per annum. Career prospects at that time for young women solicitors were strictly limited, and in common with many other professions there was a general expectation that a woman would cease to work when she had a family.

So in 1957, when she was expecting her first child, Madeleine set up in practice on her own account at her home in Ealing. Professional advertising was strictly prohibited and Madeleine only accepted new clients upon personal recommendation. Nevertheless, she soon developed a substantial practice in domestic and commercial conveyancing, trusts and probate, with a certain amount of family law and civil litigation. Her linguistic facility, 'I have always loved speaking Italian', resulted in cases being referred to her in London by lawyers in Italy. Working from home enabled her to deliver and collect her three children from school each day, look after them outside school hours and care for them during school holidays, but the accelerating growth of her practice eventually dominated her life to an unacceptable extent.

She also had a strong sense of social justice, of wishing to help those in more straitened circumstances, and while she was in practice as a solicitor frequently did work for little or no money for those unable to pay. 'I really was in general practice and found myself doing all sorts of things which did not strictly speaking constitute legal work, including helping people to fill in their UCCA [university application form superseded by UCAS] forms. This was not in my view what is now regarded as pro bono work, it is just what we did at that time. Of course it would be much more difficult now to take this attitude because legal practice in large firms is very much a big business, and as far as sole practitioners are concerned the insurance premiums are just prohibitive. I would have to think twice now before I set up in practice on my own.'

Tribunal chairman and commissioner

After 19 years as a sole practitioner Madeleine's problem was 'gradually, and unexpectedly, resolved. In 1976 I was invited to serve as chairman of the National Insurance Local Tribunal (now the Social Security Appeal Tribunals) in Ealing. I was never made aware that I was under consideration or who it was who recommended me for the appointment, but I am eternally grateful to that person'. The clerk of the tribunal, who was a former sergeant in the ATS, greeted her appointment by remarking that at last she would not have to find 'a loose woman' to sit on the tribunal panel to determine appeals relating to women's issues. As she became more experienced she was invited to sit as a substitute for the chairman at High Wycombe and in other areas, and in course of time the department sent advocates for training by attendance at hearings before her own tribunal in Ealing. 'I began to feel that in presiding over judicial tribunals I had achieved the professional goal for which my years of experience in private practice had provided the foundation.'

Gradually the public side of Madeleine's legal work expanded. In 1978 the Home Secretary (again without her knowing on whose recommendation) appointed her as President of the Appeal Tribunal under the London Building Acts, determining appeals against building regulation directions given by GLC Building Officers, and in the same year she was appointed a part-time chairman of Industrial Tribunals in the London South Region. Soon afterwards she accepted an appointment as a President of Mental Health Appeal Tribunals, which continued for 17 years until 2001, including a spell as Deputy Regional Chairman.

In November 1981 an invitation to become a Social Security Commissioner (a Group 6 full-time judicial appointment on a par with a circuit judge) enabled her to retire from private practice. Her practice was clearly successful, 'but it could be lonely working on your own, and it could also be very intrusive. People would ask for advice at the school gates when I went to pick up my children, and I was very conscious that I could often have contributed significantly to coffee morning gossip but could not of course do so because I was bound by client confidentiality'.

With her firm but courteous manner she would appear highly suitable to be a Social Security Commissioner and Child Support Commissioner. Her function as a commissioner was to determine appeals on points of law from decisions of social security appeal tribunals and subsequently from child support tribunals. In her view the social security system should exist to provide justice for the poor and disabled, and determining appeals is clearly a serious responsibility, as any subsequent appeal to the Court of Appeal requires leave.

At the time of her appointment the 15 commissioners in England and Wales were usually silks or senior Chancery juniors. Madeleine was the first woman, and for 18 years the only woman, and also the first practising solicitor to be so appointed, although appointments are now being made from a wider range of people, including academic lawyers and former full-time chairmen of social security appeal tribunals. Madeleine finally retired as a commissioner on grounds of age at the end of 2002. It was an ideal appointment for someone who is influenced by a very strong sense of social justice and who with a clear mind can sympathise with the difficulties of those who find themselves in difficult situations.

What does a commissioner do?

Such clarity of mind is necessary because the work of a commissioner involves the interpretation of complex regulations determining the extent to which the state is prepared to provide assistance in an individual's daily life. This frequently gives rise to many 'hard cases'. The first appeal on the availability of any state benefit is made to various tribunals set up under the Social Security and Child Support Acts. If claimants are not satisfied by the decision of the tribunal they may appeal to the commissioners; here the commissioners have a dual function, first in deciding whether leave to appeal should be granted and second to hear appeals in the event that leave is granted. Their function at this point is to decide matters strictly on points of law and they cannot interfere with previous findings of fact. Although there is a right of appeal with leave to the Court of Appeal only a tiny minority of cases result in appeals from the commissioners. Thus they carry the main responsibility for the implementation of social security law in the UK.

The ambit of the commissioners' jurisdiction is very wide, so that Madeleine might be asked to determine appeals from tribunals concerning disability, appeals concerning the payment otherwise of contributory or means-tested benefits, and against determinations by the child support tribunals. During her tenure as a commissioner constantly increasing legislation has made considerable intellectual demands on commissioners, who are also required to have what might best be described as 'an efficient human touch'. As well as conducting the business of their courts effectively they must be able to communicate sympathetically with claimants, while at the same time giving written decisions in a form capable of being used as a precedent or guideline in future commissioners' decisions.

Discrimination

During a professional career spanning 47 years Madeleine cannot recall many instances of being subjected to direct sex discrimination, apart from the difficulties experienced by young women in obtaining employment with any career prospects prior to 1975, a difficulty which was not confined to the legal profession, and the blatant discrimination she discovered in the statutory judicial pension scheme when she took up her appointment as Social Security Commissioner in 1981. The rules under this scheme precluded any provision for a widower's pension, although there were generous arrangements for widows' pensions. When she took this up with the Lord Chancellor's department she received a letter informing her that 'I am afraid that it is not possible under the rules at present constituted for a female social security commissioner to contribute for a widower's pension. I can appreciate your concern and your desire to make suitable arrangements for your husband in the event of your death, and your willingness to contribute four per cent of your salary. Unfortunately the relevant legislation does not contain any provision for a widower's pension to be awarded and so far as I am aware there is no immediate likelihood of legislative changes to make such provision'.

Madeleine sought the advice of the Chief Commissioner and pointed out that the differential pension provision for male and female members of the judiciary contravened the sex discrimination legislation and the provisions of European Union law, but she was advised 'not to rock the boat'. It was not until 1993 that this discriminatory treatment ended by virtue of the Judicial Pensions and Retirement Act, when the pension rules were amended, but still without any provision which would enable female members of the judiciary to make up payment for past service by way of deduction from current salary.

Madeleine has always adopted a pragmatic attitude towards life and she says that 'I don't think that I have ever been an embittered feminist. When I qualified as a solicitor it was unusual for a woman to return to work after childbirth or to expect partnership firms to provide paid maternity leave and to keep her post open in the event that she might express a wish to return. That's just how it was'. She was determined to 'bring up my children myself and not to commit them to the unsupervised care of an unqualified au pair'. She considers that she was fortunate that her solution of setting up in practice at home as a sole practitioner enabled her to satisfy the statutory requirement of having been in continuous practice for the requisite period of years to qualify for a judicial appointment, 'although at the time I had no thought of any such possibility arising'. Madeleine was told that her appointment to each of the judicial posts that she has held was on merit and not in any way because she was a 'statutory woman'.

She considers that she has been equally fortunate in her family. Two of her children, Christopher and Caroline, qualified into their mother's first choice of profession, medicine, and her other son, Oliver qualified as a barrister. It would be easy to assume that she might now retire gracefully into a round of visiting the theatre, art galleries and grandchildren (she and Geoffrey have five), but that would be to totally underestimate the vigour and energy of a woman who actively seeks hard work. She has just embarked on a new career as a 'roving ambassador' on behalf of the Minerva Trust in order to establish effective links between the Old Girls' Associations of the 25 schools within the Public Girls Day School Trust, 'because they helped me all those years ago'.

Dianna Kempe

An insolvency practitioner, Dianna Kempe has recently retired from the position of senior partner at Appleby Spurling & Kempe, a Bermuda law firm with offices in London and Hong Kong. She was the first woman to be appointed Queen's Counsel in Bermuda, and the first woman to be elected President of the International Bar Association.

Overview

Bermuda is a small island of 21 square miles with the status of British Overseas Territory and a population of 63,400. The Bermuda legal system is based on English Common Law but with its own statutory law. There are however no organised training facilities, which means that all lawyers practising in Bermuda must first qualify in another Commonwealth country although traditionally this will be England or Canada. As Appleby Spurling & Kempe considers itself very much an international firm it actively encourages its young people to go as *stagiares* (trainees on a short work placement) to law firms in other countries and takes many *stagiares* from other countries, because in Dianna's view 'you need other cultures if you're going to build a good strong international law firm'.

This, Dianna considers, makes for an interesting and challenging legal environment to some extent influenced by the island's proximity to the US. This is particularly obvious where international financial law is concerned, and it perhaps explains in part why a lawyer from such a small legal community should become the first woman President of the International Bar Association (IBA).

How to become a Bermuda lawyer

As so very often happened with women of her generation her career started off apparently dictated by men. Her father, a London gynaecologist decided that 'you are not smart enough to be a doctor, so why don't you try law?'.

Having agreed with her father that she should become a lawyer Dianna characteristically took a very direct approach and with the insouciance of a 16-year old went to ask the registrar of Middle Temple 'What does it take to come here?'. At the age of 17 and having obtained the requisite A level grades and seeing no reason to go to university prior to entering the law, she went straight to Middle Temple. She became one of the youngest people ever to qualify as a barrister and indeed had to wait until she was 21 before she could be called to the Bar.

With typical frankness Dianna admits that she did not in fact work very hard at Middle Temple. 'It was widely recognised at the time that the quality of training was truly appalling,' so she spent much of her time with her fellow students attending trials at the High Court and the Old Bailey such as the fraud trial of Emil Savundra and the drug trials in which the Beatles were involved. It was 'a very pleasant and exciting way of learning practical court room procedure and technique'. But at the same time she cannily analysed previous exam questions and studied hard enough to pass. Later at the age of 21 she moved with her husband to Bermuda because he had found employment there, even though she had not commenced her pupillage.

Leaving London without even having begun her pupillage could have been career death, but having arrived in Bermuda she sat down, analysed the law firms in Bermuda, decided on the firm which is now Appleby Spurling & Kempe, went to see the senior partner and requested that he took her on. Although he did point out that 'this was not usually how things were done'. the result of that conversation was that Dianna became the first pupil ever taken on by the firm.

Being a female lawyer in Bermuda

There are certain consequences to being a lawyer on a relatively small island. Professional survival depends on being outward looking and taking full advantage of the international financial environment. But it also has the advantage of being a community where women have always worked so that it is seen to be 'normal'. To make her point about the recognition of talent on Bermuda, Dianna cites Dame Lois Brown Evans DBE JP MP who is the present Attorney-General and Minister for Legislative Affairs for Bermuda. Aged 72 she was called to the Bermuda Bar in 1953, the first woman to be so. Dianna contrasts this with her childhood in the UK where she noted that neither her mother nor any of her mother's friends ever worked.

In 25 years of professional practice Dianna feels that she has never experienced any prejudice on the part of either her clients or her colleagues. But her election as the first ever female managing partner by the partners of her firm was 'a leap of faith on their part', especially when the business community 'did raise its eyebrows a little bit' because of her perceived lack of business experience. However, in a couple of years she had proved her competence and their reservations disappeared.

When Dianna joined her firm there was only one other woman lawyer there who left soon afterwards so that for many years she was the only woman in the firm. Now the firm has an impressive equality record, and 40 per cent of the firm's lawyers and seven out of the firm's 21 partners are women. She is proud that within two years of her becoming managing partner 60 per cent of all women qualifying as lawyers in Bermuda applied to work for her firm.

Being part of the IBA

In her three separate careers, as practising insolvency lawyer, managing partner and Bar leader she considers that she has found most prejudice in the IBA, where she was exposed on a regular basis to the thought processes of the male élite of legal systems which were far more traditional and less flexible than those of her adopted country.

'I don't think I ever understood institutional thought until I joined the IBA, but there in living technicolor I encountered institutional sexism.' She recalls with horror the experience of a French female law professor with 'a stellar CV' who had joined the IBA and who wrote asking the chairman of an IBA Committee what she could contribute to his committee. Despite having practical law experience and speaking several languages she was told firmly that he had 'filled all the slots for this year and next year' and that perhaps she could 'just come along and observe'. This rejection of someone who was so obviously competent, despite Dianna's own intervention on her behalf, was a clear example of the type of institutional thought which she considers unfortunately to be more prevalent in Europe than in other places and which she feels denies creativity and progress. It has been part of her mission at the IBA therefore to encourage lawyers to have mutual respect for each other's cultures and competences in a true international spirit.

International women

One of Dianna's reasons for leaving England was her impatience with its cultural rigidity, and it was a desire for openness which later led her to start the IBA Women Lawyer Groups. The structure that she proposed did not go down well with senior IBA members who argued that Women Lawyer Groups should be constituted in the same way as other IBA committees. What she wanted was a 'no rules' structure which would enable women to do what was culturally acceptable in each country in which they came together whether that was by having only one meeting a year or several and whether the meetings were relatively informal or of conference stature. She insisted that this 'formal flexibility' was necessary because the Women Lawyer Groups were 'intended for women who feel the need to come together with other women sharing common values with a common purpose to help women who need the support of other women professionals'. She won.

However when she organised the first World Women Lawyer Conference in March 2001 she once again encountered that institutional unwillingness to associate with anything 'untraditional'. Because most senior IBA men did not think it would be successful, only two of them attended the conference, but the truth of her vision was shown spectacularly when 900 people from 100 countries attended.

Given that she was a woman and not a passive one at that, was her election as IBA president a surprise to her? Not entirely. 'You need to know what you are doing,' she points out, 'and you should remember that in Appleby Spurling & Kempe I had been running a multi-million pound operation for 10 years and that I had the talent to make people loyal, to make an organisation work and that I could prove historically that I had done so.' In the course of spending almost 10 years doing pro bono work for developing countries and helping them to run local bar associations on just $500 a year she had got to know all the Bar leaders in the world on personal terms. The qualification to be an IBA president was simply to be 'damn good and to get on with 99 per cent of the world'.

Women leaders

Women leaders fall into two categories as far as Dianna is concerned. First, there are those who have made it to the top ('they have sort of swung to the top') without offending anyone. 'They are completely uncontroversial and so it is easy for the boys to let them have a go,' but Dianna feels that they do not really make any difference to the position of women, as they have not caused those same 'boys' to reassess any of their attitudes towards women.

There is a second category into which 'I regret to say I fall, and that is the category that gets into trouble'. Electing someone from this category as IBA president must have been a very conscious choice, because Dianna's natural candour is hard to keep in check. At her very first IBA Management Committee Meeting, her determination to say nothing was thwarted when the question of how to designate women who chaired IBA committees came up. After the usual discussion as to whether it should be 'chairman, chairwoman or chair', she was addressed by the Committee Chairman 'shouldn't we ask the only woman in the room?'.

Dianna explained that she had in fact been discussing this very point at lunch with some other women lawyers and they had concluded that 'as in most countries the word "chair" doesn't really work it might be best to ask each individual woman in the situation, and there were not many of them, what they thought'. When a male European retorted, 'So we are to decide to change any policy at the IBA on the basis of a casual lunchtime discussion by women.' Dianna pointed out in lengthy and trenchant terms how insulted she felt by his dinosaur attitude.

Despite this outburst (and there were many more) Dianna was elected as IBA president. She had been supported by Reece Smith, a past IBA president from Florida, who asked her to consider being the first woman IBA officer and then to work towards becoming the first woman IBA president. 'And he mentored me all the way through.' She notes wryly that he was her very first mentor, because for the first 20 years of her legal life she did not have another woman lawyer to talk to about her position, and indeed until Reece Smith took her under his wing no male mentors either.

Do women help each other?

Dianna believes that in general women are more prepared to be co-operative than men but she is surprised at how harshly competitive women are in the London legal environment. As an insolvency practitioner in the 1980s she frequently had to deal with women lawyers in the large City firms where she felt that the competition was 'nightmarish'. This was not as a result of any importation of American values; it was just the result of the indigenous culture.

'English women lawyers never cease to surprise me.' At the Women Lawyer Forum five years ago she felt that it was absolutely outrageous that so many women lawyers were still complaining that they were less well paid, that they had fewer benefits and that they were not making it to partnership in the way that their male colleagues were. She feels that 'they should do something about it', and it is this dynamic assertion of self-help that makes her such a staunch supporter of women's legal organisations worldwide.

Flexible working

Bermuda's size and the relatively small pool of available local lawyers partly explains Dianna's belief that people are the most important thing in her firm, but she also has a strong urge to help her staff to reach their full potential. The firm feels that it has a responsibility to try to accommodate those individuals who want to work flexibly because they have childcare or other responsibilities. Working out a remuneration policy to take account of this, particularly in the case of partners who wish to spend less time in the office may be difficult, but she sees it as merely another aspect of her job as head of a firm where she has other personnel problems to juggle because of Bermuda's limited resources.

As only Bermuda nationals can be made partners of Bermuda law firms, sensitive pay and status recognition policies must be put in place to deal with very senior lawyers who cannot progress beyond associate level because their nationality position disqualifies them from progressing further. Her overall aim is to make everyone in the firm feel valued and part of the Appleby Spurling & Kempe team, so that she discourages 'any posturing within the profession where a "deals person" expects to be regarded as in some way superior to someone who practises probate', because she has seen that this is not the case in the majority of the world.

'After all,' as she points out, 'apart from Canada, Australia, England and the USA where law is increasingly specialised and there is a dichotomy between the solicitors' and the barristers' branches of the profession, most law that is practised internationally is general practice. In Africa, Eastern Europe and most of Latin America apart from large cities like Buenos Aires or São Paulo, law is practised by general attorneys combining the functions of both solicitor and barrister.'

Young lawyers now

'The whole environment for young people entering the profession has changed dramatically. It is now possible for someone to choose what sort of legal business environment she wants to be in as a lawyer, and because of the availability of information through print and increasingly the Internet, it is possible to investigate thoroughly the legal organisations available.' This statement seems more indicative of the sort of proactive young lawyer that Dianna would be in today's recruitment marketplace than an actual analysis of how things are, but her next words are certainly spoken from a deep well of sound common sense even if they are sometimes difficult to put into practice.

'It is paramount that you should ask yourself what is important to you, and what you want to find in the law firm you want to work for. If equality and diversity are important, then you should ask the human resources department what equality and diversity policies they have in place, and almost more importantly how they operate them. It is extremely important to recognise that going to work for a firm just because it will sound good on your CV or just because it has an international reputation, but where the culture is not empathic, can be disastrous. Culture cannot instantly be changed and you will probably end up feeling dissatisfied.'

But with a smile she points out that although she did research all the available firms in Bermuda when she arrived there, she did not exactly have the freedom of choice that she would like to feel is available to today's young women.

Cultural and generational stuff

Despite the sound advice about choosing a firm in tune with your beliefs, Dianna takes the pragmatic personal line that if there has ever been anything about the culture of an organisation that she did not like, then it was up to her to change it. She is slow to take umbrage at what she calls 'generational stuff', even though much of it could be characterised as sexist or prejudicial by many other people. She seems to be able to get over incidents motivated by such bias unless they are injustices perpetrated on other people such as the French law professor. Three examples will suffice.

When her twins were about four years old the then senior partner of Appleby Spurling & Kempe commented avuncularly that 'as you have been married for some time you might be thinking of having children soon'. When she gently pointed out that she had two children and that they were four years old, 'he had no idea'. Neither was she unduly upset when the senior partner's wife, who was not used to women working, and making conversation at a staff function asked her 'And whose secretary are you, dear?'. This, as she points out, was 'all generational stuff'.

At an informal office lunch with a Saudi in-house counsel Dianna was present and took her turn at serving from the buffet. When she excused herself early to go to court the guest commented that although he had realised that Bermuda was a fairly free and easy place he was surprised that they had allowed their housekeeper to have lunch with them. Far from taking offence Dianna considered this as 'a purely cultural misapprehension'.

To Dianna these are not vast problems, they are little local difficulties, intellectual challenges which require a little bit of thought to be overcome. If someone's conduct is inappropriate she would rather think of ways to make that person aware of it themself rather than have a huge blustering row. Her view, even on the occasion when she was not consulted as a member of a committee because she was new to it, is that nobody is being 'super nasty to anyone else', it is just an example of thoughtless casual and easy exclusivity. 'A group goes only to the people that it feels most comfortable with and forgets the people on the outside that it feels less comfortable with, with the inevitable result that even though those excluded would come to the same decision another layer has been built on a wall of alienation which means that people lose their self-confidence and they won't give you their best potential.' That is why she tries very hard to break down what she sees as barriers of negligence because if repeated they become 'institutional thought' whose rigidity 'can border on a sin'.

Advice to young women

So what advice would Dianna give to young women entering the profession? There is no hesitation; it comes in two words 'know yourself'. If you don't know what is important to you, you are likely to have serious problems. 'Because you are a woman you have to consider whether marriage and children are important to you and you need to try to work this out as these events get closer. It can be potentially disastrous to go into a law firm and think that they will change their culture just to accommodate you; now there are so many organisations which employ lawyers that young women have so much choice. The status, for example, of in-house counsel has improved enormously and for some women this may be a way of combining a satisfying career with having children.'

In Dianna's view before a young women even starts her articles she should be conducting 'a personal audit'. Law schools too have a responsibility and should be much more proactive in facilitating this and should spend much more time helping their students before they apply for articles. She chuckles that the most successful people in her firm are the ones who have interviewed the firm rather than vice versa. She has for example one very bright and successful woman associate who from the very first day stated that 'I want you know that I will work devotedly for you while I am here but I may want to have children. Do you still want to hire me?'. As Dianna says 'everybody knew upfront what her position was. She is now a happy employee and we are very happy employers'.

Physical coping

In order to cope with a schedule which has meant working 60 hours a week for the last 30 years and travelling for maybe 85 per cent of her time for the last two years, she considers that she has had to be 'relatively positively organised and relatively blessed'. Until her children were 21 she employed a full-time nanny; this may seem surprising but, as she points out, 'if you live on aeroplanes it is really not good enough for there not to be some sort of continuing day-to-day care and support'. Since then she has had full-time housekeepers to take care of 'the basic stuff'. As for everything else she 'just fits it in'. Stamina and good health are of paramount importance, and the ability to encourage loyalty in others. In all her years at Appelby Spurling & Kempe she has had only three secretaries all of whom still work for her in some capacity or another.

Dianna admits to being 'solution oriented' when there is a problem. She recognises that she 'lives by lists' and as far as clothing is concerned 'if you see it you buy it'. And also she tries not to buy in Bermuda. 'It is such a small place that everybody would know where you bought it and what it cost.' It is important 'to have people around you who care for you' and in her case to have a husband who is understanding about a wife who goes globetrotting fairly constantly.

Having spent so much of the past two decades in intense activity first as managing partner and then as senior partner of the only law firm that she has ever known, working for some of that time with simultaneous enthusiasm in senior IBA positions, Dianna took the decision that that she would retire from the firm in 2003 at the age of 52. She is too young and energetic simply to retire to a garden full of hibiscus and is fully alert to the next new challenge which might, she ponders, be in the international diplomatic or human rights field.

Helena Kennedy

Helena Kennedy QC was made a Life Peer as Baroness Kennedy of the Shaws in 1997 and practises predominantly at the Criminal Bar. She is also chair of the British Council, President of the School for Oriental and African Studies, a Fellow of the Royal Society of Arts and is chairman of the Human Genetics Commission, as well as being the author of *Eve was Framed*.

Beginnings

Somewhat surprisingly for a young woman who grew up in the 1960s in a working class Scottish family Helena Kennedy was called to the English Bar in 1972. She had originally intended to read English at Glasgow University but changed her mind at the last minute and decided both to read law and to postpone university for a year. Realising that 'having a traditional gap year would have been a total indulgence which my family could not afford', and drawn by the lure of the great metropolis, she set off for London 'to work at anything for a year', with the intention of returning to Glasgow to study law the following year. But she did not return.

The Scottish Education Department helpfully funded her three-year course at the Council of Legal Education in London, but despite the additional grant paid for London study she found herself very impecunious in the first year and was forced to take a succession of part-time jobs. Still she considers herself more fortunate than today's young working class students with legal ambitions. The lengthening of the educational stage of training (now a degree plus Bar School) coupled with the attenuation of the grant system has made it almost impossible for working class students to come to pupillage unsaddled with vast amounts of debt. She has therefore become increasingly concerned that her profession will return to the élitist status which it enjoyed when she became a pupil barrister.

Legal London

A bright girl, her steepest learning curve was the social one of adapting to the 'weird world of the Bar' and those who practised in it. Her father was a despatch hand in the newspaper industry and she had been brought up in a close Catholic community in the Pollokshaws area of Glasgow. She certainly felt herself 'a bit of an outsider' because she was a woman and working class and felt that she was straying into 'an Evelyn Waugh novel'. At Bar School it was drilled into her by some very bright people whose ambitions had been thwarted by their social background that her lack of 'connections' would preclude her from ever being able to practise at the Bar. However as the Finals approached that same questioning spirit that had drawn her to London three years previously made her realise that 'I wanted that experience of going to court.' She applied and was accepted for pupillage by Montague Sherborne QC.

For a long time Helena found it difficult to believe that she actually was a barrister and in common with many women constantly felt that 'I would be found out. It took me 10 years until I was probably in my early thirties before I felt that I had some sort of entitlement to be there'. Her practice was, and remains, very much at the Criminal Bar, where her concerns about miscarriages of justice and unhelpful judicial practices, persuasively set out in *Eve was Framed* (about injustices against women in particular), have led her to focus on the much wider field of civil liberties and human rights. Speaking to her it is easy to see how she not only secured her niche at the Bar, but also became a QC in 1991.

She has a clarity of expression that is able to get straight to the heart of an issue and to encapsulate a point briefly and often trenchantly. When speaking about the right of the state to retain DNA samples taken voluntarily in criminal investigations or for health research, she formulated the test as being 'to what extent do we have a right to genetic privacy'. And speaking on the reform of the judicial system she stated without any persiflage, 'The Lord Chancellor, a member of the Government, sitting in the Cabinet, should not be appointing judges or QCs'. Expediency or tradition are simply insufficient justifications for continuing with behaviour that is contrary to a right to basic civil liberties.

Promoting women

Despite public statements of concern by the legal establishment Helena feels that 'we still haven't got it right about promoting women in the profession and that the Lord Chancellor's Department has not got it right in promoting women to the status of Queen's Counsel or to the judiciary'. There may be public calls for women to apply but there is insufficient recognition that women on the whole don't have career plans and that they wait for invitations to apply for promotion. She herself did not apply for silk until she had been 'jockeyed' by her colleagues and particularly encouraged by younger women. When she did take silk at the age of 40, having applied only once before, she received several letters the gist of which were 'not before time'.

She is very conscious that women don't measure success in quite the same way as men, a difference she has noticed when conducting staff assessments at the British Council. Women tend to describe how they are doing the job and whether they are doing it well but men on the other hand ask 'What's the next rung on the ladder for me?' and gauge success by how much they are earning. Women's choice of legal specialism is more likely to be motivated by their assessment of its intrinsic interest rather than its potential for cash generation. At this point she smiles and indicates that this is something she understands because 'money has not interested me at all'.

Despite all her other responsibilities Helena still practises at the Bar and would be extremely reluctant to give it up. But being involved as a director in other organisations constantly looking at staffing issues she is also made aware that 'women do come at things very differently and are more concerned with getting the balance right than being driven by pure ambition'.

As chairman of the British Council, for example, where she manages more than 6,000 people in an organisation with a turnover of £500 million per annum, she has considered very carefully how equal opportunities policies might be implemented. Women on the whole suffer, she has concluded, from the twin handicaps of constantly underestimating their skills and having a strong aversion to risk. To some extent she contrasts this with her own character which is one of constant willingness to take on new challenges and risks.

To encourage people, and not just women, who have found it difficult to follow the traditional educational path, to take on one particular sort of risk, she advocated easier access to higher education for mature students in her report *Learning Works, Widening Participation in Higher Education* and is a patron of the Helena Kennedy Bursary Scheme for 'second chance' students.

Family life

Because barristers are self-employed the childbearing decision has perhaps a more acute financial edge for women who are barristers rather than solicitors. Their decision does not relate to potential partnership prospects but to the possible complete disappearance of a livelihood, and it was not until she was in her 30s and enjoying enough success professionally that Helena felt reasonably confident that her career would not disappear if she had children; her three children were born when she was 33, 36 and 39. 'Anxious that I would be forgotten,' and conscious that only eight per cent of those at the Bar in her generation were women, she took only three months off when her first child was born, but with each subsequent child she felt able to take increasing amounts of maternity leave. She now regards taking only three months off as 'machismo mothering' and would counsel women that career destruction is not an inevitable consequence of maternity leave.

Helena is married to a busy practising surgeon, but feels very strongly about the difficulties confronted by single parents who try to hold a family together as well as managing some sort of career or job. 'It is not easy to do this if there is no one at the end of the day to share the stresses and the good things with.' Having a full-time nanny for her children has enabled her to pursue a multi-faceted career but at weekends she restricts dinner parties or social occasions as far as possible to those which include her children. Although she cannot replicate exactly the solid family background where her mother was constantly present, she values the concentrated time that her own family can have together during the holidays. The whole of August off is designated as 'real family time where I take on the traditional mother's role' in the family's annual visit to Cape Cod. The preservation of 'a sense of focus and order in their lives' is clearly important to her and is encouraged by 'going back to the same place at the same time every year so that the family spends every New Year and Easter in Scotland, because families are about creating memories'.

'Having excellent support staff is important in maintaining the family structure, because it is very hard on the children if you have too much change.' Her staff have always stayed for a long time and in 14 years she has had only two nannies for her children. Given that stable background, there are, she thinks, certain advantages to children in having a working mother. Going to local state schools (many successful lawyers send their children to boarding school) has reinforced her children's sense of certainty and local involvement, and they have become 'pretty independent'. Meanwhile their parents are occupied with very interesting things which can give rise to lively debate round the dinner table. Helena's involvement in government and 'arts things' (she was chairman of the London International Festival of Theatre) has also added to the rich mix of conversation and experience which they encounter.

The future of women at the Bar

She is very encouraged by the prospect of 'so many fabulous young women' going to the Bar now. So many of them come to speak to her and tell her about their experiences and she enjoys their vibrancy and intelligence and the fact that 'they seem to have a much clearer sense of what they are about than women had 25 years ago. They are more competitive and tougher than they were then, but in some ways their experience can be just as difficult when they decide that they wish to have children and to bring up families, simply because having young children cuts a woman out of whole swathes of the informal information gathering system that appertains in the after work wine bar culture'.

Perhaps because a greater percentage of the Bar is female than previously, Helena feels that the structures now in place are much more supportive and that all 'obvious' discrimination has been reduced. 'The difficulty for women is that there is an intensity about working at the Bar now which produces a pressure cooker feeling and means that women still have a battle to reconcile their professional and domestic lives.' This will only be relieved if there is a general change in attitude. The struggle now should be for a better accommodation of family life for all professionals and not just for women.

She was much encouraged recently when in the robing room before a case she heard some young male barristers asking each other about their babies and their young children, something you would never have heard 15 years ago. Valuing everybody's rights within the workplace 'simply makes good business sense, because there will inevitably be better performance if the other aspects of someone's life are taken care of'. Unfortunately she feels that barristers' cost-sharing arrangements make family friendly arrangements more difficult in chambers than in law firms. Women barristers who are self-regulating can be much harder on themselves than women in big law firms who may more easily be able to negotiate flexible hours. She has noticed that when flexible working options are available in large law firms it is the women who take them up; but the men who have not taken advantage of this opportunity often complain that trainees who need direction go to the qualified male solicitor in situ rather than phone up their female principal who happens to be at home but who might be perfectly willing to be disturbed.

Diversity

Helena's life has been one of constant reappraisal and readjustment, 'very important if you are to have an interesting career. I'm still that ridiculous person who doesn't plan a career ahead' because she feels that life has so many new opportunities to offer. She enjoys a ferocious energy which enables her to travel the world with the British Council, then to speak on behalf of a multitude of organisations and causes such as the International Planned Parenthood Federation and to write articles in support of international justice as well as maintaining her Bar practice. She also possesses an impressively acute recall which enables her to absorb not only the factual information necessary for a practising barrister with high profile non-legal positions, but also to remember to their delight most of the people that she meets in her various roles. Success does not mean pulling up the ladder behind her, but remembering what it was like to be young and confused and deciding that she might just be able to help.

Her period as chairman of the British Council will end in 2004 but she will continue to chair the Human Genetics Commission, which is involved with some very interesting areas of the law. Helena sees this as 'fascinating work', because the law to her is a tool to be used to safeguard the rights and liberties of the citizen and not merely to be revered as an erudite study. The stealing of a sample of the DNA of an American millionaire to settle a paternity suit was condemned by Helena, even though others may have thought that it was, as she put it, 'rough justice'. Everyone, even those of whom we disapprove or fear has a right to justice and access to justice, including those suspected of terrorism or bombing, for whose legal rights she is an outspoken advocate.

She is clear that whatever she does, the retention of her own integrity and holding on to basic 'absolutely non-negotiable' principles is paramount. She has an ambivalent view about the possibility of high political office. 'I have political views, and I have been on the fringes of government and I have been involved in some issues which are highly political such as the Guildford Four appeal, but I would find it very hard to take up a purely political office which could require the defence of a party line which ran contrary to my principles.' Being a member of the House of Lords has for this very reason not proved to be an easy position. She does feel hugely privileged to be in the Lords and to be part of the legislative process but 'I do question how far the expectation of party loyalty should go'.

This has been recently tested by the Government's recent promulgation of the Criminal Justice Bill, which she feels could result in a severe curtailment of the individual's access to justice. She is totally opposed to the proposal that a judge will be able to hear cases without a jury, such as those involving serious fraud, because she feels that the right to a jury trial is fundamental to the concept of justice in this country. The proposed abolition of the double jeopardy rule in certain cases, such as murder and rape would in her opinion be an unjustifiable erosion of principle which gives too much power to the state. Quiet dissent is not her style, and her criticism of the Bill in the media has been articulate and certain. Her public life retains as its motivation a concern for the underdog, the poor or those less fortunate than herself. She simply wants to make life better and richer for others, and her chosen honorific, Baroness Kennedy of the Shaws, is a proud reminder of what she herself gained from a less than financially privileged upbringing.

Carolyn Kirby

Carolyn Kirby was the first woman to become President of the Law Society of England and Wales.

Legal beginnings

Carolyn Kirby, the first woman to become President of the Law Society was, like many others of her generation, influenced by the courtroom drama television series that she watched as a child in the 1960s. *Perry Mason* was a particular favourite, which she now finds 'quite bizarre' as it bears so little resemblance to the reality of criminal court work in this country. With no solicitors in her family it was indeed probably Mason's cool intelligence which influenced her choice of career, although ironically the firm that she chose for articles was a small firm in Swansea with no criminal law practice. In retrospect she considers that she might have enjoyed court work; but fate conspired to keep her out of the courts for, in common with many articled clerks, her main experience of civil litigation was minor debt collecting. Motivated as she is by an interest in working with people rather than organisations, debt collecting 'definitely did not cut it for me'.

By the time Carolyn qualified she was married, after six months she joined the Swansea practice owned by her husband and brother-in-law and was soon installed in their new office in the Gower peninsula; eventually she was to become a partner at the firm.

Again and again Carolyn has made it clear that she is a lawyer for people rather than organisations. Her legal career has been spent as a 'private client' lawyer in small High Street firms in the Swansea area. 'Private client' for Carolyn is not confined to a narrow definition of wills, trusts and probate; it means working from the personal perspective. She gains her interest and satisfaction from 'making life easier because of something I have done. A private client for me is an individual who wants to do something in terms of his assets, family or his or her own ambitions', and thus her work also extended to acting for small companies and partnerships.

Mental health

It is not surprising that someone who can say that 'purely legal problems do not interest me. I am interested in a legal solution for people's problems', would feel acutely sympathetic to clients who had suffered from illnesses or disabilities. With several years of experience of assisting those whose legal situations were exacerbated by age-related, physical or psychiatric disabilities she was more than ready to accept the invitation in 1990 to become non-executive director of a health authority, which involved her ex officio in being hospital manager of a local psychiatric hospital. Six years later she was appointed as a member of a mental health tribunal, an unusual step as she had not previously represented patients in front of such tribunals.

After only another two years she accepted an appointment as chairman of the Regional Mental Health Tribunal for Wales. It is Carolyn's wider almost philosophically practical legal concerns which were at work here. Involved with the Welsh Assembly through Law Society devolution work, she was very aware that various parts of the Government of Wales Act would be bringing in the Human Rights Act in advance of its introduction in England. She rightly saw this as an opportunity to assist in a cutting edge legal area; 'I felt that I could be of help as the new legislation would inevitably deal with the human rights of patients with psychiatric difficulties'.

Carolyn has been a member of the Law Society Mental Health and Disability Committee for three years, and spoke on the proposed new mental health legislation at the 2002 Law Society conference. The committee has been lobbying 'not so quietly' for 15 years for an Incapacity Act and recently the Law Society jointly with the British Medical Association and the Making Decisions Alliance launched a charter entitled *Mental Capacity and Decision Making* setting out criteria for new legislation in this area. Unfortunately, as Carolyn pointed out in her speech, not only does the draft Mental Health Bill contain many things which the Mental Health and Disability Committee consider to be unhelpful but the Government does not seem at the present moment prepared to introduce an Incapacity Act. As Scotland passed the Adults with Incapacity Act 2000 as one of the first acts of the new Scottish Parliament Carolyn is mildly outraged, 'They've done it. Why can't we?'.

Being a President

Representation of the whole profession is implicit in the office of Law Society President. Carolyn rejects completely the notion that the focus of concern of someone who has spent most of her working life in Wales in a small practice might be restricted to small firms and to the Principality. 'One of the strengths of the Law Society almost by coincidence seems to be a rolling programme of people coming from different backgrounds. It's one of the strengths of the role that Law Society Presidents come from different geographical areas, doing different types of work, from different firms and with different experiences. In fact, the previous president, David McIntosh, who came from a large City firm (Davies Arnold Cooper) was very supportive of criminal practitioners.' Carolyn quotes a medical friend who told her that, 'you don't have to be ill to be a good doctor'.

She is very clear that Law Society office holders are there to represent solicitors in their role as solicitors of the Supreme Court regardless of the nature of 'the pieces of paper they push around a table'. When as President she found that issues of importance to City firms required more intensive briefing she would obtain this through discussion with City practitioners and reading extensive briefing papers often late into the night in bed.

Valuing the opportunity to progress from being Deputy Vice President through Vice President to President, Carolyn considers that orderly structure is far more beneficial both for the individual concerned and for the profession than contested elections at every level. A President in waiting learns by watching and sharing so that when the presidential year begins he or she is already fully involved and committed and any firm which will be losing the services of a partner to the presidency for a year will have been able to make advance preparation for the loss to the firm during that year.

The inevitable question on what difference a woman can make to the role of the President is met with Carolyn's amused comment that one of her favourite books is *Why Men Don't Listen and Women Can't Read Maps*. Although she does not believe that the thought processes of one sex are better than the other, she considers them to be different. Women simply do not necessarily go about things in the same way as men, in particular they are not as competitive, but do have a facility to 'look at the common good in the round'. She hates macho politics where 'I've done this' gets in the way of actually getting things done at all. When one or two men suggested to her that as President she needed to be 'more robust', she considered quietly that there was 'more than one way to skin a cat', and that a more subtle approach often wins in the long run.

First woman?

Women all over the country were justly pleased to have a female President of the Law Society for the first time, coincidentally in the same year that saw the first Association of Women Solicitors (AWS) designated council seat, the launch of the Law Society Equality and Diversity Initiative and the 80th Anniversary of the first woman to qualify as a solicitor in England and Wales.

Carolyn herself would not read too much into this as she sees herself very much as a solicitor first and a solicitor who happens to be a woman second. She is however aware that things have changed from the early days when there were probably only three or four qualified women solicitors in Swansea. As the first female articled clerk in her firm she was aware that she was 'something of an abnormality' who felt not deliberately but rather casually excluded when the other articled clerks sat around at lunchtime talking endlessly about rugby. What she did learn and recalls with some gratitude now, was how to cope with working long hours, as articled clerks' noses were kept 'pretty much to the grindstone'.

Confronted by a young woman some clients were slightly surprised, but it was very seldom seen as a problem except for one day when she attempted to answer a telephone enquiry in the absence of her supervising partner. To the client's loud response that 'he wanted to speak to a partner and not some damn typist', she replied feistily, 'I am not a typist but I would take great exception to being spoken to in that way if I had been one'.

It was an experience that she did not forget. In later years when as a partner she could see that one of her staff was having a difficult time with a client on the telephone, she would take the telephone, listen to the harangue for a few minutes and then say sweetly, 'Well, Mr X, it's Carolyn Kirby speaking'. People she feels should be treated properly and not in demeaning ways by others who are too ready to stick labels on them, and that if anyone should be shouted at it should be the most senior person in the organisation.

Agenda for a President

Carolyn had extraordinarily clear ideas about what she wished to achieve in her year as President and what she would wish to be remembered for other than being the first woman President. It was a happy coincidence that the Equality and Diversity Initiative was launched at the beginning of her year. She pointed out that it had had a long genesis and was conceived as the result of an Equal Opportunities Committee paper in 1997. However she was more than happy to take the Initiative forward as it is something that is central to her thinking.

Being a provincial solicitor she is very aware of the feeling of many rural solicitors that the Law Society is a remote London based institution. She therefore decided to focus a major part of her year on better communications – all sorts of communication. She wanted the profession as a whole to realise the value of the Law Society specialist committees in terms of law reform, on examining legislation for unforeseen consequences and on advising the Government. 'As so often this is well known to those involved but largely unknown to the rank and the file of the profession because it is not communicated to them.'

It is a sadness to her that many solicitors are presently not associated with local law societies or Law Society groups. Improvement of Law Society communication with its members is therefore imperative and one way she feels that this can be done is through electronic communication so that the Law Society can tell solicitors more efficiently 'the things it needs to tell them, because it is essential that the Law Society becomes more proactive in finding ways of communicating with its constituents'. Part of the information which will be required as part of the new practising certificate form is a solicitor's e-mail address, which could then be used to direct appropriate information to solicitors who have indicated an interest in a particular area whether it be mental health or building defects.

Carolyn is a staunch advocate of local law societies and Law Society groups including the AWS, and she feels that part of the Law Society's function is to help the groups and local law societies by demonstrating to the main body of solicitors what value they can obtain by sharing their common interests geographically and through common work. 'What frustrates me is that so few people know about the good work the groups and the local law societies do, and the contribution I can make is to communicate the value of that work.'

The next generation

Carolyn has had a varied career to date and even though she would not dwell on it she obviously has become used to being 'the first woman who . . .' which led her from the clear air of the Welsh coast, where she enjoys strenuous walking, to the confines of Chancery Lane and London for most of her presidential year. It is a career that she has obviously enjoyed because of her interest in people and the possibility it has given her to help them in positive ways.

'Clearly I would always advise any man or woman to go into the profession. But one of the difficulties with law is that so many young people have preconceptions of the legal profession which are not always borne out by reality. Many of these preconceptions would not exist if the aspiring solicitor first found work experience in a solicitor's office or actually went to court to see legal services being dispensed.' It comes back to informed decision, to communication, to helping people to choose appropriately.

Final thoughts

In her professional role Carolyn presents a studied dichotomy between the private and the public person, but the public persona is very much motivated by her private convictions of fairness and justice in the widest sense, which Carolyn considers can be facilitated by her legal skills and those of her chosen profession. She does not believe that people should be judged by their apparent commercial role and even worse be treated in an aggressive or demeaning fashion because of their apparently low social status. This informs her belief that those with mental or physical disability should not be assessed negatively, but that they should be looked at positively and appreciated for what they can do. And it is probably why Carolyn Kirby, the first female President of the Law Society wants to be remembered not as that, but as a President of the Law Society who has made a difference.

Margaret McCabe

Margaret McCabe is a barrister who founded the Women Lawyer Forum in 1995.

In July 2000 Margaret McCabe and Cherie Booth pleaded a case before the United Nations Human Rights Commissioner against the Australian Government regarding the mandatory sentencing laws of the Australian Northern Territories, and challenged the 'three strikes' provision that adults be sentenced to minimum periods of imprisonment for set offences.

Why should Margaret McCabe, who is an English qualified commercial barrister, have been involved in this case? The answer lies partly in her background and partly in a conscious decision to redirect her career.

Origins

Margaret McCabe is in fact an example of Australian energy applied to the traditions of the English legal establishment. Born in Queensland, one of six children whose father was obliged to leave school at the age of 10 to support his mother and family, Margaret has herself worked since the age of 13 in order to finance her educational ambitions. Her parents' desire that she train for a 'proper job' as a doctor was thwarted because of her squeamishness, but equally they refused to condone her pursuing a theatrical career. Law was the family compromise containing the possibility of both financial security and histrionic fulfilment.

In the early 1970s at the University of Queensland she discovered that although the misogynistic head of the law department accepted 'girls', women were required to attain a mark of 75 per cent to pass exams whereas men required only 50 per cent. But success as so often changes all and now she is proudly listed as an alumnus in their visiting lecturer website.

English legal education

After graduating from the University of Queensland and after a year's round the clock work as a waitress she arrived at King's College in London where she married another Australian equally imbued with the Antipodean spirit of adventure. On one extensive travelling trip they drove through the Soviet Union long before the Iron Curtain was lifted, traversing terrain where no maps were available so that the almost inevitable Russian tailing them was often helpful in getting them back on track when they were unable to decipher the Cyrillic road signs.

By the time that she graduated from King's Margaret appeared to be destined for the Bar; advocacy could enable her to combine her love of law and of theatricals. But again she almost fell foul of entrenched attitudes. Attracted by the echoing splendour of Middle Temple Hall where Shakespeare's Twelfth Night was performed for the first time, she applied for Bar School despite the Middle Temple student adviser stating that she would have no hope of success at the Bar because 'you're a woman, Australian and have no connections' and insisting on returning Margaret's fees. After the fees cheque had travelled backwards and forwards over the desk a few times Margaret gave up (only temporarily) and set off for articles at Lovell White and King. It took less than a year for her to decide that, although she could do nothing about being a woman or being Australian, she could do something about 'connections'.

This determination carried her through a successful interview for acceptance to the Middle Temple and through her Bar Finals, but the next step was pupillage, 'and I had absolutely no idea what pupillage was'. Still with no idea she had a chance meeting with a barrister in Stone Buildings, where she remembers that everything was in Dickensian disorder and covered in 18th century dust. After attempting to dissuade her from applying on much the same grounds as the Middle Temple student adviser, the friendly barristers' clerk eventually conceded that if she were really determined he 'could organise it for her'. At last she had the courage to ask, 'Well, what is pupillage?' It was with some relief that she learned that it only meant training with a barrister for a year.

Being a barrister

Although the first six months were dominated by sorting out her recently divorced pupilmaster's disorganised domestic life, she is also grateful for the vast amount that she learned about strategy and practice management. But the next step of 'finding a tenancy' exposed her to an invisible level of discrimination as she searched for a set of chambers where she could become 'the token woman', the only hope for an outsider in the early 1980s. She wrote to every single set of chambers in London. Hundreds of letters. Many interviews. She was astonished at the varying degrees of quality of the interview, and outraged by the frequent question, 'and what about marriage?'. Obviously she did find a tenancy, for many years was extremely successful at the Chancery and Commercial Bar and was proudly acknowledged by her clerk as being 'part of the First XI'.

She was prepared to absorb herself completely in her cases and revelled in the emotion of the courtroom. 'If you ask people who have been cross-examined in court they will tell you that it was the worst experience of their lives; for the barrister on the other hand it is one of the most intense. You have to be totally focused on what you are doing.' In court you are totally exposed with no time for reflection and little opportunity for retrieval. She quotes her early mentor Tony Scrivener, 'It's like being in a river full of piranhas. They eat you alive if you stand still, but if you survive it's fantastic'. How far this is different from the sense of exhilarated satisfaction that many people who work under short term public scrutiny, such as actors and professional sportsmen, experience when they are successful it is difficult to know but it is clear that Margaret feels that there is a distinct difference between academic work to give advice and the sustained emotional and intellectual intensity of court work.

Commercial work was 'what I thought the law was all about, why I came into the law'. It provided the twin pleasures of intellectual challenge and the opportunity to sort out problems. 'My clients were large companies mostly with deep pockets and the issues were largely concerned with financial strategy, about who had the money and who wanted to get it.' The emotional intensity at this stage in her career was supplied by the experience of the legal process, not by empathy with clients who had been abused or assaulted.

As she points out, 'a case is not just for a day, it may last for months or years and I have worked with many QCs who expect their juniors to be on call 24 hours a day for the whole of that time'. This pressure is created partly by the way that the Bar is structured. 'Six per cent of all the work at the Bar is done by a small number of huge earners whose high profile cases make the news and who are sought after by high profile and wealthy clients.' It is in the interests of chambers' clerks to concentrate on promoting these particular barristers as they themselves have traditionally been on a percentage of those golden fees. Being favoured by chambers' clerks and promoted towards high value cases is what 'being in the First XI' is all about. And having the intellectual and physical stamina. And the emotional freedom.

The chambers' culture

But all this changed when her daughter was born. The same clerk who had been so proud to work for her used his enormous informal power to 'clerk me out' by telling clients that 'Miss McCabe could not unfortunately give you the time that you need for this case because she has a child'. As Margaret pointed out 'he knew nothing about my pretty formidable organisational skills and the strong support and back up that I had arranged at home and did not bother to enquire about it. He spoke purely from deep-rooted prejudice'. As helpful as this clerk had previously been he was culturally unable to cope with the concept of women with children not being at home. Margaret's early arrival at work every morning to work efficiently in peace counted for nothing against the prejudice encapsulated in the words 'Doing a half day, are we?' if she left promptly at 6 p.m.

Margaret is the first to admit that it is difficult for women at the Bar when they have children. A barrister is to some extent in the same position as an actor; the show must go on even when there are problems at home. And having even five per cent of your mind astray thinking of your child can be detrimental to courtroom performance. Unlike actors, barristers are also faced with huge amounts of additional work when not in the courtroom, mastering briefs and keeping up to date. In this latter respect they are no different from solicitors, but the added pressure for commercial barristers is the knowledge that other vastly expensive salaries are dependent on their appearance. Here is where the analogy with the theatre most thoroughly breaks down; in the theatre an understudy may save the show for a night if the principal actor cannot appear. But in the court because the barrister very rarely gets a second chance to present his case, the performance of a substitute can have a much more deleterious effect on the outcome of a case than the effect that the occasional performance by an understudy will have on a play's financial success.

In Margaret's case her clerk quite simply, and without any reason apart from his own ingrained prejudice, took the view that a woman's reliability is inevitably affected by her maternity and he was no longer prepared to promote her. Consequently her income dwindled from the very substantial to dangerously close to insufficient to cover the large childcare costs. Even when faced by the managing clerk's admission of discrimination ('he knew that he had been doing it, but just could not help himself'), it didn't occur to her head of chambers that he should take appropriate disciplinary action. Joining another set of Temple chambers seemed a good solution to the difficulty because they were aware both of her reputation and of her domestic circumstances, but it turned out to be 'another disaster'. Despite being given a tenancy because of her 'connections, background and experience', she was excluded from marketing outings, forced to find all her own work and given very little support. When she finally left, the managing clerk wiped all records of her fees from the computer just to get even.

The Bar for women?

These experiences have led Margaret to conclude that being at the Bar is a fabulous career for women but true equality for women barristers will require a complete change of culture including the chambers' structure. Even some 10–12 years after these unfortunate experiences able women are still giving up when they have had children because they feel that any difficulties in arranging suitable childcare will be compounded by the intransigence of their clerks. 'In other professions an employee making a mistake will be disciplined.' In chambers if a clerk, who is an employee, is in error it is the professional, his nominal employer, who may well be forced to move on. Management in 'all but the very best chambers is run by clerks who are often totally unskilled'. Her response has been to set up her own chambers moving from that traditional structure to be clerked by clerksroom.com capable of access from anywhere in the world. This, she feels, is the future.

She has very firm views on the structure of chambers which she considers to be outdated and very badly arranged. 'In reality barristers are sole practitioners who need to be independent. They are obliged by the professional rules of conduct to be self-employed and it makes no sense for them to be lumped together in chambers. Barristers are analogous to medical specialists who operate on their own via a referral system and are subject to self-regulation.' She explains that the present situation has come about because originally barristers could practise only from the Inns of Court where chambers rapidly became overcrowded, and thus premises had to be shared. Because of the requirement for independence the chambers' structure permits only expenses but not profits to be shared, and also makes it difficult for many practitioners (often women) to organise themselves properly. The more enlightened chambers she considers have made the structure work well for them, because they have acquired a 'brand name'.

Change of focus

The birth of her daughter, and the consequent discovery of the 'unlevel' playing field resulted in a definite change of legal direction.

Some people crumble under adversity, but others like Margaret assess the situation and use the experience as a springboard to the future. 'I needed to earn a living to support my daughter,' she says pragmatically, 'but I realised one Saturday when I brought my daughter into chambers to do yet another 10 hour day that life could not continue like this,' even with the excellent nanny that she considers to be an absolute essential in the life of every working mother who is a lawyer.

Her subsequent move into public law was a response to endemic discrimination in the commercial field, but it also enabled Margaret to use another part of her skills set. Her open down-to-earth manner, persuasive skills and ability to communicate with anyone are exactly what those who really do not have a voice require in a lawyer. And this partly explains why she became involved with the Australian mandatory sentencing case.

She considers that in common with many Australians she had been brought up in an environment imbued with racist attitudes and that at the time when she was growing up Australians were certainly institutionally racist, evidenced by the 1969 referendum to decide whether aborigines could be permitted to have passports and citizenship. Returning to Australia she became aware not only of the potentially unequal access to justice available to aborigines but of the full horror of the experiences of the 'stolen generation' of aboriginal children who were removed from their aboriginal mothers because their fathers or grandfathers happened to be white.

As she points out it was circumstances that got her involved in 'all this human rights stuff' but it is now something that she has completely embraced because 'I am good at getting things done'. An example of this is her setting up the European Women Lawyers' Association and the now mainstream Women Lawyers' Forum (WLF) which has now been running successfully for 10 years. In conjunction with Charles Purle QC she is completing a practitioner's book on privacy, confidentiality, and rights and remedies under Article 8 of the European Convention on Human Rights. 'I have been waiting for this area of the law to get interesting,' and she is now clearly excited that it has become sufficiently so to merit a book.

Women Lawyers' Forum (WLF)

It is clear that she abhors discrimination of any kind. Where others might have caved in because of the unequal treatment meted out to her, largely by the present organisation of the legal system, Margaret assessed the situation and created a new expertise and a new reputation. As well as her publicly recognised human rights work including the NSPCC Justice for Children campaign set up to help victims of paedophile crime, which was, she points out, 'a lawyers' self-contained initiative', she has also recently been appointed as a member of the International Human Rights Watch Committee.

The Women Lawyers' Forum (WLF) she conceived as an opportunity for all women lawyers, whether solicitors, barristers or legal executives, to get together to discuss those issues that were of most importance to them, to hear inspirational speakers and to seek and to implement positive solutions to the difficulties and inequalities that they faced. Increasingly the WLF has been attended by men because of the sheer quality of the participants, and indeed Peter Goldsmith, the chairman of the Bar at the time and now Attorney-General, wrote to the Sex Discrimination Committee and said that this conference will most likely be judged as the most significant event that had happened to the legal profession during the 20th century. Margaret noted this compliment but takes it with a pinch of salt!

One of the most significant achievements of the WLF, for which she takes full credit, is the setting up of the Joint Equal Opportunities Working Party in 1997. 'Under Lord Irvine this committee has tackled all the difficult issues facing the profession and made significant changes, again too slowly but they are changes nevertheless. We have to thank the indefatigable and wonderful Judith Lennard without whom it would not have been possible. This committee led to the appointment of Sir Leonard Peach and is able to take full responsibility for the appointment of Sir Colin Campbell as Chairman of the Commission for the Appointment of Judges.'

Mentoring?

Margaret considers that she could not have achieved what she has without helpful male mentors who 'took me under their wings. Women,' she adds, 'are not good at supporting other women. Senior women often see themselves largely as more in need of help than being able to give it. Even the most senior women often struggle to keep at the top of the pile'. One of her most treasured accolades comes from 'a brilliant female pupil that I had a few years ago who told me that I had been the best pupilmaster that she could have had because I developed the potential of younger women. That struck a pleasing chord'. She is particularly concerned that she does not work in a diverse profession and that change is taking too long.

She sees the WLF as going part of the way to providing an opportunity for senior women to help those younger and less experienced than themselves, but it will not address the more intransigent problem of the dearth of senior women judges. And 'as well as the requirement for more women judges I see the QC system as being in need of urgent modernisation. It needs to be dragged into this century to reflect the talent that it takes to be a leading lawyer and if that happens it will inevitably include more women. This will involve a redefinition of the merits test.'

Final thoughts

Despite the hard work and setbacks, Margaret says that she 'loves the job. It's very important for individuals to have access to justice, and I feel that women are ideally suited to the law'. In the present climate she would not advise a young woman to become a barrister because the Bar is still dominated by white, male, middle class, public schoolboys. 'Become a solicitor,' she advises, 'It provides a much better quality of life, the workplace is more meritocratic and it is now possible to practise advocacy at all levels.'

Lesley MacDonagh

Lesley MacDonagh is the managing partner of Lovells, the world's eighth largest law firm. She was voted Legal Business Managing Partner of the Year for the year 2000.

In her eighth floor eyrie looking down Holborn Viaduct in London Lesley MacDonagh works 20 minutes from home and her children, in the same building as her husband and, as managing partner of Lovells since 1996, she is in charge of 27 offices, 333 partners and 1,600 lawyers worldwide.

Before Lovells

'My mother worked in the RAF for a while, so perhaps she was a bit of a role model,' says Lesley but points out that there are no legal connections in her family. Neither was her career path dictated or even suggested by her father, a Dorset businessman. It was 'a complete outsider' who suggested that she might have some legal talent. Qualified for university but rather too young to go, she went to work for nine months for 'a very forward-looking local authority, where I was given what was in effect a sort of internship. Being moved from department to department, architecture, weights and measures, with a stint at the abattoir, and finally with the town clerk, it was a very privileged commercial training'. It was the town clerk who suggested that she could qualify as a solicitor by taking the old five years' articles route sponsored by the local authority, which would also pay her College of Law fees.

'To be completely honest I was attracted by the prospect of a job with money. They gave me £3,000 a year and I could afford a car. The local authority was very cutting-edge, engaged in all sorts of activities, very switched on and it had an intense degree of service towards its clients, so that it would go the extra mile. By chance I was involved in the environmental and planning side where there were big developments at this time, re-designations of land use and compulsory purchase orders. I was very lucky to be able to get stuck into this specialist planning type of work, so that when I came to Lovells I already had a very good idea of what it was to work for a commercial organisation.'

Lesley has a breathless way of imparting facts which appears conversational, but on reflection has delivered a great deal of information about her reasons for the choice, focus and benefits of her first job. In negotiation it would be easy to be lulled by her friendliness only to be brought up short by a question or statement left suddenly hanging in the air. She paused and the depth of her gratitude to her first employer was very clear. When, newly qualified, she applied to Lovells (then Lovell White & King) after seeing an advertisement in *The Times*, she already had desirable experience of specialist planning issues.

Career analysis

Today's trainees have a very different set of skills to offer. They may be the same age that she was when she arrived newly qualified at Lovells but what they bring through the front door is very different. 'It is a bit of a truism to say that although they are very talented, when they first arrive they do not come with experience of applying the law. But they do adjust pretty quickly, and they do work very hard at making that adjustment.'

'At that time, things were different. I applied for the position without even researching the firm, turned up at Serjeant's Inn for interview and liked the partners I met.' She was instantly placed in the department specialising in planning and environmental law. She had no grand personal career plan, she was merely happy to be working in London in the late 1970s, but the firm was 'very far-sighted, they recognised a specialism of the future, and I was lucky that my previous experience matched what they required'. She was happy to be directed and says that she did not feel that 'it was such a substantial change from local authority work' because the work was very familiar to her.

'Nowadays young people are much more clued up from the start and much clearer as to what it means to be a litigator or a corporate lawyer and have a much clearer idea of what their own career is about. There is also a change in attitude in the firms themselves, and there is much more effort to accommodate the wishes of trainees than there was before when they were simply told which seats they would have.'

This increased choice does of course place a greater responsibility on the shoulders of a trainee or newly qualified solicitor. 'It's a very obvious point, but speaking to young people you almost give them different sorts of advice for different areas of the law. There are so many different areas of the law, and the important thing is to know yourself and to match your skills and your stamina to the right area of law for you. The law may be one profession, but it has lots of sub-sets, and you should play to your strengths and whatever suits your stamina.' Some young people will revel in negotiation, whereas others would happily solve technical problems behind the scenes. It is very much an issue of self-recognition.

She also feels strongly that mistakes are retrievable. 'It's so important to choose what you like and what you can do. If you have made a wrong choice, you should admit it, because the law is so diverse, and sometimes all that it takes is a move two degrees to the left to find the correct niche for you.'

Managing partner

In effect Lesley found two niches at Lovells, the first as a planning and environmental lawyer and the second as the firm's managing partner. Lesley was not the first female partner at Lovells; the year before she was made up Harriet Maunsell OBE, now the chairman of the Occupational Pensions Regulatory Authority, was also made up to partnership. She did not feel that this was unusual, or something which she had had to fight for other than by being a good lawyer, because she has 'genuinely never felt any sexism within the firm'. She did not feel her elevation seven years ago to managing partner was unexpected in the context of the firm's natural character, but she was surprised by the 'external attention' although in retrospect she realises that it was perhaps 'a bold move in the market context' to elect a woman to her position. She made the general comment that 'people were very kind' and particularly the senior management in other law firms; 'I was disproportionately fussed up and I enjoyed it.' She is also proud of being elected as the first woman member of the Justinians, a previously all-male legal dining club.

During her watch as managing partner of Lovells the number of offices and the number of staff have both doubled. In the last three years there have been mergers with firms in Germany, the Netherlands and most recently, France. Managing this empire could be a punishing task, but Lesley has worked out a way of dealing with the diversity just as she has found a way to give attention to the request from her younger son that she view his assembly performance as a singing banana.

It would be easy, but Lesley considers unproductive, to spend too much of her time on aeroplanes visiting international offices when modern technology can provide so much to facilitate meaningful communication. What she looks for all the time is a way to expand communication beyond the two-dimensional. 'Videoconferencing helps because you can see the person on the other end, and I prefer voicemail to email. I am a great fan of voicemail, because you can sense in the other person's voice just how anxious they are or how urgent the matter is or whether the response can be deferred. So many people don't edit their emails before they send them because they are in a hurry and all sorts of misunderstandings can be created. The crispness of the keyboard can sometimes detract from the real meaning. So, I'm a voicemail addict.'

Armed with the technological means Lesley considers that it is no more difficult for a woman to manage an international office than for a man, although there may be initial difficulties of acceptance because of domestic cultural differences. However by way of compensation she considers that 'women generally', and she pauses, because she knows she is about to make a statement that might be construed as sexist, 'are more attuned to the differences in the way of doing things that are important to other people'. The skill of being a good manager in these circumstances is to be able to 'pick up on what is best in each different jurisdiction rather than to impose a way of working from a single office. A multicultural firm has a lot of strengths. When our clients are doing a deal which crosses borders we are not restricted to recommending lawyers in other firms that we barely know, we are using our own people, whose quality of work we do know because we are a single firm'.

Lesley clearly feels that Lovells has formed 'something new' by integrating into 'international practice areas. We encourage people to think on international lines by organising international "retreats" for each practice area, by sharing know-how and taking every opportunity to get to know each other'. This integration strategy and its implementation has been the most important thing on her agenda for the past few years. For the last eight years she has done no legal work, which she recognises could be viewed as a serious problem for a lawyer; 'there are people who return to practice and attempt to take up the threads of legal work again, but it's very difficult to do that. When you take on this job it's a personal decision that you have to think very hard about'. She looks out of the floor to ceiling window of her new office in her new building and says, 'but it's a very fun train-set, the most fascinatingly varied role. Apart from the excitement of the mergers the largest project that I have been involved in is the building of the building'.

The Building as Metaphor

As Lesley describes it, the project and the result deserve the initial capitals. 'I knew that if we got it right it would help Lovells as a firm both in terms of client perception and in terms of helping the lawyers in the firm. I was involved in every design decision. I was passionate about it.'

An island site was chosen so that the whole building could be suffused with as much natural light as possible; all fee earners' offices either face to the outside world or into a huge central atrium which is dominated by the largest indoor water sculpture in Europe. The concept behind this reality was of an office where people could look out and see 'each other coming and going' rather like the inhabitants of a small town, who can be in touch with each other easily, and who are 'aware of the size of the firm that they are part of'. The lightness of the building strikes an outsider as a visual metaphor for 'maximum visibility, of being part of something'.

The detail of this design and the part that the managing partner has taken in it is surprising. There are 'sleeping pods, rather like Travelodge rooms on site, not because we want people to sleep here, but just in case they are in the middle of a deal in the middle of the night and they can have the opportunity to catch a couple of hours of sleep, then they can take it, get up and have a shower and feel a whole lot better'. This is the sort of detail, like the collection and delivery of dry cleaning to and from the office, and the discount tickets at theme parks available to all the staff ('there are some areas where our sheer size makes it possible to use our bargaining power to benefit everyone, and why shouldn't we use it?'), that Lesley thrives on provided that it will make life easier for her staff. 'And our clients.'

Unlike many other firms the reception area is not at ground floor level but on the 11th floor up in the clouds and staffed by 'people who have been trained in the airline industry, who are used to fixing up videoconferencing, sorting out laptops and making alterations to clients' travel arrangements for them if meetings overrun. It's good for our lawyers too because they feel properly backed up, knowing that the clients are getting the best support service that we can give'.

It's clearly about pride and efficiency, pride in what you are part of, what it looks like and what you can offer, and the efficiency that comes not only from things working but knowing that they work. Described by someone else as having 'a human touch with just that hint of steel' Lesley is determined that the new building will work for her staff and that everyone will feel that they have a part to play.

She is even involved with the choice of receptionists' uniforms. She is a little shy about this, 'perhaps that's a level of detail that I need not concern myself with, but it's also about keeping a relationship with all members of staff going and not just with the lawyers who work in the firm'.

Up close and personal

She herself enjoys her 'feminine' side and does not feel that a woman needs to ignore it to succeed. Between caring for her firm and caring for her family of four her time is nearly all allocated. She does find occasional time for herself, not as much as her 18-year-old daughter thinks that she should have but every now and then she has what her husband, also a partner at Lovells, calls a 'hormonal shopping burst' when 'he knows that my Amex card is going to be blitzed for two hours at Harvey Nicks'. She admits that she is very fortunate to be able to buy what she likes when she sees it, 'without going away to think about it', but there is the shrewd suspicion that she would always have been as focused about clothes shopping as she is about building design.

Lesley is in the very unusual position in the City of having a husband who is her working as well as her domestic partner. The firm is so large that she does not see this as a problem, 'we communicate a lot by voicemail during the day', and the situation means that he understands perfectly the background to the pressures of her job. When for example the annual partnership conference is in the process of organisation 'I turn into some sort of werewolf for about three weeks beforehand, but then he can see and understand when he attends the conference what I have been spending all my time on'. For her, working in the same firm 'takes a whole layer of irritation out' because in all aspects of their lives they are working for common goals.

She would not pretend however that this is the complete answer to being a successful working mother. Not entirely seriously she says that 'maybe to stagger when you have your children is a useful tip'; her four children range in age between four and 18. Her recipe for combining family and work has two main ingredients – efficiency and luck. You have to be lucky, 'lucky certainly to have found the work that you really want to do, but the real luck is in having children who sleep through the night. If you can have your sleep you can try anything, and I've been very fortunate that all my children have been good sleepers'. You also need to have a partner who fully understands your ambition so that you can work together for the common good. It sounds very much like the way that she would describe partnership relationships within the firm.

Efficiency in her view is not just about doing things quickly and well, but in analysing what life decisions have to be made to ensure maximum flexibility, because bringing up children is 'an ever changing scene'. As soon as Lesley learns of any dates involving her children they go straight into her diary, 'if you don't do that immediately then you will never be able to prioritise them. With enough notice you can do anything that you need to do, and I am quite proud that I have never missed a nativity play at any of my children's schools'. Being rigorous about diary dates may be relatively simple advice, but ensuring a proper family life goes much further. She has eschewed 'the rolling acres' of country life and a daily commute to and from the home counties, which one might think were emotionally more beckoning to a Dorset girl, for a home in Marylebone so that she can be home in 20 minutes if there were an emergency 'I've only had to do that twice in 18 years', and arranging for her sons to go to St Paul's Choir School only 10 minutes from the office so that 'I can go to events if necessary'. In the middle of the German merger she was faced with having to use that privilege, wondering if her new German partners would understand, 'but they were fine about my asking for a 20 minute break. They all went outside for a walk and a smoke and I was able to do what I had to do at my son's school'.

This sort of flexibility might be all very well for a managing partner, but it is a view of life that Lesley would encourage in her partners. Lovells has a part-time partners' scheme, which several women, but no men yet, have taken advantage of. The firm clearly perceives that it is better to lose some of someone's time and attention than to lose that person entirely. She herself does not suggest that juggling family and work life is easy. In order to make it work, you have to 'love your work and love your family' to the extent that you can exclude the necessity for 'room to one's self' and take great satisfaction from making it work for everyone else.

Dame Judith Mayhew

Judith Mayhew is chairman of the Royal Opera House and is also deputy chairman of the Policy and Resources Committee of the Corporation of London. She was created a Dame in June 2002 for services to the City of London.

Upbringing

First of all there is Judith's mother, who through hard work and determination became a headmistress and adviser to the Department of Education in her native New Zealand. 'I had a very strong woman as a role model who instilled in me a love of history and reading.' High standards were required both in terms of school achievement and domestic responsibility, which included being a 'little mother' to her younger brothers, even keeping them quiet in her own class-room as their school day ended earlier than hers. Judith's father had died when she was five, leaving her mother the awesome task of bringing up three children aged five, two and 10 months on her own. Because of her mother's need to earn money to maintain her small family Judith says that she was, 'a latch-key kid at a time when that did not have the stigma that it carries now'.

Judith's first taste of school was in a very tough primary school where survival in the playground was the first necessary lesson and coping with the frequent corporal punishment was another. Five-year-old Judith was frequently 'belted with the tawse' (a heavy leather strap) for writing with her left hand instead of her right and initially her ability to read at the age of four was not acknowledged. She was permitted to be in the classroom but not to read, until she was found to be helping herself to 'all those marvellous books in the teacher's cupboard' and her skill had to be recognised.

The Otago Girls' High School followed and 'a superb education based on the Scottish model of discipline and hard work'. Judith was unwittingly following in the footsteps of the first woman solic-itor in New Zealand, Ethel Benjamin (probably one of the first woman solicitors in the Commonwealth) who was not only edu-cated at Otago Girls between 1883 and 1892 but also read law at

Otago University in the 1890s, before becoming a lawyer after the passing of the Female Law Practitioners Act in 1896. When in 1910 she left New Zealand for London she had to wait until 1919 to be permitted to practise officially as a lawyer in the UK. Judith was more fortunate when she moved to London and was later to produce a television programme on Ethel's life.

Legal education

Judith knew that 'I did not want to become a librarian and definitely not a teacher because I had seen how hard my mother worked', an ironic comment from someone whose working days often last from 7 a.m. until 11 p.m. At the last minute she chose law over economics and found herself as one of only two women in the law class of her year.

By the time she graduated in 1972 half the law faculty intake were women. Again New Zealand was ahead of its parent country in terms of legal emancipation as in 1977 only seven per cent of solicitors in England and Wales were women, which she notes wryly may partly explain the paucity of women in their late 40s in City partnerships.

A teacher after all!

In September 1973 Judith came to England to the law faculty at Southampton University, where 'I was astonished that the nights were so short and dismayed by the length of oil-slicked pebbles that was called a beach' after the wind-swept cleanliness of a semi-rural Dunedin. She had been offered the position 'by post' without a formal interview.

Indeed Judith is very short on interview experience, as the only formal job interview that she has ever had was for the position of Lecturer at King's College London in 1976. When she left 13 years later she was Sub-Dean of the law faculty and had developed with the Sorbonne the first genuinely joint degree in law in Europe. This required supreme organisational skills because of the French Government's insistence that the course was not only to be evenly split with two years in English Law and two years in French Law but that the English Law should come first sequentially. She was faced with 'unpicking the French thing', weaning young French students off the formalism of French education and teaching them how to think freely. Her colleagues on the other side of the Channel were some of the best legal minds in France, who, askance that the

English had put forward a young foreign woman without a doctorate, considered that she would not have the intellectual rigour to carry the project forward. But after they were told by their own students that, 'It's the woman who's the tough one', she was accepted.

She is obviously proud of this degree course. Not only did it hone Judith's managerial and administrative skills but it also gave her her first taste of setting cutting edge policy at an international level.

The practical lawyer

Judith narrates her career as though it were totally governed by serendipity, and has a disarming way of summing up the steps, 'I was visiting a friend at Titmuss Sainer Dechert and I walked out an hour later with a job as an employment lawyer and director of training' or 'I happened to meet the senior partner of Clifford Chance five times in one week and eventually he asked me "What can Clifford Chance do for you? And what can you do for Clifford Chance?" So we discussed it and I got the job of special adviser.' She does in fact know a lot of people, is willing to take on a challenge, and is always looking for further opportunities for personal development.

Titmuss Sainer Dechert brought her 'the steepest learning curve of my life' and some 'searing experiences'. Because New Zealand lawyers are regarded as qualified after they have completed a law degree and are not required to serve articles Judith had not even worked in a legal office before she began to practise there. She rapidly learned that there was a substantial difference between teaching 'black letter law' and putting it into practice to solve client problems which inevitably are always messier than artificial case studies. She started out with an academic knowledge of sex discrimination but quickly found herself learning to draft, negotiating dismissal settlements and advising on the tax implications of share option schemes. After six months she realised that many employment law matters could be solved by the application of common sense. 'Then it got better!'

Not being a natural litigator she worked out a distinctive non-confrontational way of operating. She refused to take on employer clients unless they were prepared to treat their employees fairly. She would suggest to solicitors on the other side in dismissal cases that as they both knew what the settlement figure should be, give or take a small percentage, settling claims expeditiously should be their aim. In her view time spent in litigation prevents an individual from looking forward into an alternative future, and is a distraction for the employing company which could be better spent on its core business.

Women she feels have a pragmatic organised approach to bring to the law. She recalls with affectionate pleasure the one occasion that Titmuss Sainer Dechert fielded by accident an all woman team on a major transaction. It was, she thought, 'a miracle of organisation and efficiency because we treated it all as a housekeeping exercise, and we didn't play silly macho games'.

Eventually Judith was headhunted by Wilde Sapte to fulfil the same role of practical lawyer and director of education in a wider sphere. She feels very strongly that legal education must be practice relevant and negotiated a Wilde Sapte in-house legal training course which was accredited by the Law Society. While there must be an element of choice in what is taught at law college and on university courses trainees must acquire a sound grounding of the law of tort and contract because, 'Contract is the essence of what we are doing as lawyers'. The emphasis on tort is partly tied up with her strong views on the ethical position of solicitors; 'It's what distinguishes us from the accountants. We must always remember that we are Solicitors of the Supreme Court even if we never appear in court'.

Another string to the bow

Parallel with her legal career is a strong commitment to public service. In 1986 she was elected to the Court of Common Council of the Corporation of London. She was later appointed chair of the Education Committee and has used her position to influence and assist all sorts of educational establishments from deprived primary schools in Hackney to the Women's Library in London Metropolitan University. Setting up a parents' room in a primary school in an area with a high Bangladeshi population resulted in 25 per cent of the mothers moving into education themselves. 'This is one of the greatest achievements that I've had.' Although the funding given by the City for the Women's Library was regarded by some of Judith's male council colleagues as 'her little indulgence', it helped to turn a collection of packing cases on several disparate sites into an organised research library.

'The area which embodies the wealth and privilege of London should act positively to improve its poorer neighbours,' is an idea that motivates her as deputy chairman (she stepped down from the position as chairman early in 2003) of the Policy and Resources Committee. 'I feel that my role is to build on the strengths and achievements of my predecessors to facilitate the regeneration and economic development of the poorer boroughs surrounding the City.' So important is this wider view of society that she has in the past rejected career opportunities which she considered would not have left her sufficient time to pursue her political work.

The wider community

Until recently Judith was also special adviser to the senior partner at Clifford Chance. Part of her role was to put together a coherent and mutually beneficial strategy for community affairs, by providing free advocacy for children's tribunals and arranging for corporate, property and banking lawyers to act as governors and trustees in the local community. Involving secretaries and support staff across the firm in mentoring activities within local schools is 'wonderful for team-building across the firm', because as well as helping the young people in the local community the staff feel that the firm values their skills in a wider context. The firm also supports young artists and actors to go into the local schools to provide first class additional teaching, because where you can make school an unexpectedly interesting place which can be shared by a whole community the horizons of children are raised way above their apparent conditioning.

At the other end of the spectrum she operated to facilitate Clifford Chance's dialogue with British universities and the European Union at all levels from student to senior relatonships.

Being a Dame

It is not only for personal reasons that Judith is very proud of the honour that was bestowed on her in 2002. In her eyes it represents the achievement of the City in supporting the poorer boroughs surrounding it, and the process of integration through education that she advocates.

But typically Judith sees this recognition as something to build on and not to recline on. She is already looking to see how her 'Damehood' can be used to advance the public profile of other women. 'There are not enough women in the commercial world who have been honoured for what they have achieved.'

Summing up

The question remains of how a slender woman with a soft voice and a taste for delicate Victorian jewellery has managed to operate so successfully in a man's world?

First, she is non-confrontational. 'I hate conflict and aggression. I have always worked for consensus, for ensuring that the maximum number of people are happy with the outcome and to get the most out of scarce resources.' Understanding the dislocation of the immigrant she simply made the resources available for Bangladeshi women in the non-threatening environment of their children's school so that they too could learn and contribute to their community.

Second, she operates by inclusion. Mention to Judith that you have a particular project and she will not only reel off the names of several people that you should meet, but she will clear the ground in advance with those who can really help you. She is also quick to celebrate and praise the achievements of others as she does so.

Third, she is realistic. 'I could not do what I do if I were married, let alone combine that with having children.' But what she does, combining what for many people would be two full-time occupations of public service and commercial enterprise would also be difficult for a man. She has been driven she says by 'the breadwinning imperative', the force which keeps men on the career track, although 'a lot of men do feel trapped by that breadwinning macho culture'.

Fourth, she considers that she has been fortunate in having 'champions rather than mentors. A mentor may be a useful person to talk things over with; a champion will not only open doors for you but will also push you through them'. Not unsurprisingly she lists her mother as her first great champion, but admits that after she left New Zealand those who filled that role in her life have all been men. Whether they occupied positions in the academic, business or legal worlds they were undoubtedly men. 'The truth is that there have just not been many women in positions of power and influence, but there are a great many men.' This is something that she would like to change by encouraging young women, particularly lawyers, to make the most that they can of their chosen careers.

By deciding to devote so much of her energies to public service Judith has chosen not to work 'flat out at the commercial side of things, even though I know that I have taken a financial hit in doing so'. Questions about her achievements are neatly deflected into what she has helped other people to do, and that skill to encourage and facilitate is clearly one of her great strengths. She does not have a boring list of 'cases that I have won' and 'Masters that I have persuaded' in her repertoire. It is perhaps that gently intelligent approach that has helped her to succeed, and has enabled her to see the advantages in being a woman. 'In some ways you have a head start because you are not taken hugely seriously at first. So you are not blocked and by the time that the chaps realise that maybe they should block you, it's too late.' Interestingly the qualities that she lists as being essential for success in the big wide world of business are almost exactly those that are expected of a successful mother – the ability to be flexible, to be determined, to do without much sleep and to be physically fit.

Barbara Mills

Barbara Mills is the adjudicator for the Inland Revenue, Customs and Excise, Public Guardianship Office and the Insolvency Service. She was formerly the Director of Public Prosecutions.

Beginnings

Organisation is one of the key concepts in Barbara Mills' life, a necessary attribute in someone who has acquired four children and seven grandchildren in the course of a highly successful professional life. All the more surprising that she has no idea why she wanted to become a barrister. 'This is something that I have never been able to explain satisfactorily either to myself or to anyone else. All I know is that at about the age of 14 I knew that I had a burning desire to become a barrister, and only a barrister.' With no lawyers in her family and no desire to go on the stage she speculates that it was nevertheless the idea of advocacy that attracted her.

Whatever the reason she was intensely focused on her career path, electing English, History and Latin as her A level subjects, 'you had to do Latin if you wanted to be a lawyer at that time'. and her parents and her school were intensely supportive of her ambition, 'although my school (St Helen's, Northwood) had very few pupils, only about four in a year, who were destined for university. They were a bit baffled by my choice of career, but were very helpful'. At that time the chairman of the Board of Governors of her school was the Principal of Lady Margaret Hall (LMH), Oxford, so she decided to apply there.

Barbara also applied to Cambridge but rejected any idea of studying law there when she was told firmly at her interview in 1958 that 'women can't be barristers'. When Barbara arrived at Oxford she found that she was one of only two girls at LMH reading law and that there were no law dons in LMH which at that time was a women only college. Now she says with obvious pleasure, 'the LMH law faculty is very strong'.

Being a female student at Oxford at that time was a good experience. Her tutors were all men who 'taught, marked and viewed their women students equally'. She experienced no prejudice because of her gender and the ratio of 10 men to every female student ensured that the social life from a woman's point of view was excellent. This was of course the time when post-war austerity was receding and the ideas of American feminist writers were becoming topical currency. Barbara's conversation does not suggest much of this. For her there simply were no indicators of prejudice. 'It did not occur to me that women would be any different and I felt that I was treated in exactly the same way as the male students. It was not until I went to the Bar that I understood what discrimination was.'

Motherhood and the Bar

Barbara met her husband at Oxford and married him six weeks after her Finals' exams. In a rush to get on both with her professional and personal life ('we had decided that we would like a large family') she succeeded in fitting in study for the Bar exams while pregnant with her first child, 'Sarah was born between my taking the exams and receiving the results. At that time although there were some classes run by the Council for Legal Education, it was possible to do most of the preparation on your own and as I was pregnant that was what I did. What was needed was a good memory because the exams at that time tested rote learning rather than the ability to think'. However she was forced to accept that with a young baby doing pupillage at that time 'would be pretty impractical'. As well as having another daughter 18 months later she 'did a bit of lecturing to keep sane, although it was pretty irritating to watch my contemporaries progressing at the Bar while I was not doing what I really wanted to do'. The irritation of an energetic woman who had won scholarships at both Oxford and Middle Temple is easy to imagine.

When she did decide to progress her career obtaining pupillages did not prove too difficult but 'it was when I was looking for tenancy, that I found out what prejudice was all about. There were few women at the Bar at that time, even fewer women with children and the clerks who controlled the work-flow controlled everything and did not welcome women into chambers. You couldn't win. If you had no children, you would be going to have them and if you did then you would not be dedicated to the job. It took me a long time to find a tenancy'. In Barbara's view one of the attributes of a good advocate is to be able to take a complex issue and to simplify it for the jury. Her succinct explanation without examples of this time in her life is clearly the distillation of many petty instances of slight and rejection.

In 1967 she joined the chambers of Edward Cussen, which was regarded as one of the top six criminal chambers at that time, acting both for the prosecution and defence in a range of criminal cases, from 'general knockabout crime involving minor driving offences to large murder and fraud trials'. Fortunately for Barbara 'they had a bit of a backdrop of women tenants as they had two women tenants both of whom had combined having children with successful careers'.

Prosecuting and defending

She perceived the criminal, rather than the commercial, Bar would offer her the clearest opportunity for deploying her advocacy skills. 'I would have hated being at the Chancery Bar spending my time on drafting.' She was instructed to act for both prosecution and defence, and rapidly came to the conclusion that different skills were necessary for each.

'As a prosecutor it is mainly a question of simplification, of being able to present the issues to a jury so that they can understand them and not being side-tracked, whereas defending on the face of it is pretty different. There you have the challenge of making the best of the material that you get. You have a closer relationship with the client and the solicitor and have the task of keeping up the morale of the client, and making sure that you give a realistic estimate of what is *likely* to happen, not what *is* going to happen because you can't know that, but what is likely to happen so that the client can be prepared.'

The position of the prosecutor is much more analytic. 'First you have to consider whether there is a realistic prospect of a conviction on the evidence, and if so whether it is in the public interest that this person should be prosecuted. It is at this second point that a prose-cuting barrister might have some impact, but to a large extent the decision as to whether to prosecute or not someone who might be called socially inadequate, is dealt with by the solicitor and the police. When I became Treasury Counsel I was involved at a very early stage in the decision as to whether or not to prosecute, and it can be very hard to have to tell the police that there is simply insuf-ficient evidence for a likely conviction when they are assuring you that they are certain that this person has committed some outrageous crime and is likely to do so again. But the job of Treasury Counsel is to assess the likelihood of conviction dispassionately as well as to prosecute in court later.'

In 1977 after more than 10 years at the Bar Barbara was invited to become in rapid succession, Junior Prosecuting Counsel to the

Inland Revenue, then Senior Prosecuting Counsel, a part-time job, involving prosecuting four or five cases of a serious nature a year, but 'one which suggests that you have been noticed'.

It was the eventual move to becoming Treasury Counsel at the Central Criminal Court at the Old Bailey 'which really changed my workload. It was very, very hard work involving not only the most serious cases of rape, murder and pornography but also serious fraud because this was in the days before the creation of the Serious Fraud Office (SFO). I had an extremely heavy workload and I think that it was the time in my life when I have worked hardest. I would start at the crack of dawn, be in court all day and then would leave court only to have to take a conference and finish up with drafting'. It is not surprising that Barbara developed 'juggling' skills, 'I don't like that phrase but it does encapsulate what it is like to be a working mother'.

From the Old Bailey to the Serious Fraud Office

After taking silk in 1986, and undertaking a massive amount of defence work to broaden her practice, Barbara was asked in 1988 to prosecute the defendants in the well-publicised Guinness trial, where several prominent business figures were accused and eventually convicted of playing a leading part in an illegal scheme to boost the value of Guinness shares in the run-up to the company's £2.6 billion takeover of Distillers in 1986. 'I spent the better part of 18 months doing that case, working in a team of four barristers.' As the trial was drawing to a conclusion she received a telephone call which was to change both the nature of her professional work and the press's view of her right to personal anonymity.

Barbara had always been, in common with most barristers, self-employed, and it had never occurred to her to become employed. However, when the incumbent head of the SFO had agreed at short notice to become Director of Public Prosecutions (DPP) in Hong Kong, Barbara was invited to enter the open competition to become the new SFO head. Barbara analysed the situation. She was 50, had worked at the Bar for more than 20 years and felt ready for a new experience, even one which would require a very steep learning curve indeed. 'I felt that I needed a change, and more or less as I finished the Guinness trial I began as the head of the SFO with little or no experience of managing either staff or budgets. At the Bar you stand up in court and you make your reputation, that's how you survive at the Bar and your chambers' clerks deal with almost everything else.'

From managing very little she took over an organisation with 120 staff and a budget of £15 million. Her role gave her responsibility for both the management and the case management side of SFO work. 'Fortunately I was able to rely on very good people with experience in finance and personnel on the organisational side, and on the case side three or four counsel were deployed on each case.' But ultimately she had to become familiar with all SFO cases in case of crises, 'and these were major cases, because we took no cases which involved less than £5 million'. Her new status put her in the peculiar hybrid position of being an employed barrister with no rights of audience. The other important change was that 'it was much more of a desk type job as opposed to the long hours that I had previously spent in court'.

Aware that the move from self-employment to employment was a substantial and to some extent unknown step she negotiated a three year contract, the minimum permissible duration. Her tenure was however to be very brief. After 18 months the post of DPP unexpectedly became available. 'I had a hard decision to make, because I had always felt that this was a job that I would like to do, but I realised that the time frame was such that if I did not take this opportunity I would probably be considered to be too old when the post next became available.'

Crown Prosecution Service

The move to the Crown Prosecution Service (CPS), an organisation which had existed only since 1986, brought a new set of challenges. 'It was still suffering from being a new organisation and it had gone through a period of severe recruitment difficulties.' She now had responsibility for 6,000 staff, of whom 2,000 were lawyers, in 120 different locations and a budget of £300 million. To some extent the recruitment position was ameliorated by the economic downturn of the early 1990s but of course not all applicant lawyers had criminal expertise and recruiting lawyers with little or no experience in that area brought its own challenges. 'Lawyers as employees have their own professional standards and many find it difficult being employed in a large organisation. Some like it better than others, but it is a different way of operating.'

She herself had many new things to learn. 'I had never worked at the heart of government before, and I now found that I was the accounting officer for the CPS responsible to Parliament, with the title of Permanent Secretary.' Although given the rank of Permanent Secretary, her position was different from that of other permanent secretaries who work very closely with their relevant Secretaries of

State. So that she would be able to brief the Attorney-General at short notice on the progress of cases on which he might be questioned she was required to be very familiar with about 30–40 of the most important of those cases at any one time. There were inevitably many crises, and her role extended beyond case management and people management to becoming public relations' spokeswoman for the CPS, dealing with the media, writing articles and giving speeches as well as, 'a lot of evening social life. Fortunately I had lots of good staff to help. It was truly a seven day a week job, and even now, four years later I can't break myself of the habit of letting everyone know where I am all the time'.

Barbara is notoriously tidy, but this was a time when inevitably 'crisis piled on crisis, and just when one ended and I thought that I would be able to get all the other stuff cleared up, there would be another overlapping crisis. I had to recognise that as DPP I could not be tidy minded and tidy all the time. I had to learn to have a good sense of what is really important at any one time', and because the CPS was the target of some very public criticism during her tenure, 'to have a very thick skin'. What carried her through was her very palpable enjoyment of the job.

Believing that 'in general you should not do anything for more than about five years', Barbara had decided to move on when her five year contract was up, but agreed to stay for another two years, which was in retrospect 'a moderately good idea'. However, 31 October 1998, 'I remember that it was Hallowe'en,' was her last day at the CPS. The new Labour Government had plans for a substantial reorganisation of the CPS to increase the number of CPS jurisdictional areas and to make them coterminous with police force boundaries. Barbara felt that it would be unfair on her staff for her to commence such a substantial and long-term project knowing that she would not be there at the completion, and informed the Government that she would remain only until a suitable replacement could be found.

Women and the law

Barbara considers that she and other women of her generation were very much pioneers and points out that she qualified and spent many of her years in practice before the passing of the Equal Opportunities Act 1976. 'The world has changed a lot since the late 50s and 60s although not in all its fundamentals. There was no other woman at the Bar with four young children. Now even the Bar is more sensitive to the difficulties that women face, and most organisations are better at recognising that they benefit from implementing proper equal opportunities' policies and enabling their staff to have a proper work-life balance, another phrase I hate although it does say what it means.'

She has clearly thought very carefully about what it means to be a woman at the Bar, where she had to pay her full share of chamber's expenses when taking time off to have her children. 'The real difficulty for a woman is to decide when to have children. I had four by the age of 30 and although it was very difficult at the time, it was probably better than having them later. Women now tend to marry later and to have children later and this can create a difficult situation as motherhood coincides with seniority and the opportunity to take on more demanding cases. This is why women are dropping out of the profession.' These difficulties and the lack of support are not she considers confined to the Bar. 'In many City firms there is still underlying prejudice, and bonus and payment issues are still not fairly worked out. We are still short of women judges and it is still not very representative at the judges' level. Unless we keep trying it won't change. Leading by example undoubtedly gets the numbers up. You can see how that operates in sport, where if your country is successful in a particular sport there will be lots of young people who will take it up. And if you get the numbers up then you are treated differently, treated for what you are rather than because of your gender.'

The qualities that make a good lawyer are very much the qualities that might be attributed to being a good mother, although Barbara has always tried very hard to keep her professional and her family life separate. 'It's attention to detail, attention to detail and more attention to detail, which is very important whichever profession you are in. You need enormous stamina, and the ability to make things simple for your clients or a jury, you must preserve a sense of humour about the whole thing and must have the ability to make the clients feel that they are in good hands. I suppose that is rather like being a doctor.'

Family life

Far from considering that being a mother has in any way held her back in her career aspirations Barbara presents the professional and family combination almost as a positive force. 'I like to have the contrast, and I used to say just give me 10 minutes' adjustment time when I get in the door and I'll be happy to listen to all the lost gym shoe problems.' Her solution to one domestic difficulty when appointed as Treasury Counsel suggests that she also has formidable persuasive and man management skills. 'I just came home one day, and said to my children, who were 18, 16, 12 and 10 at the time that either they learned to draft indictments or they would have to agree to making one meal a week each and I would undertake dinner on Fridays. I've always believed that if you have a lot to do you either do it by operating in a disorganised way or in a totally organised way, and I'm in the latter category. My desk is always tidy, because I can't work in an untidy office, and at home my husband and I have allocated responsibilities. I take charge of the food and he takes charge of the wine and together we make sure that we are never without.'

She is very conscious that her own personal skills would not have been sufficient to ensure a balanced life for herself and her family. 'I have been very fortunate that my husband has always wanted me to pursue my career, not just been supportive but has actively wanted me to do it, and we've been able to come up with practical solutions to difficulties.' She acknowledges that it has felt at times like 'muddling through' even with a dedicated nanny and there 'has always been anxiety about illnesses. What you need is total discipline and perfect organisation'. Typical of her application of available resources to an apparent problem was the decision to alleviate the ongoing financial drain of a full-time nanny when her children were at nursery school age by setting up her own nursery school in the bottom floor of her North London home which ran until the children all went to school.

Now

Barbara's present main role, because she has many others, occupies her for two to three days a week. She acts as the adjudicator, whose office now acts as ombudsman for the Inland Revenue, Customs and Excise, the Public Guardianship Office and the Insolvency Service. 'Now I don't have crises, I am much less in the public eye and my job is much more flexible.' From being very much an advocate either in the courtroom or as the public face of two important governmental organisations, she finds herself almost in a judicial position 'holding the ring between complainants and government agencies, because I deal mainly with Codes of Practice and accusations of maladministration'.

At this juncture in her life she feels 'enormously lucky'. Possessed of a sharp anticipatory intelligence she finishes the question what would you 'have done differently? Nothing. I had a good education, enjoyed university, have been married to my husband for more than 40 years, have four children, several grandchildren, lots of interests, I play tennis, go to the theatre and the opera and I have had a fascinating career'. This is clearly not over. 'I am never going to retire. I can't see any point, because I get a great deal of pleasure out of working.'

Diana Parker

Diana Parker is the chairman of Withers Bergman LLP and also a practising family law partner. She is a co-founder of the Family Mediators' Association and a Member of the International Academy of Matrimonial Lawyers.

Diana Parker is crisp. Crisply dressed, crisp in her responses but with an endearing professional friendliness. She has just come from court, has a conference to attend at the end of the interview so that time is neatly defined and it becomes easy to see how it might just be possible to combine chairmanship of an international firm with maintaining a practice as a family law specialist. She is extraordinarily focused, giving her complete attention to the task in hand.

Why study law?

Born and educated in Newcastle upon Tyne, Diana cannot remember any defining moment when she decided to become a solicitor. Her father, who was a chartered surveyor, and who died when Diana was nine, had given her a book called simply *A Young Man's Guide to the Law*. It somehow became part of her view of herself that she would become a lawyer, an ambition that was further refined through reading the novels of A. P. Herbert and books concerning forensic science, 'with all the gory bits', to an ambition to become a barrister. She also had the shrewd thought that being at the Bar might be best suited to her argumentative personality.

So without too much introspection she ended up at Cambridge reading law, an occupation which she gradually concluded was 'a waste of time' as far as having an 'education' was concerned. 'Now I would not advise anyone who wants to become a lawyer to read law. It's much better to read something else first.' Her second degree, an M.Phil in criminology, she saw as 'compensation' for the aridity of the traditional Cambridge law degree. It did not denote any intention to pursue a career in criminal law, although it sharpened her interest in psychology, and she took full advantage of being less intellectually constricted by coming top of her class.

Somehow or other the ambition to become a barrister was lost along the way, probably because by the time that she left Cambridge her focus had moved. Legal practice was now not to be the ultimate goal, but was now to be an economic safety net because 'I thought that I would end up doing something like Harriet Harman and Patricia Hewitt, who were running the National Council for Civil Liberties at the time, but I thought that I would sign up for articles just in case my courage failed me'.

Articles

Diana's applications for articles went only to firms ranging from the small to the very tiny, including Withers which at that time came within the definition of 'small' and resided in Dickensian offices in Essex Street. Diana's only temptation to leave the firm during the ensuing 20 years was when it was suggested to her by one of her partners that they might leave to set up their own niche practice – 'the thought of clean modern offices was almost too much for me, but I realised that I would miss the buzz and the camaraderie that you get in a larger firm'.

Now Diana is proud of what she considers to be the 'quirkiness' of her firm, personified in the efficient minimalist structure behind an almost rococo façade near the Old Bailey. But all those years ago, a feisty young radical, she turned up for interview prepared to turn her nose up at what she thought would be 'unacceptable green welly values', an impression temporarily confirmed when one of the other interviewees turned out to be the chairman of the Cambridge Beagling Society, but she was to her surprise attracted by the breadth of training offered and the sense that this could be an opportunity to join a firm which was 'seriously one-off'.

It may seem surprising that Diana did not star from the start, but she spent the first three months of articles in an aura of uncertainty, unhappy that 'I was being asked to do something that I found very difficult but that everyone else seemed able to do, and in fact that I did not actually approve of. Every day I would come in with the intention of resigning, but by the time that it got to 3.30 p.m. I would say that I could go at 5.30 p.m. and I would do it tomorrow. In this way we got to Christmas when I was taken aside by the person with whom I shared a room, and told over the space of three hours how seriously misguided I was in being an articled clerk at Withers and how he thought that my attitude was morally reprehensible in working for clients that I had no sympathy with'.

'After that it was alright,' she concludes, but rejects any suggestion that she then decided to 'show them what I could do'. She acknowledges that her experience is one that is repeated by many trainees who find the transition to the workplace initially strange but who after the first Christmas break, and perhaps fortified by telling their families about their experiences, return with a feeling of 'coming home'.

The family lawyer

Diana also rejects any notion that she has had a planned career. 'I take a long view on things. I like to do things now and then move on in the belief that things will fall into place.' That having been said she almost instinctively leaves herself a safety net. Retaining her own family law practice is to some extent an insurance against the day (because, in her mid-40s, she is still very young) when she may no longer be chairman of her firm. When asked by the head of department to make family law one of her seats she agreed, but only on the basis that it would be restricted to three months. Extraordinary arrangements having been made to secure this, 'after two months I had to eat humble pie and admit that I really wanted the whole six months'.

'With hindsight I should have realised that this would be an exciting area of law for me, because of the link with psychology and because it is highly political.' This is not most people's immediate concept of family law, but as Diana explains it is 'at the heart of politics because everyone is part of a family, involving consultation and negotiation about the place of the family in society, the provision that should be made for children, how to ensure that absentee fathers should finance their children, what constitutes a family and at the moment the whole raft of discussion on the position of cohabiting couples and same sex couples in relation to all aspects of property, whether taxation or tenancy or inheritance rights'. It is a breathless list over which she appears to have supreme command.

A founder of the Solicitors' Family Law Association (SFLA) she feels that in a previous incarnation she would have been 'functioning in an Istanbul street market', because what she really enjoys is 'cutting deals'. In her present life she sees her function as being to manage expectations and to understand the psychodynamics of a situation so as to produce the best outcome for her client. Her priority is to ensure the best possible financial settlement on divorce, and this may involve persuading not only the other side but her client as well. She smiles at a suggestion that some women can be disadvantaged due to the fact that their husbands have always managed their financial affairs because her experience has made her aware that people often have what she calls 'compensating qualities' which get them through life. 'You can always get someone to manage your money and it's often the dizziest women who get the best settlements because they can look helpless to the judge.'

Diana clearly derives great personal satisfaction from the personal aspect of her specialism, 'from being very close to people at a period of dramatic change in their lives, because change management whether for an individual or for an organisation is always a challenge'. That latter comment is a clue to what she so obviously relishes in her dual role, changing the lives of individuals or changing the orientation of her firm.

Senior partner

Diana was elected to the position of senior partner of Withers in 1999. At the time she was not only the only female senior partner in a Top 100 firm but was the youngest senior partner as well, so that by the more traditional the firm could be seen as taking two 'risks' simultaneously. Diana does not find this surprising. She speaks of Withers as a separate entity with an ongoing life of its own, not 'my firm' but 'the firm' and in this case as 'the firm was a long established professional firm which does do things that are refreshing. If any firm would have gone for it, it would have been this firm'.

Indeed she says that she found only support from the informal club of City senior partners. She did not find her position at all uncomfortable 'but then I suspect that if I were sent to prison I would be more comfortable in Wandsworth than in Holloway'. With two brothers Diana has always found herself more comfortable in mixed or all male groups than in all female ones. She can offer no detailed explanation for this; it is simply one of those things that immutably is, like the idea that she would be a lawyer.

A flexible practice

In case this lack of explanation sounds like a classic Queen Bee statement from a woman who pulls up the drawbridge after she has attained her own pinnacle of achievement, it should be noted that Diana is very proud of Withers' flexibility, and her first and immediate response to a question concerning the desirability of law as a career for women is that 'it is highly compatible with family life'.

This does not only mean that female solicitors at Withers have won the part-time working battle that so many large firms are still engaged in, but that some of the partners at Withers are part-time partners, and one of them is male.

'No one has been held back in the partnership stakes simply because they have children. They may rule themselves out because they have children but that is a different issue. The firm would even consider making someone up to partnership who is pregnant without there being a cast iron guarantee of that person coming back, because as you know in that situation there cannot be certainty.' She says proudly that a third of the partnership in the London office is female, a proportion which certainly helps to drag up the UK large firm average.

The role of chairman

She puts her own flexibility down to 'having a very short attention span', plus one suspects a very high energy level. This could also be interpreted as the ability to focus with extreme concentration for the appropriate and sufficient length of time on one factor or topic before moving seamlessly on to the next. It is certainly an attribute which must be of inestimable value in an Atlantic-hopping chairman. Withers merged with Bergman Horowitz and Reynolds in December 2001 and Diana was elected chairman of the merged firm. There are two managing directors, one in New York and one in London, although the new organisation also has offices in Milan and New Haven, Connecticut.

The unusual title of 'chairman' is forced partly by the new limited liability partnership structure which is a first for a UK firm (the partners are now called 'principals' to distinguish them from old-style Partnership Act partners) but even before that, when 10 years ago a structural change was being discussed within the Withers partnership she was very firmly of the view that a senior partner should be non-executive, and should if possible retain a fee earning responsibility. 'If you don't have that then the temptation is to meddle, and that is not what a senior partner should be about.' Senior partners, or chairmen, are about taking the wider strategic view, about seeing beyond the firm and 'having an instinct for being able to catch the balls before they drop'.

This she does by 'being able to prowl around the building and talking and observing', which has been made immeasurably easier in London by the move into the Old Bailey building but more difficult because of the merger. Diana tries to spend six weeks every year at a stretch in the New York office with lesser amounts of time in the two subsidiary offices. She has no illusions about the difficulty of what she is doing but has a calm certainty that she can manage her time to ensure that most of the time it will work out. She has allocated one hour to me, she arrives one minute late and apologises, apologises again because the meeting will be reduced to 50 minutes because of the conference, we have two minutes of acquaintance touching chit chat and then total attention for the allocated time, swift re-focusing from interview to the personal while she sees me to the front door, and then she is off to the next thing, catching up with her voicemails before the conference. Crisp. She has also acknowledged the receptionists in passing and all in all it is a polished and very professional performance.

As the public face of Withers, as the chairman and as the family lawyer Diana is polished and she is professional, but the toughness and the argumentativeness and the sharpness are bedded in something else. She refers several times to the quirkiness of her firm, to its camaraderie and the support it has given her. She speaks of its 'spirit' which is to act for internationally wealthy clients and their businesses. It is a 'personal' firm, which although it does act in substantial money transactions, would be unlikely to be acting for a 'large faceless corporation'. There is always a 'personal angle'. Looking back Diana recognises that she might not have had such a fulfilling career at the Bar because 'it is not involving enough' in terms of a long term relationship with clients, and it might also be lacking in that friendship and sense of common purpose which she appreciates at Withers.

Final thoughts

She has very clear words of advice for young women contemplating the Law as a career. Read another subject first or read law with something else and try to find articles with a well-established broadly based practice with a high reputation. This will enable you to experience law in practice, so that later if you decide not to stay you will have a good springboard either into high intensity City firms or into High Street firms and law centres, 'Withers solicitors have gone on to all of these, and finally remember that you should be able to combine the law with family life'.

She had earlier listed the necessary qualities in a good family lawyer, 'good sense of humour, objectivity, distance coupled with a high degree of empathy with the client, and a great deal of financial nous'. and in that brief interview I consider that I was given at least a glimmer of all of these. Except perhaps the financial nous. But then again sitting in a slickly organised meeting room in a new but 'quirky' building perhaps I should take that on trust.

Alison Parkinson

Alison Parkinson was unanimously chosen as the first woman to occupy the designated AWS seat on the Law Society Council. She is an in-house legal adviser with Network Rail (formerly Railtrack) and has been national chairwoman of the AWS and also president of the Holborn Law Society.

In-house

Being an in-house lawyer for a large organisation like Network Rail is rather like being a conduit for legal services. As the first line of legal advice for the whole company concerning property and telecommunications issues Alison's team divides its time between giving timeous legal advice and managing the external panel solicitors who carry out transactions for Network Rail. Her team act as a filter in this process, accepting instructions from the board and giving instructions to the panel solicitors. The team is also responsible for negotiating the letting of railway arches and for selling off surplus land (the famous British Rail hotels having gone a long time ago). Under the old British Rail regime all the nitty-gritty of this work was carried out in-house, but the break up of British Rail into the train operating companies like South West Trains, Virgin Rail and Network Rail which is responsible for the infrastructure, caused a review of legal services' provision. Hence Network Rail lawyers are now responsible for the allocation to and supervision of the work of other lawyers rather than the drawing up of individual leases and conveyances.

Alison considers that contracting out many of their legal requirements provides a better deal for Network Rail. First, many of the panel firms, centred in Bristol and Derby have a mutually beneficial arrangement to do much of the lower level work at very good rates because this provides a dependable flow of work for their trainees and junior assistants, and second, Network Rail gets the benefit of the experience acquired by panel lawyers acting for a wide variety of other clients and thus a better quality of work. 'Legal work is about quality and not just about cost.' This concentration on outsourcing explains the relatively small size of the Network Rail legal department of 14 lawyers.

In addition to property work Alison also specialises in telecommunications. This may seem a strange focus and unrelated to the movement of people and goods, but the break up of British Rail left the new rail companies with ongoing relationships with regard to signalling equipment and communications systems, which still need monitoring. In addition Network Rail land being to some extent already 'blighted' provides ideal sites for mobile telephone masts, which again requires the negotiation of contracts and licences with the mobile phone providers.

Why be a lawyer?

Working in London for one of the country's largest employers is a long way from Yorkshire and a family with no legal connections whatsoever, where both parents left school at 14. Although her father studied hard at night school for further educational qualifications his aspirations were thwarted when he contracted tuberculosis during his National Service; his application for one of the university places which were allocated for ex-servicemen was refused when he left the Army because his early death seemed inevitable. Alison grew up with parents who were thus eager for the best possible education for their children, and were supportive of her own ambitions for a university education.

'You don't want to be a teacher, do you? Why don't you do law?' was her father's response to her initial suggestion that she read English at university. By the time she sat her A levels Alison was destined to be a lawyer, although 'I didn't realise at the time how steered I was being by my father because of an unspoken but very real wish that he himself had entered the law'. Her immediate personal reason for going into the law was altruistic. She wanted to help people and wanted to do legal aid work.

She recalls that 30 per cent of her law class at Birmingham University in 1971 were female, and by the time she qualified as a solicitor in 1978 the rapid expansion of the number of women in the legal profession was well under way. She and her fellow students were very much influenced by the full flourishing of the feminist movement in the UK and had a sense of opportunities opening up to women and of anything being possible.

Articles

Graduation brought confrontation with reality. In one of the law's cyclical downturns it was quite difficult for anyone, male or female, to find articles, but she was fortunate that a friend of her father's offered her articles with his firm in Leeds, where she became the first woman articled clerk in the firm. Although she did not have to pay a premium, her acceptance of a meagre salary of £15 per week meant that she was actually worse off than she had been as an undergraduate. Babysitting and working as a barmaid two nights a week supplemented her income, although it was often midnight before her second job finished and she could snatch a few hours' sleep before getting up the next morning to return to the office. Perhaps it is this early moonlighting training which has enabled Alison to juggle family life, paid career and public service.

Like many other firms in Leeds the one she worked for was a fundamentally Jewish one. If pressed her principal would come into work on Jewish holidays, but it was Alison as a non-Jew who would sign any letters going to other Jewish solicitors so that they would not know that he was working in prohibited time. Alison speaks warmly of this small general practice in the city centre of Leeds because it had a good spread of work, and she was given 'whatever came through the door and could be delegated' – family law, trust work, commercial property, legal aid work, but not criminal matters because her principal did not think it was suitable for a young lady to go to prison and interview clients in the cells.

This experience has given her a very sound understanding of the concerns of her constituents when she was President of the Holborn Law Society and now in the very broad church of the AWS. But she might equally have been trapped in one area of the law because at that time there was no requirement to experience 'three seats' during articles; while she was jumping rapidly from one area of law to another, her husband whom she had married at university, spent his entire articles doing criminal work.

Alison's main difficulty during articles was not with legal knowledge or practice or with clients or the male solicitors in the office, but with the secretaries, many of whom were older than Alison and were unused to taking orders from a 'woman boss' who felt that their position was being subtly undermined. But at least they worked for her. Years later the speaker at an East Midlands dinner related how the secretaries in her office had gone on strike when she arrived and simply refused to work for her.

Being a provincial solicitor

Her articles convinced her that she was not suited to be a 'lawyer's lawyer', someone who gets down to the detail and is willing to spend months if not years seeing a case from start to finish. When she alighted on in-house legal work she felt that she had found the niche that suited her 'butterfly mind', and she still becomes bored if she has to work on a large transaction for more than four weeks.

Following her husband to a small-town practice in Shropshire put her initially into a very straitened legal environment. Perhaps she should have read the runes better when she was offered a position in the firm which employed him on the grounds that it would be totally unacceptable and lead to potential breaches of client confidentiality if she were employed by any other firm in the area. Client confidentiality was in their view not capable of surviving domestic chit chat.

She soon found that this type of legal life was not at all to her taste. She did not so much encounter direct prejudice resulting from her female status as feel excluded. There seemed to be a well-established local social mafia to which the male partners belonged and where business was done at the golf club or the local Round Table, which being a woman she was not permitted to join. When it became clear that no partnership would ever be on offer for her, she bravely set up in partnership with another woman. Predictably very little work came from 'the local movers and shakers'. The new firm's work consisted mainly of legal aid and conveyancing matters, which, unfortunately, although fitting in with Alison's general view of life that justice and legal services should be available to all, was never going to produce much of a living.

Moving in-house

Two years later Alison began her provincial in-house career. Her varied experience encompassed working for Redditch New Town on a short-term contract, for a subsidiary of Christian Salvesen, then the Commissioner for New Towns, which relocated her to London before she made the move to work for British Rail at Paddington when her son was five years old.

Aware of the perceived lower status of in-house lawyers in the eyes of some private practitioners, has she ever considered applying for work with any of the large City firms? She says that she considered this but that even in 1988 she was aware that the motivations and ethos of the larger firms was changing rapidly as a result of the abolition of the 20 partner rule. The private client centres of many old City firms had begun to wither and were being replaced by large corporate law practices and the long hours' culture, which she decided would not sit easily with her responsibilities as a young mother. Now she feels that in her case the much lower base salary that she accepts for being an in-house lawyer rather than a City lawyer is at least partly recompensed by the additional benefits of generous holidays and pension and free or highly subsidised rail travel both in the UK and in Europe.

In fact she considers herself to have been very fortunate. Because of the expansion of City firms in the late 1980s and 1990s and the consequently high salaries that they offered, no one wanted to work for British Rail at that time. Alison worked part time for three years expecting the usual fate of many part timers, to be allocated the work that no one else wanted, but staff shortages meant that she had consistently good work which stretched her abilities and enhanced her experience, and ensured that she was prepared for promotions when they were offered.

From her present position further promotion prospects within the company are limited. Network Rail is a heavily engineering biased concern so that promotions from the legal team to the board are unlikely. However as far as Alison is concerned that is not a drawback as the main satisfaction in a legal career is to be found in 'work which you find interesting, that attracts your way of thinking. Personally I like things being so old and deeds being on parchment'. Many of the titles to Network Rail land are unregistered, as 'there has never been any reason why in the past we would want to register and pay for the registration of title'. However the Land Registration Act 2002 may change that with its insistence that all leases over seven years should be registered — Network Rail has over 2,500 historic leases.

Alison has never regretted her move to being an in-house lawyer. Quite apart from being able to operate within her 'butterfly mind' syndrome, being an in-house lawyer has enabled her to develop a comfortable long-term relationship with her 'clients'. The role requires 'enhanced management skills, an ability to identify the issues quickly and to decide equally rapidly whether there is a straightforward quick answer or whether the matter should be delegated to one of Network Rail's retained legal firms'. She finds that solicitors who have come from private practice often require a considerable time of 're-education' as in-house clients want an operative answer quickly not a reasoned disquisition on how the answer was arrived at.

Public service

Alison has an extensive commitment to public service in the sense of improving life for other people and particularly women lawyers. She had been a member of the East Midlands AWS while working in Shropshire and on arrival in London considered that joining the

AWS would enable her to meet like-minded women. It was not long before she was encouraged by Eva Crawley to become a member of the AWS committee, then AWS national chairwoman where she was responsible for separating the social functions of the London AWS from the policy concerns of the national committee, and for fostering links with international women lawyers' organisations. It was in recognition of her work for the AWS that she was awarded the second Eva Crawley award in 2000 and was unanimously proposed as the first AWS council member on the Law Society Council.

In parallel with this she has been an active member of the Holborn Law Society whose President she became in 2001. Alison would recommend being involved in such associations at a high level to any woman, as it has enabled her to meet people whom she would not otherwise have met and to obtain a wider view of the world generally and the legal world in particular.

Women in the profession

Asked whether there is anyone who has acted as a mentor apart from her father whose thwarted ambition obviously impliedly dictated hers, Alison points to Karen Aldred, the 2002 AWS national chairwoman, who 'was my boss at Redditch. She was always telling me to try something or to go for something. It was the best kind of informal friendly mentoring'. She is a strong advocate of the AWS mentoring scheme because the sort of support and advice that she received from Karen and later Eva Crawley is not always available on a more casual basis.

Alison feels that the position of women in the profession has changed but has not changed quickly enough. She considers that the legal profession now operates too much as a money-making business and not enough as a public service, and that this has been detrimental to the progress of women. Some very senior lawyers have told her that many of the people going into the profession now are 'people who would formerly have become accountants, less interested in helping people than in making money'. Consequently they feel little loyalty to their employing firms and little interest in the softer aspects of legal work. The emphasis is on doing deals which involve substantial amounts of money and therefore provide substantial salaries for themselves. In order to achieve this they are willing to collude with the long hours required of them so that partners may produce large profits. The result for women is that it has become more, rather than less, difficult to provide the flexibility necessary for them to obtain a balance between the demands of work and family life.

Alison is concerned that the position of women in the profession has not been helped by their apparent inability to promote other women in the wider, mentoring and supporting sense. She feels that she was fortunate to have encountered women who encouraged and advised her, but in general women have not so far succeeded in evolving a culture where it is seen as appropriate and 'a good thing' for an older professional to introduce younger colleagues to clients and contacts with a view to promoting their careers. In the new macho long hours' culture it has become even more difficult for women to take the time to assist their younger female colleagues.

Another difficulty for women was pointed out to Alison by a senior male colleague. When she wondered why it was that the young men who had been at law college with her, and who had apparently espoused the concept of female equality, were not sympathetic to flexible working requirements, he pointed out that those men were competitive among themselves and consequently saw their female contemporaries as threats to their economic well-being rather than as allies. All of which is very confusing for young women at the start of their careers.

The future?

So, would Alison advise today's young women to go into the law? The answer is that she would hesitate to do so. She would not positively advise anyone to enter the law, which on reflection she feels is very sad as she still retains the belief that the law is a necessary requirement of a civilised society which regulates the relationships of its citizens and which should therefore require the best practitioners. However as an incorrigible optimist she thinks that it is possible that the practice of the law can change sufficiently to make it attractive again. 'This needs a change from the long hours' culture and a reconsideration of the work-life balance in favour of life.' It also means that law firms would have to accept lower profits for a time, but, Alison believes, 'firms will find that better investment in their staff will bear fruit in the future and those firms will succeed'.

Eileen Pembridge

Eileen Pembridge is the senior partner of Fisher Meredith, the South London firm which she co-founded in 1975. A family law specialist with substantial generalist experience, she is also the General Editor of Sweet & Maxwell's *Legal Aid Practice Manual* and has been a member of the Law Society Council since 1990.

First impressions

You can often tell a lot about a legal firm from its reception area. The boxes of books and toys in Fisher Meredith's Family Department reception are there 'because clients often cannot come without their children'. Eileen Pembridge is nothing if not realistic about the difficulties that her clients face and intensely practical in her approach to helping them. She has 'some time free for an interview before Christmas because people are either trying to patch things up in a spirit of goodwill or they are having one last Christmas together for the sake of the children, but after Christmas', she comments with an air of sad realism 'I shall be very busy'.

The two cultures

Eileen did not set out to be a lawyer. Fascinated by the discovery of the double helix by Watson and Crick, and undeterred by the small number of women studying natural sciences in the early 1960s, her ambition when she went up to Cambridge was to become either a chemist or a biochemist. At a time when C. P. Snow was decrying the split in intellectual life into 'the two cultures', Eileen still believed in the Renaissance concept of the educated man (or woman) who understood both the arts and the sciences. She chose to study sciences for A Level 'because of the love of it', but Latin which could not be fitted into a scientific timetable she pursued in her own time along with the Russian she learned at night school.

An intellectual crisis of sorts eventually arrived when she decided that she was not good enough to be 'a top scientist'. She says with modest candour that 'you could be given a B.Sc after two years at

Cambridge', so she quietly pocketed that degree and refocused her attentions on a language diploma followed by a postgraduate degree in French and Russian. This plus the UN Diploma in Language Studies left Eileen exceptionally well equipped to be an interpreter for the Atomic Energy Authority in Vienna, who were 'desperate to find interpreters who could understand science'.

Foreign travels

At a time in the late 1960s when London and the UK were buzzing with Mary Quant, the Beatles and the new youth culture Eileen was faced with a city of tradition and regulation and she quite simply hated it. She moved about Europe doing freelance interpreting from French and Russian for UN agencies (World Health Organisation, UNICEF and UNESCO), where she also 'picked up' Spanish as well as translating scientific and technical publications and doing consecutive interpretations at meetings, a skill which requires great confidence in the two languages being used. She subsequently worked in Africa (at the African Development Bank in Abidjan in the Ivory Coast) where she interpreted and made reports on meetings attended by both anglophone and francophone speakers from throughout the continent.

All this indicates an extreme adaptability, agility of mind and exceptional memory, all qualities which a good lawyer should possess. The African experience also bespeaks a concern for those who are less fortunate than herself, although Eileen would not present herself as in any way a pious do-gooder. She is quite simply concerned with justice.

But after four years of international travel, including a year teaching science in Mexico, she became weary of 'always coming and going and always reporting what other people had said', and so returned to London where she had kept a small flat in Battersea, and found a job with Release through Bernard Simons, a friend from Cambridge, and by now an up and coming civil rights solicitor.

After about a year of doing 'CAB (Citizens' Advice Bureau) type stuff and constantly ringing up lawyers for advice', with typical self-confidence Eileen concluded that she could do just as well herself and should therefore 'get qualified'. This is not said with any degree of arrogance but simply matter-of-factly, she saw that for her Release was a step rather than a destination and that she had better get on with the journey. And with typical speed. She passed Law Society Part One in three months by correspondence course, followed by six months at College of Law where she obtained a distinction, and two years' articles with Bernard Simons led to qualification in 1975.

The new firm

At this point many people might have taken a big sigh of relief and settled down to learn about legal business in an established firm but certainly not Eileen. While still keeping on her African conference work she was introduced to Mike Fisher, another young solicitor only two years' qualified, through Helena Kennedy, a mutual friend, and the two of them set up in partnership in Mike's modest flat in Streatham. Fisher Meredith (Meredith was Eileen's married name) now has over 60 lawyers and a total of 105 staff spread over four buildings at a crossroads in Stockwell. It is poised to move into large new offices 'where we can all be together' in Kennington. Such audacity would not be possible now but in 1975 newly qualified solicitors could start up their own practices without waiting for a mandatory three year period first. In an era before faxes with only rudimentary photocopiers and one phone in the office along with a secretary who came in the mornings, Eileen assured me that it, 'was not really scary. It was more a sense of Here We Go in capital letters! After all, women are naturally good at multi-tasking'.

She feels that setting up in practice in 1975, before new technology increased the speed and pressure of communication and the burden of new legislation became oppressive, was in some ways easier. 'It was more a case of finding the right forms and applying legal principles and professional rules. Keeping one step ahead of what was required was more straightforward then.' When they started 'we did not have much idea of what was meant by client care and management'; *The Guide to the Professional Conduct of Solicitors* (now in its ninth edition) was not fully developed and the Investors in People Award which her firm was awarded in 2000, let alone the Lexcel award they achieved in 2003, had not been invented. But to someone with Eileen's energy, analytical mind and natural concern for other people these were not obstacles to growing a successful practice.

The partners between them covered the waterfront of crime, family law, adoption procedures, conveyancing, shipping law, personal injury and medical negligence, as well as music and dance licensing and company formation. This breadth of practice where you have to fall back on and be very confident of basic legal principles is 'not something that is possible for young solicitors now because they are forced into specialisation'. Her advice to young lawyers is that they should seek out firms which not only give them breadth of experience in their training contracts but also permit them if possible to practise in more than one field after qualification so that they can make a truly informed choice when they need to specialise. A rounded lawyer in Eileen's opinion is definitely a better lawyer.

From the start Eileen was involved in the women's movement, principally to assist less fortunate people to ameliorate their situation mostly, but not always with the help of the law. She participated in women's groups along with Harriet Harman, Patricia Hewitt and Anna Coote, and was particularly incensed by instances of sexual discrimination and most of all by acts of violence towards women. It is Erin Pizzey who grabbed the headlines in the 1970s by setting up refuges for battered wives, but Eileen was also involved in this radical initiative. By finding unoccupied properties and squatting them her group was able to set up informal refuges for battered wives, while at the same time organising marches and lobbying the House of Commons to argue for legislative change such the Domestic Violence Act which was passed in 1978. It clearly angered Eileen that before the Act was passed violent husbands could be excluded from the matrimonial home only by using the law of trespass and assault and that many county court judges were very unsympathetic to the use of the law for this purpose.

A fair hearing

Eileen has always had a stern eye for injustice and unnecessary legal procedures, and has always been willing to take on the whole legal establishment on her client's behalf. Before she was even qualified she took a deportation case by way of habeas corpus all the way, in three months, from the High Court to the House of Lords with the assistance of Stephen Sedley (now Lord Justice Sedley); discovering the nuances of civil bail applications as she rushed from court to court in sandals and long skirts (it was the era of flower power after all!); and experienced the sadness of having to say 'I did my best' because the House of Lords ruled that her client's appeal should fail.

There must have been many such cases when Eileen has not been afraid to take on authority or to go against public opinion because she believes that everyone is entitled to a fair hearing and to the best representation that his or her lawyer can give. Although she has been financially successful in it, the law for her is not a mere moneymaking enterprise. In 1990 she acted for Sonia Sutcliffe, the wife of the Yorkshire Ripper, in her highly successful defamation cases against *Private Eye*. In 1977 the little partnership had acted for nearly all those arrested in the scuffle following an anti-Nazi demonstration in New Cross to prevent the National Front marching through Lewisham. This latter action was probably the cause of their offices in Lambeth being torched during the first break that she and her former colleague had had for some time. The office was effectively destroyed, and those law books which they managed to save 'held the odour of charred paper for years'. It was this conflagration that led to the speedy acquisition of their first Clapham Road premises by Stockwell underground station.

The Law Society

Eileen was well known among family law and legal aid practitioners but, although she had sat on the Law Society's Courts and Legal Services Committee from 1987, she had not been at all involved with her local (South London) law society. Nevertheless when the incumbent member retired in 1990 she stood and was elected. Until then she did not know 'what council membership would entail, but by that time I felt that I had got on top of my subject, on top of my firm and was looking for something different'.

The Law Society certainly got something different. Much has been written about the 'traditional' practices at Chancery Lane which have only gradually been broken down over the years. Eileen points out that 'until 1977, following the implementation of the Sex Discrimination Act women were not allowed into the main building of the Law Society at all. Indeed one day I went to Chancery Lane with a fellow articled clerk and a qualified Hong Kong solicitor who was in London for the purpose of training to be a judge. We were challenged and the trainee, who happened to be a white male, was asked to escort the Chinese lawyer and myself off the premises'. It was therefore not likely that she would accept unequal treatment at the hands of the Law Society in 1990 whether deliberate or inadvertent. When she discovered that a large cloakroom was available for male council members but none for their female counterparts she quite simply insisted on using the male facilities until another cloakroom was provided five years later, a room which the first black female Attorney-General of Alabama, a lady with a sense of humour, designated on a visit as the 'Pembridge Memorial Loo'. This is perhaps frivolity but it does make the point that Eileen is willing to take a principled stand to ensure that what should be right is right.

Determined to play a full part in her new role she was surprised to find that although welcoming, the council was still very male oriented, with a certain macho style which could be summarised as 'urbane, pompous, jokey, golf-clubby and stiff', a place where it was hard for women 'to find an appropriate voice between soft-spoken agreement and stridency'. Fourteen years later she has mixed feelings about the increased council membership introduced as a result of the Stevenson Report. On the one hand the council's increase in size and heterogeneity makes it much easier for women to operate effectively, but will at the same time she believes make it much more unwieldy and less efficient in getting the full picture and holding management to account.

She was of course the first woman to challenge the established hierarchy by standing for election in 1995 against the official candidate for the presidency, John Young because she felt strongly that 'the Buggins Turn principle was producing very inappropriate results and that it was time for women's voices to be heard'. At the same time Martin Mears challenged the Society's practice of selecting its own candidate and in their very different ways they appealed for backing from the profession as a whole. When John Young was eventually advised to stand down, Henry Hodge was chosen as the official candidate. The first and only countrywide electoral campaign then involved the three candidates travelling to speak at meetings hastily convened all over the country to set out their individual visions of the future of the profession. Eileen recalls the challenge of a large meeting in Manchester at which she was the only visible female presence 'happily highly unlikely now, only a relatively few years later'.

Although no longer viewing the presidency as a goal Eileen is still very active in council work. A member of the access to justice committee and the law reform board, she has also been for many years the chair of the equal opportunities committee. She spent many years on the international human rights working party and led the reputation working party before the new governance reforms. A former chair of the family law committee, she has been one of the authors of the family law protocol, and co-authored the Society's policy document on the reform of the laws of co-habitation and ancillary relief.

The present

Eileen's firm, Fisher Meredith, is still 70 per cent financed by legal aid work, although the reforms and restrictions which have been introduced over the past few years are making this increasingly difficult. Eileen is very much against these budgetary restrictions 'because it makes it more and more difficult for the ordinary person to get access to the justice system. Now it is impossible to run a practice solely on legal aid – in London anyway. Unfortunately we have to spend a lot of time turning people away because we simply cannot afford to take on any more of that type of work'.

Unusually for someone of her age Eileen has two children aged 15 and five. Asked about the generic children question, she smiles and says 'That's easy'. A strange response, but here comes the pertinent analysis again. 'Either you have children when you are very young, so that by the time that you are well established they are grown up, or you get established first, so that by the time that you have your children you have the home and the income and you can afford the nanny, and,' a quirky smile, ' in my case the gardener as well.' But one can't help thinking that if she had had triplets at the age of 27 she would still have coped. This is after all a senior partner who cycles to work, who deals with domestic and social tasks (her husband cooks) and who finds the time to attend evening functions such as the Human Rights Awards and the AWS 80th Anniversary Reception because she knows that it is important for the Law Society to show their appreciation of the efforts made by the profession.

Since she has had the children she has stopped working at weekends. Shopping? Her approach to that is unfailingly practical. 'Try getting the five-year-old into Gap with the 15-year-old and then see how much time there is left for shopping for oneself.' She finds that 'upmarket mail order' is invaluable for personal and present shopping, and she has an unusual take on Christmas presents for adults. 'I don't give them presents as such. I match them up with what I think are appropriate charities and then send them a card telling then that I have made a donation to their individual charity.'

Eileen clearly feels keenly about the human rights of people all over the world and in the 1980s was willing to go to Nicaragua at her own expense to see that the elections there were carried out in a fair and honest way, and to report back in the Bulletin of the Haldane Society.

However, while spending almost all of her off duty time with her family she has become passionate about sailing, and takes her dinghy out in the Solent whenever she can get a few hours to herself, although 'gardening, walking and camping in remote places are much more fun when done with the girls'.

Looking back and looking forward

There is no sense that this energetic woman is ready to make the traditional 'I want to spend more time with my family' retirement speech. Indeed, 'I foresee another seven years of practice, and then I would like to go into the House of Lords in its new incarnation'. She still feels that she has very much to give and that her roundabout way of coming to the law was an advantage. 'I would not have wanted to go into the law any sooner.' In comparison with young women today 'my generation was lucky. We were the first generation to have the benefit of contact lenses, tights and the Pill and also local authorities who were financially willing and capable of funding postgraduates to go to the College of Law. We could set up when we were newly qualified and it was possible to be entrepreneurial in business terms and at the same time to care passionately about access to justice'.

She was part of that period of transition from lawyers practising over several areas in small practices to ones requiring macro-management and development as specialists, becoming expert in ever smaller areas of expertise. She feels that there is now too sharp a dichotomy between legal aid and non legal aid practices. It is she says wryly 'often a choice between feeling worthy and poor in a legal aid practice or miserable and rich while acting for corporate clients'. This is not an idle ill-informed comment but one made by the senior partner of a firm which does in fact attract refugees from major City firms who feel that they want a more rounded way of life. It is a comment from someone who feels that original art and flowers in cut glass in the reception are not always an indicator that the best service will be provided where it is needed. Indeed she makes a point of stressing to clients that 'they are paying for the legal service, not the marble atrium'. They come to her firm for its value for money.

She herself has increasingly specialised in family law, finally giving up defamation for financial settlements, and now heads up a department of 17 fee earners, including a dedicated children's law team. In her own family law work she has been recognised in the various legal directories as a 'leader in her field' and now gets clients from all over the country and abroad, and while still taking on legal aid cases 'where it is really important to do so against a wealthy opponent', she is usually now dealing with Magic Circle firms but is not tempted to join them.

As she surveys her now substantial firm her final thought is 'I know I have a good firm with good colleagues and a good reputation and have learned that nothing works without trustworthy partners of like mind, and these days, best management practice'.

Barbara Roche MP

Barbara Roche MP qualified as a barrister and is the MP for Hornsey and Wood Green. She was, until June 2003, a Minister of State at the Office of the Deputy Prime Minister.

Law and Politics

In 1965 at the age of 11 Barbara Roche read two short books, 'probably no longer in print, and they both featured men. The first was about becoming a MP and the second was about becoming a lawyer. The second book featured two brothers, one who became a solicitor and the other who became a barrister'.

These two books may not have instigated the twin ambitions that have informed her professional life but her obvious pleasure in the memory of them is a clear indication that she had decided on her career path very early on in life. 'I think I always knew that I wanted to be a lawyer, and I definitely wanted to be a barrister; perhaps it was a sort of frustrated dramatic instinct, but it was certainly the courtroom that appealed.'

About her parents Barbara explains 'no they were not lawyers, teachers or doctors', when I say that many of the parents of successful women lawyers were, 'but they were certainly very supportive and very keen on education'. The general media representation is that she is the child of immediate immigrants. Barbara points out that 'all four of my grandparents were born in this country, and I am very proud of my background and my Judaism'.

The struggle between politics and law was won by politics at university, for Barbara read philosophy, politics and economics (PPE) at Oxford, but immediately on graduation she embarked on legal training. Although she evinces a great deal of sympathy with the proffered advice of some that those who wish to practise law should study something else at university first, this was not her motivation in her choice of degree at Oxford. At Oxford she had been a woman of strong views, delighting in debate, and had been elected as the librarian of the Oxford Union and the JCR president. The transition to the Bar seemed a natural one.

Being a barrister

She 'did all my core subjects in about a year at the Inns of Court School of Law before I did the Bar Finals, and I was very fortunate in my chambers because I got lots of work very quickly. It was a general common law chambers where there was a lot of domestic violence work. I always knew that at some point I would want to try to be elected'. She had not chosen her pupillage chambers with the idea that the experience that she gained there would be useful in law centre work, although 'I had always been attracted to the work that law centres did', so her time of practising at the Bar was shortened when an opportunity at North Lewisham law centre came up.

Nevertheless in the late 1970s and early 1980s working in a law centre was very rewarding in its excitement, and she was able to put her legal skills to good use. Barbara did most of the centre's advocacy, and on one occasion took a case to the Court of Appeal, though she can't remember the exact details. I am interviewing her on a day when there are difficult political decisions to be made by her party and by the Government and her politician's protective armour is evident; ransacking her mind for the detail of an event that must have been of some moment to her as a young barrister is not at the top of her agenda. Her mind is understandably partly elsewhere. Her apparent forgetfulness also gives an insight into a character that is more interested in what is to come than on dwelling on the past. Still, she comments that the law centre's existence was a precarious one, 'we nearly had our grant cut off, before we were funded by the local authority. But it was a very good time, and many of the friends that I made then are still friends today'.

Being an MP

Gradually the political campaigning that she had begun at university and carried on as a qualified barrister became focused on election as a Member of Parliament. Her first and doomed attempt was in the safe Conservative seat of South West Surrey, where she challenged the sitting candidate Virginia Bottomley, but then, after one unsuccessful attempt in 1987, Barbara was elected in 1992 as Member of Parliament for Hornsey and Wood Green, a constituency she has represented ever since. The seat is multiracial and multicultural and contains people from many different socio-economic backgrounds.

With her East End background she is well able to understand their concerns, but that still leaves her with the problem of how to translate that understanding into tangible assistance.

Here she feels that her legal training has been of immense assistance, particularly for constituency work. The analytical skills that she acquired as a barrister are invaluable when conducting local surgeries as an MP. 'They help me to ask what is the problem and what do I need to do to be able to solve it? It's also useful in my work as a minister. My legal experience tells me that it is as important to know where to get the answers as to know them in the first place, because I know that I can't know everything.'

The ability to assess masses of information in a brief period of time is not only one that is essential to a barrister who is presented with a brief only a short time before a court appearance, but is also an extraordinarily useful attribute for a politician who has served in several government departments as diverse as the Home Office, the Treasury, the DTI and the Office of the Deputy Prime Minister. Her legal training shows in her often careful responses, short and to the point, considering whether to amplify them and often deciding not to. It is also clear that a legal training teaches a sense of order. The coffee table in her ministerial boardroom is covered with serried lines of the newspapers of the day obviously read and set aside in case further reference is necessary. Her immediate staff of three PAs are efficient and busy, reflecting the character of her ministerial office in Whitehall, a former Admiralty building where Nelson lay in state after the Battle of Trafalgar. Although she observes that 'I'm not sure that I would claim any special position for lawyers in Parliament. Teachers and lecturers are just as likely to succeed', there is an implication that an ability to analyse large amounts of material, to ascertain what is important and to be able to communicate it to others are the qualities which are required in a good MP.

In the public eye

Her life as an MP is subject to public scrutiny, and she has developed an ability to separate the public from the private. This potential public scrutiny is something that 'comes with the territory. If you go into politics you know that your life is going to be in the public domain, so as soon as you start thinking about running for public office you need to think about what that is going to mean in terms of being criticised. But it's a gradual thing, it doesn't happen overnight and you have time to get used to it. What you do need to do is to learn to take the good things that people say about you in the same way as the bad things'.

Like Kipling's injunction that you should 'meet with triumph and disaster and treat these two imposters just the same'. It is also necessary in her view to work at 'getting the balance right' and absolutely crucial to behave professionally.

Family and family friendly policies

Barbara clearly values the family life that she shares with her husband, another barrister, and her daughter, who is now 14. 'My husband has always been very supportive of what I have done, and we share the domestic chores. We do share the cooking. We had help with childcare when my daughter was younger, and I am still in touch with many of them.' She is very clear that 'if you are going to be a mother and have a career you do need support, but having a family helps you to get your priorities right, and a family is so important in getting things in perspective'.

She was working only part time when she was elected and the whole family (her daughter was then only four) had to adjust to the situation of her more than full-time work as an MP. As the Minister for Women, only one of her governmental roles (for she was also responsible for the government's social exclusion policies, homelessness and the Neighbourhood Renewal Unit), she was and continues to be a strong advocate of family friendly policies, 'even though MPs are the last people to preach about these things, considering the antisocial hours that we work'.

Nevertheless one of her department's initiatives of which she was most proud, was that those who value women's skills and experience should be officially recognised. In March 2002 the government set up the Castle awards, named after Barbara Castle who was instrumental in the passing of the first Equal Pay Act 1970, and which recognises those employers who are committed to treating their whole workforce equally. Encouraged by the 'very good take up' in the first year of its operation Barbara is proposing that the awards should be developed 'for use as a kite mark of excellence'.

Even though the gender pay gap has reduced considerably from the days of the first Equal Pay Act (from 34 per cent to 18 per cent) Barbara feels that this is not enough and she emphasises the findings of the Equal Opportunities Commission (EOC) study on salary disparities which followed a group of university graduates and found that several years after graduation there was still a substantial gap between the salaries earned by the male graduates and those earned by female graduates. 'This is troublesome, because this was a few years after graduation.'

This is of great concern to her, but she takes pride in the improvement in the situation relating to domestic violence. As a young barrister she acted in many domestic violence cases and 'Things, I'm glad to say, have moved on since then. The attitudes of the police and the judiciary now are not perfect but they have improved a lot, because some of the attitudes that the police and the judiciary had then were pretty outrageous.' The twin threads of her legal and political lives are at work here; as a barrister she tried to obtain justice for the individual victims of violence, then as the Minister for Women she was in a position to influence and if necessary to promote legislation to improve the position of women and children as a whole. Realising that mere rhetoric in this area was not enough she launched research into the annual cost to the economy of domestic violence so that a sound business case could be established to back increased resources for this area. It was clearly one of the benefits of her position as she saw it to be able to promote the interests of women in this way.

For the future, and she is always thinking of the future, she would like to see 'many more women coming through the glass ceiling in big firms and many more women becoming judges. We need to highlight flexible working, because that is so important, and to criticise the long hours' culture. There is an agenda here for men as well as women, as it is equally important for men to be able to take part in their children's lives'.

I asked about the advice she would give to new graduates. She suggests that 'It is always a good idea not to rush into things. Think about where you are going. At university on the milk rounds ask about the gender pay gap in the different organisations you are speaking to, and ask about their equality and diversity policies'. And as I leave, she tells me that her way of relaxing is to 'read obscure detective fiction and go to bad films with my daughter'.

Sandra Teichman

Sandra Teichman is the UK Legal Counsel of
Unisys. In 2001 she also became the first
female board member of Unisys UK.

Background

Several decades ago Barclays Bank ran a scholarship programme for
gifted children in Ghana; unusually the programme's administrators
sought out children not from the well-known private schools but
from small village schools, at one of which Sandra's grandfather was
headmaster. As a result of this entrepreneurial educational venture
Sandra's father received part of his education in England, was called
to Middle Temple and practised in London for several years before
returning to Ghana with his Barbadian born wife and his only
daughter, Sandra, who was then aged five.

Part of her father's motivation in returning to Ghana was his concern
that spending all her formative years in England would distance his
daughter from the culture of her ancestors. She did not find the transition difficult, 'because I am fairly adaptable, and in any case education in Ghana is modelled very much on the English system. I
went to a girls' boarding school from the ages of 11 to 17 before
I came back to England at the age of 17 to attend university'.

Returning to England was much more problematic. In Ghana she
had lived in an international environment mixing with German,
Swiss and Scots neighbours, and 'as we were very much an international family I was taken to a variety of foreign countries with my
family during the school holidays to visit friends and relatives'. All
ex-pats in Ghana were white and middle class, so that her expectation of England was that it would be populated by white, middle
class people, who spoke in a particular and identical way, much as
she had herself learned to speak in Ghana. Ghana is a country of
many different languages and dialects where English is the lingua
franca and where a certain type of old-fashioned Queen's English is
the preferred language of the middle classes.

When she arrived in England, she had to make a rapid adjustment to a multicultural country where skin colour was no indicator of place of birth. 'I had to learn a few cultural things very quickly. I used to ask black people where they came from originally, and some of them took considerable offence because they had been born in the UK. I learned that it was better to ask where their parents had come from.' She was also surprised by the prevalence of 'Estuary English'; she still finds the use of ungrammatical English by people who have lived in England since birth very odd.

Why law?

Sandra's father did not force his legal ambitions or opinions on her, but undoubtedly he was an influence. 'I loved reading; I was such a voracious reader that my mother enrolled me in the local library at the age of five. I also used to go to court to listen to my father speaking, because that was very exciting and often we would sit down together and watch the *Rumpole of the Bailey* videos which he had imported from the UK. But my father never said that he wanted me to become a lawyer.' Her father's other involvement in a successful seafood and cocoa export business meant that her upbringing contained a very intense mix of the legal and the commercial, probably influencing the direction of her own legal career.

From an early age she rejected her mother's profession of nursing 'as I am really quite squeamish when it comes to other people's injuries. I also discovered that I was no good at maths and physics, so becoming a doctor was ruled out. In fact I realised quite soon that I wanted to follow my father into the law'.

Back in Ghana her mother had been very protective of her only child and her boarding school had ensured that she never had '100 per cent freedom', so that coming to Essex University was quite a 'shock to the system'. Being on campus had a superficial resemblance to being at boarding school, but 'there were no rules and no curfew. I went a little bit mad. What saved me was the mid-sessional exams at the beginning of the second term. Like many students I had never failed anything and indeed had done rather well in my A Levels'. But between arriving at Essex and the exams 'I really hadn't done a thing'. She cannily did not tell her parents that she had failed all four papers, but her failure was 'my wake up call'.

Sandra clearly had idolized her father; 'I put him on a pedestal', and the thought of disappointing him was unbearable, as her life plan when she came to England involved sitting the Bar exams, then completing her pupillage before returning to Ghana to practise with her father. Training as a solicitor was not considered. In Commonwealth countries training as a barrister is often perceived as the better option because it gives access to higher rights of audience, and in Ghana the legal profession still operates very much as a split rather than a fused system. So just as her father had done she applied to and was accepted by Middle Temple.

However, whereas she had loved the research and the detail of law at university, and had found it easy to absorb large amounts of information, 'I got through by learning all the cases and the principles parrot-fashion, when I went to Bar School I had to change the way I studied. All of a sudden I had to look at a problem in an analytical way and had to advise clients. I found the shift from university to Bar School a little bit difficult. And I also missed the cohesion of campus life. At Bar School people came from all over the place, and we all belonged to different Inns. I would not say that I enjoyed Bar School.'

Pupillage

'In those days,' and we are not talking about so very long ago, Sandra is only 38, 'you were given a little booklet with the names of all the chambers, and told to sort out your pupillage. I knew that some of my white, male Oxbridge friends were having difficulties in obtaining pupillage, and I thought that it would be even more difficult for me.' Typically her research into the composition and the work of chambers was detailed and she decided to offer herself to the chambers of Michael Hill QC, 'which was very much in the limelight at the time for representing *The Star* newspaper against Jeffrey Archer. It seemed like a forward thinking place, which had a strong corporate and white collar crime practice. So I went along and told a somewhat bemused clerk that I was looking for pupillage and just at that moment Michael Lawson QC was walking past. He asked to see my CV, had quite a long chat with me and I think that when he realised that we had a love of the same books, such as the novels of Thomas Hardy, it influenced his decision to offer me six months' pupillage on the spot. You can't of course pick up pupillage just like that now'.

Sandra admits that she had the idea at the back of her mind that after six months' experience in chambers she might return to Ghana to work with her father even though she would not have obtained her formal qualification, but simultaneously another line of reasoning was at work. She was conscious that in her short lifetime there had been three coup d'états in Ghana. Although the political situation had settled down rapidly afterwards and Ghana is, she believes, a stable and friendly place she had noticed that those Ghanaians who had been forced to leave had not always found it easy to find well-paid employment in Europe even though they had held down responsible positions in their home country. It might, she thought, be sensible to work for a few years in England before returning so that if ever forced to leave Ghana she would have a better understanding of the world of work in the UK.

It did not take her long to realise that she did not like pupillage. 'Temple Gardens was like a rabbit warren, the rooms were tiny, people were sitting on top of each other and many had very fixed old-fashioned views on women and black people. Many of the remarks that were made in chambers could have given offence to many people, but I was really grateful to my father who had taught me not to be upset by such things. I also did not enjoy trawling round the courts, it was very unglamorous and not at all like *Rumpole* or *LA Law*.'

Her feelings about this period in her life are clearly ambivalent. On the one hand she felt cut off from the clients; 'I think that I was probably only ever present at one conference with counsel', a hard position for an outgoing, intellectually curious young woman. On the other hand some of the mainly white collar criminal work with which she was involved was 'fascinating stuff. There was one case where an American couple had perpetrated a fraud on *Marks and Spencer*; as the case progressed we discovered that they had come to England in the first place because the wife had killed her parents and buried them in the cellar'. This case also made her realise that straight criminal law would be difficult for her 'because I did not enjoy looking at pictures of dead or mutilated bodies', an extension perhaps of the feelings that decreed that she would not become a doctor. What she was looking for was 'a more dynamic and commercial environment' something that a change of chambers would not accomplish for her as she had come to believe that the Bar in itself was 'old-fashioned and fusty'.

Commerciality

Three months into her pupillage she was headhunted to join Fujitsu-ICL who were looking for a young lawyer 'to be moulded'. She saw a clear choice in front of her. She could continue with the Bar and most probably return to Africa where her father would welcome her, but after a little while would expect her to marry, produce children and never to work again, or she could do something completely different. As a child and young girl Sandra had been 'a bit of an athlete', she was used to being ambitious, to 'asking what am I doing here? Where am I going next? I was used to looking forward and not backwards'.

Although she had no idea about computers, little about commercial contracts and none at all about IT contracts she chose the position at ICL, 'because what I did know was that it was very much a niche area of law. You still can't go to Joe Bloggs in the High Street if you want someone to deal with an IT contract. You have to go to a firm like Allen & Overy or Shaw Pittman. I joined ICL because I wanted to be in something new and dynamic. And when I arrived at their offices in Putney I realised that this was where I wanted to be, because there were computers on their desks for a start, rare for those days'.

She remained at ICL for three years 'starting at grass-roots level, until in 1990 I saw a job advertised in *The Times* which was pretty much for what I was doing at the time, but for a lot more money. I decided that I would just go for it and see because if nothing else it would be good interview experience. The company advertising was Unisys'.

The interview went well, most probably because as Sandra says 'this is where personality can really help you'. In the short list of two she was up against a young male Oxbridge graduate with an MBA. Later her new manager told her that the young man was 'fantastic on paper', but that he just would not have fitted into the culture of the company. What they were looking for was a young lawyer with some experience but most importantly a willingness to work hard and an ability to communicate with the company's technicians and sales-people. 'Unisys has a culture of fun,' Sandra explains, 'because it has so many young people working for it. Although the senior man-agement are not young they are not very old either; the average age of the board is late 40s, early 50s.' Sandra joined as 'a baby lawyer' with another steep learning curve ahead of her, reporting directly to the UK general counsel to whose position she herself succeeded five years later. For the past two years she has also been a member of the UK board.

The future?

As to the future? 'Well I have hit the wall as far as Unisys in the UK is concerned. The next step up would be either becoming European general counsel or going to Unisys in America to take up a role in the office of the general counsel there.' The former she would reject because it is a purely management role overseeing the work of lawyers in the European jurisdictions where Unisys operates and 'I like to be involved, I enjoy the commercial work. What I really like to do is to wheel and deal, negotiate the big deals. I'm very proud that the company allowed me to negotiate high value contracts right from the start and now the contracts that I negotiate are business process outsourcing deals with revenue values of a minimum of £500 million. They can take months to negotiate during which time I am working with the real crème de la crème of lawyers in my field. I feel very good that I am entrusted to do that'.

A move to the American headquarters of Unisys would make promotion to the board of the parent company possible. An opportunity to work in America has been offered to her and Sandra might have contemplated this before her marriage and her pregnancy. 'I know that this is a big potential sacrifice, but I feel that it is such a blessing to be happily married and to be about to become a mother. The feminist brigade probably won't like what I am about to say, but I'll say it anyway. Because the environment in which I work is very competitive and very hard ball, I need to have a husband that I can look up to. Perhaps this is because of my culture, I'm not sure.' What is certainly true is that Sandra will give her husband and her child a very high priority – although she would be unlikely ever to become a stay at home mother. 'I don't think that I have any aspirations to be Superwoman, although I do know a few very senior women with families who work exceptionally hard, and who made no concessions to their working hours when they became mothers. I'm not sure that I see myself being quite like that.'

On the plus side Unisys is a company which is geared up to home working. Sandra already has all the necessary technology in place and considers it possible to divide her work between working in the office and working at home, which is only 15 minutes' walk from the Unisys West End office. 'But to make this work, even with my mother who is at hand living in the same street, I'll have to change my style.' To Sandra the company is a village where it is important to speak to people, to be aware of the grapevine, to be tuned in to what is happening.

Being general counsel

As general counsel Sandra's responsibility extends further than the wheeling and dealing contract negotiation that she loves. She is the first filter for the company's legal problems, being consulted by other board members about what is legally possible when a new deal is mooted. Unisys is very much 'a sales-oriented company, and it is important that the sales people realise what they may legally claim and what they may not, and that they are aware of the requirements of the non-disclosure agreements. Part of my job is to educate people, and I do a lot of in-house legal training. I'm in at the very early stages of any deal, although at that point it is usually not too time consuming. But when the customer does not agree to our standard terms and I have to put the contract together that is quite different'.

Not all the company's legal work is carried on in-house. Employment matters are dealt with mostly in-house, but mergers and acquisition work and property matters are usually outsourced. One of her roles is to manage the outsourcing, to build good relationships with the law firms that Unisys uses, and to monitor costs. 'Some of them still think that we are living in the 1980s with an open chequebook.' The Bar she considers is a cheaper option and able to provide advice of just as good a quality as solicitor's firms. She is impressed by 'New Age barristers' who are prepared to work in the same way as solicitors, but with lower overheads. 'They're prepared to come to my office, they do their own research, type their own opinions and tie their own pink ribbons.' She is clearly pleased that her erstwhile if somewhat brief profession is fighting back in the face of the attack by solicitors on the barristers' court monopoly. Personally she feels more affinity with barristers, who she considers to be disadvantaged in not having the supportive infrastructure of solicitors working in City firms.

'I love the law,' is Sandra's final summation of her position, 'it is an amazing foundation to have even if you don't stay in it. It is a wonderful starting point for so many things.' That part of the Bar training which required that she be filmed in mock trials before judges has been particularly helpful. 'I have found this invaluable, as it got me over any fear of giving public presentations. And I love the area of law I'm in because it's so fast-moving.' Such a hard won qualification should not be cast away lightly she feels. It is highly inadvisable to embark on an alternative occupation immediately after qualification without having acquired at least a minimum of practical legal experience if there is any intention of going back to law later. 'It will be too late,' she says simply, 'without practical experience you will not be at all marketable.'

Sandra's enthusiasm for an IT company seems surprising from someone who was not comfortable with maths and science, 'although I was very good at biology'. She seems slightly surprised herself when she considers the question, ponders and then decides that 'I don't find my lack of science a problem because I find the products that we produce so fascinating. I could not programme anything or develop any software, but I do have a good knowledge of what the products do. It's not like being a doctor or a chemist, where you have to be aware of formulae to do anything. I only have to understand the products in a "sales-y" way so that I can learn how to improve the business'.

However she admits that 'if you work in a commercial environment you do need to learn how figures work, and that took me a long time. In some ways it's useful being a woman in an environment like this because you can ask the questions that men won't ask. Often when I have decided that knowing the answer to a question is more important than the impression that I give by revealing my ignorance, I find that half the men did not know the answer either but were certainly not going to ask'.

Women in commerce

'People are the key to success in a commercial environment and it's important to be a good judge of character because some people will help and some people who appear helpful will definitely try to pull you down and there women's intuition is a big advantage.' She is grateful for having been helped by several very good male mentors in the company, the usual dearth of women in senior positions had as usual precluded being mentored by a woman. But from observation she feels that women need to be careful about their relationship with mentors. 'There is a fine line between mentoring and seduction, and you need to be careful that you can recognise if your mentor intends the relationship to be anything other than professional.'

Even now it is difficult to obtain a woman as a mentor. Obviously there are still not many women in senior positions, 'and it is unfortunate that some senior women often want to be seen as special and want to be alone. When I was young and attended a Unisys conference where I was one of only two women I had a sense of pride that I was one of those two, and it did not dawn on me that there should in fact be more women there. However as I have got older I have realised that this can't be right, and now I want my company to pursue diversity. When I was appointed to the board I said to my fellow board members that this was now the time to appoint another woman. One woman was not enough.'

Advice for in-house counsel

Sandra has several key pieces of advice for in-house counsel, some of which would be usefully transferable to any work environment. Being gregarious she will not find her first injunction, to get to know everyone, very difficult. 'Don't stick to one particular group of people. People move around and you can then find yourself very isolated. You also have to realise that everyone plays a part in the success of an organisation. If you are the sort of lawyer who looks down at people below a certain level then you will be the person that the postroom will not help when you need a courier after five o'clock.'

Commerciality is important. 'Your non-legal work colleagues are your clients, and nothing irritates this type of client so much as a lawyer who sounds like a lawyer. You need to realise that the client may have no idea about the law. Sometimes you have to be technical, but if you can avoid it you should not spout case names and legislative references at them. Equally don't tell them what they know.' The law is there as a tool to create solutions and it is the solutions that the client wants to hear about, not the legal reasoning.

A little anecdote which she tells at her in-house training sessions for salespeople sums up what for her constitutes a bad in-house lawyer; 'A chap in a hot air balloon was lost, but when he arrived above a farm and saw someone below he shouted down and asked where he was. "In a hot-air balloon above a farm," came the reply. "Are you a lawyer?" asked the balloonist. When asked by the man on the ground how he could possibly know that, the balloonist tartly replied, "Everything you say is factually correct, but no use to anyone!"'

An in-house lawyer needs to be a team player, and she advises that being an ivory tower lawyer who just gets involved at the end of the deal will not get you anywhere. 'If you are not involved at the beginning you will get by-passed all the time, which will not be good for the company and certainly it will not be good for you.'

But at the same time lawyers need to maintain objectivity and to remember that their first loyalty is to the company. Lawyers must be careful not to be bullied by their colleagues, who might like the law to be other than it is. Sandra has heard that she herself has the reputation of being 'friendly but won't take any rubbish'. Socialising with colleagues is part of the job, because apart from anything else being in the gossip circle is important, but an in-house lawyer must be careful that socialising with certain groups of people, and particularly senior people, does not put her in a compromising position. 'This is especially important post-Enron, because you must be free to confront and to make other people confront ethical issues in relation to the company. You need to be able to take the knowledge that you are good at your job to the party, so that if there is a serious confrontation about an ethical issue, you can not only threaten to resign but feel that you are able to resign because you will surely get another job.'

Juliet Wheldon

Juliet Wheldon is the Treasury Solicitor.
She is the first woman to be appointed to
this position.

Juliet Wheldon considers that the Government Legal Service (GLS) of which she is the official head occupies an interesting interface between politics and law. Indeed the word that she would use to sum up her work, her career and her colleagues would be a stronger one, 'fascinating'.

Although her grandfather was a solicitor she had no intention of becoming a lawyer when she went up to Oxford University in 1968, that ambition developed not by family influence but through her growing fascination with the political and constitutional history which she studied. By the time that she graduated she was not only sure that she wanted to be a barrister, but almost certain that her future lay with what is now called the GLS. Her father was surprised. He had her marked down as an academic, and although always supportive and understanding considered that it was 'the most surprising thing, a puzzling choice' that his daughter would wish to become a civil servant.

This was not a derogatory observation. In his view, and he had worked with senior civil servants, they 'worked very hard, were ill-rewarded for what they did and operated in circumstances of grey anonymity which meant that they were not recognised for what they achieved. But these days if people think that they can count on complete anonymity they have made an incorrect judgment because increasingly everything that we do is subject to public scrutiny. I also rapidly found that my colleagues were not at all grey and that they have a fascinating range of skills and experiences'.

From Bar to GLS

Undeterred by her father's concern Juliet qualified as a barrister after two six-month pupillages at the Chancery Bar, 'doing pretty classic old-style Chancery work for six months where I did trusts and even rights of way, and then a more commercial mix for the second'. She had made it clear that she would not be looking for a tenancy on qualification as her aim was to enter the civil service as soon as pupillage was completed. At that time there was no GLS training scheme, but even if there had been it is doubtful if Juliet would have taken advantage of it. 'I would always have chosen the Bar first anyway, just to see what it was like.'

This statement probably suggests another aspect of her character – curiosity – which has been amply satisfied in her long GLS career. Although her first posting in 1976 was to the Treasury Solicitor's department she has been in and out of that department so often that she finds it difficult to give a snap assessment of the number of times, although she can give the figures for the numbers of her staff (1,761 in the GLS) and the wastage rate of the GLS without a millisecond's hesitation.

She very rapidly explains that the Treasury Solicitor's department has a misleading title. Although the department does operate as in-house advisers to the Treasury it is also the department which 'provides legal advisory and litigation services to government departments like the Ministry of Defence (MoD) and the Department for Education and Skills (DfES) as well as to other major non-governmental bodies in England and Wales. She speaks warmly of that first 'very happy time' there, where, first under a Labour Government and then under Mrs Thatcher she was involved with the first modern privatisation programme involving the sell off of a tranche of Government shares in British Petroleum (BP), and later advising the Treasury on gilts and on governmental finance issues such as the operation of the Exchange Equalisation Account Act 1979 which consolidated and extended the legislation concerned with the management of sterling. It was heady stuff for a young barrister because the BP flotation was the first equity issue that had to meet both British and American listing requirements simultaneously. Then she is quick to point out that she was very junior in the scheme of things and that of course there were also major City firms involved as solicitors to the offer. She regarded herself as 'performing the intelligent client role'.

The words that Juliet uses to describe the role of government lawyers and civil servants in general are very carefully chosen. 'I am nervous about saying that we provide stability for ministers because that would imply that we could do the job that they do all by ourselves and that is patently not the case. What the civil service does supply is support to the ministers of the day in the sense that not only can we carry out the necessary research, but we contain the folk-memory and the lore of government.' She cites as an example the change round in thinking when she was first at the Treasury Solicitor's department as a new recruit. 'I joined in the last days of the Labour administration when the Government was advocating pay restraint and then when the Conservatives were elected, the focus was increasingly on privatisation. We suddenly had to re-calibrate. I knew very little about company law until Mrs Thatcher became Prime Minister, and then when the Labour Government was elected in 1997 my focus shifted to the Human Rights Act and its implications for government.'

Professional distance

This short description obviously raises two questions. How difficult is it to move from one area of scrutiny and political policy to another and how difficult is it to maintain a distance between one's personal and professional personae?

Juliet 'does not find it at all difficult making the switch between serving one government or another. I find it rather exciting, but then when you decide to make this type of legal work your career, you must recognise that governments can change, and that therefore the focus of your work can change'. In a sense that is what the whole GLS training prepares its lawyers for. 'In private practice lawyers become quite tightly specialised because it is what clients want and expect. But in the GLS we sell ourselves as offering the ability to move between specialisms and between departments. In many ways we remain generalist.'

But then a civil service caveat. 'I must not exaggerate. What we are dealing with is mainly administrative law, which I suppose is itself a form of specialism.' Within that framework however GLS lawyers are encouraged to move around every two to three years either between departments or within their departmental teams with the object of encouraging flexibility of mind and approach. Juliet regards her own career as not atypical. She points out that her initial position in the Treasury Solicitor's department involved not only Treasury work but also advice for the department of National Savings and the National Gallery, 'which meant that I could switch interests while sitting at my desk'.

Being tapped on the shoulder

The Attorney-General's Office does not maintain its own 'conventional' legal team, and because of the type of work, its intensity and the overarching confidentiality requirement, secondment to this department has traditionally been seen as a fast-track route in the GLS to senior legal appointments. 'All the great legal issues of government arrive at the Attorney-General's office and being seconded to the department is definitely a career development move.' This opportunity was previously dispensed by the 'tap on the shoulder' method, but those days have passed. The promotion process in the service has changed dramatically over the years. 'We now encourage people to organise their own careers, to suggest moves that would benefit them, and we trawl senior posts within the whole of the GLS so that all those qualified can apply for them. We no longer have any shoulder-tapping. It's all part of a move to make decision making more transparent.'

Apart from a stint at the Home Office, Juliet's career has 'zig-zagged between the Attorney-General's office and the Treasury Solicitor's department. In fact I spent eight years as the senior lawyer in the Attorney-General's office before I was appointed as the Home Office Legal Adviser and then to my present position in July 2000'.

Juliet feels that she 'was always envied by my colleagues because I was able to work with such nice people. I worked for Sir Michael Havers, Patrick Mayhew and Nicholas Lyell. The role of the senior lawyer in the Attorney-General's office is partly that of devil for Counsel (a term that would probably not be commonly used in the Bar these days) and a senior civil servant. As well as doing research and preparing notes of advice, I also took notes of meetings. My position was very much to be in support of the Attorney-General. It would have been quite inappropriate if someone phoned up and asked for my opinion on something that the minister was commenting on to say what the Attorney-General intended to say. The most that I could say was what advice I intended to give the Attorney-General but that is not the same thing. It is the law officers who must be giving the advice not their legal civil servants because this is the apex of the government legal system'.

It is fairly clear that anyone who did not understand the distinction between advice to a minister and advice from a minister would have pretty short shrift from the Treasury Solicitor. Listening to her describe the attributes required by a senior legal civil servant it is easy to see why the term 'Treasury Mandarin' was coined. Intellectual flexibility is a given, but a friendly inscrutability must be a considerable asset in ensuring that no hint of government policy or decision is disseminated to the wrong people or at the wrong time. If it seems a misnomer to call someone of such intellectual élan a 'servant' it is the old-fashioned concept of service and not any inferior slavish concept that must be borne in mind. To be truly effective a civil servant must be comfortably able to maintain a complete dichotomy between the personal and professional, and to be able to maintain this even when an overnight change of government or minister requires a concomitant change in political policy. Perhaps this explains, and Juliet is no exception, why senior civil servants find the theatre and opera, which often deal with such *bouleversements* or peripety at arm's length so attractive. In any event Juliet says that 'I do not find this difficult. It adds to the interest of an already interesting place'.

As the Attorney-General is not only legal adviser to the government but also in charge of the Crown Prosecution Service and the Serious Fraud Office, Juliet thinks that there is an argument that the incumbent of the senior legal position in that department should be a criminal specialist. She was not, but it was to her 'another challenge, another interesting area of work to come to terms with'.

The ambit of the Treasury Solicitor's department

Now that she is Treasury Solicitor, what does that mean? She is not a solicitor and her area of operation is not confined to the Treasury. A very clear explanation was given in a *Hansard* Written Answer on 27 July 2000 by the then Solicitor-General, that the Treasury Solicitor must 'be able personally to give advice to ministers on a range of legal issues, often of a highly sensitive nature; be able to act as the Chief Executive of the Treasury Solicitor's department (TSD), which is an executive agency; be able to act as head of the Government Legal Service with overall responsibility for recruitment, training and career development of . . . government lawyers, and finally to be able to implement the Modernising Government programme within the Government Legal Service'.

Although she is head of the GLS, Juliet is not responsible for lawyers in the CPS, the Foreign and Commonwealth Office, Parliamentary Counsel or the Scottish and Northern Ireland legal teams. Her main task is to ensure that the right support and co-ordinating arrangements are in place for the 1,800 qualified lawyers and legal trainees in 40 government departments as diverse as the Office of Fair Trading, Department of Health and Customs and Excise. Most GLS departments are now co-located with the government departments with which they are most closely associated but the litigation function for most departments resides with the TSD, which means that part of

Juliet's brief is to manage the litigation process. Government legal teams are divided into 'in-house counsel type' advice and litigation work. It is a 'classical way of organisation' and Juliet must ensure that 'it works in the most efficient and most effective way'. She enjoys being able to 'dip into' those aspects of her department's work she finds most interesting at the time. She is conscious that the ability to do this is very much a privilege rather than a responsibility.

The TSD also has responsibility for instructing counsel previously nominated by the Attorney-General to be on panels of counsel used by government. The process of such selection she indicates must be transparent so that 'patronage is used in a proper way. There is very serious money to be spent in litigation so that the Bar and the judges need to be sure that we are using counsel in a proper way'.

Juliet is also responsible for the morale of the organisation. When she says that she feels that it is in a very good state and 'very comfy' at the moment, this is not a complacent remark, but an assessment of its fitness for the purpose both of government and for the people who work in the service. The figures which she has at her fingertips are very persuasive. 'At the end of the 80s we were haemorrhaging lawyers but in 2002 we lost only 4.5 per cent of our staff and that included retirements.'

Government lawyers

Why the 'stickability'? Juliet has identified several factors, but perhaps the most important one is choice. Most GLS recruits are already qualified and potential trainees who apply will find that training at the GLS is not an easy alternative to articles or pupillage. There are only about 30 trainee places per annum, and although there is no guarantee that trainees will be kept on following qualification in practice most are offered posts. Of those who choose not to remain very few find difficulty in transferring their skills elsewhere. Surprisingly, until you realise the wide range of its responsibilities, the GLS has sufficient variety to enable it to fulfil Law Society requirements for diversity of training by moving trainees within and sometimes between departments. Indeed 'we take a pride in the quality of our training'.

However the bulk of GLS lawyers join at some time after qualification. The GLS draws from City firms and the Bar as well as from local authorities and smaller firms. 'We are a very diverse group of people, government lawyers train a lot together and the week-long induction courses that we have are a brilliant way for us all to get to know each other across departments.' She considers that the main

reason for the long-term nature of GLS careers is the sheer fascination of the role. 'There really is variety and we have the interest of
being involved in the headline stories of the day, and they are the
headline stories because they really do matter to people. It is hugely
rewarding.'

Conclusions

So was her father's assessment of the civil service 30 years or so ago
accurate and are his assumptions still relevant to GLS staff?

Whatever the expedient benefit of the anonymity of its civil servants
to a government, the lack of profile is of some concern to its lawyers
and therefore to the Treasury Solicitor. Lawyers have a notoriously
gossipy streak and GLS lawyers are not only restricted in their gos-
siping but are also unlikely to feature in any personal way in the
legal press. Not for them the short listing of 'the most taxing deal' or
'the most transatlantic deal' beloved of certain legal publications.
'There is a reputational thing about the anonymity question,' Juliet
reflects. 'When lawyers join the service they are surprised at what a
low profile we have. I have a little bit of a concern that we are quite
so anonymous as a group. The lawyers inside the service certainly
feel that they are insufficiently recognised as a group, and that is a
self-confidence issue.'

Perhaps surprisingly Juliet has less apparent concern about remuneration. 'People make a conscious decision when they come into government work that they are not going to be mega-rich. If you are
aiming for the million pound earnings of some barristers and City
partners you will not join the GLS. But City salaries can be exaggerated, and I know from those who join us in mid-career that there is a
huge salary spectrum in the private sector and that there are many
lawyers who do not earn vast sums there. You must also remember
that by joining the GLS you are buying into a total package, including
an index-linked pension, which has become increasingly important.'

And as to the hard work. 'The government is a good employer which
respects your private life. We have a good work-life balance record.
People certainly have to work hard but they don't work City hours
or routinely at the weekends. It's not an absolute dawdle; it would
be wrong to think that, but we do try to make part time manageable
even for senior people. In fact the senior lawyer at the department of
Culture, Media and Sport is a woman who is meant to work a four
day week, although I'm worried that she will end up working more.
We give career breaks of up to five years, and we accept job shares
as well. Home-based IT support is available depending on how far

advanced a department's own IT capabilities are. TSD does offer remote access for example but I have to admit that the DfES systems are much better.'

Asked if she would recommend the GLS as a career for women, Juliet smiles, 'I would recommend it as a career for anyone. Personally I have never experienced any sort of glass ceiling in the GLS and I think that the figures speak for themselves. Just over 53 per cent of lawyers in the GLS are women, and at the more senior grades in the civil service equivalent to partnership level in legal firms, 31 per cent are women. That is quite a comforting thought if you are entering as a woman'.

Juliet was appointed very early, at 50, to her position and so it is too early to consider what she might do next. 'Open to offers,' she jests and is amused by the thought that some other interviewees much older than she are looking for the next challenge. 'I find that very inspiring.'

Rosalind Wright CB

Rosalind Wright was the Director of the Serious Fraud Office from 1997 to 2003. She is also a Bencher of Middle Temple, a member of the Bar Council and most recently a non-executive director of the Office of Fair Trading and chairman of the Fraud Advisory Panel.

The Serious Fraud Office (SFO) occupies the ninth floor of a building just north of High Holborn in London overlooks the fringes of the City, at the centre of the UK business world whose probity the SFO constantly monitors. So comfortable and cheerful does Rosalind look in this office which seems to comprise almost equal proportions of books and family memorabilia that it is tempting to consider that she has always been there and always will be. Still full of lively energy she did in fact retire summer 2003.

Rosalind's father was a solicitor in sole practice who 'did a lot of big company stuff'. Unusually he did not encourage her to become a solicitor; Rosalind suspects that he felt that her dramatic character would alienate his clients in the likely event that she might want to go into practice with him. In retrospect she considers that his attitude was 'somewhat patronising' because his considered career advice to a daughter who enjoyed acting was that 'you would love being a barrister because you could dress up and declaim in court and indulge your thespian side'.

Life at the Bar

Rosalind was called to the Bar in 1964 and practised in the chambers of Morris Finer QC for almost five years. As her father had predicted, she did enjoy court life and wearing a wig, building up a general common law practice, including doing county court possession summonses and hire purchase repossessions. She did not feel that her position as the only woman in chambers was difficult except in so far as she was completely ignored by the clerk whom she overheard saying to a client on the telephone one day: 'You could have Mr X or Mr Y next week and I suppose that you could have Miss Kirstein as a last resort.'

His unconcealed misogyny probably reflected not only the low number of women barristers in private practice in 1964 (only 100) but also the 'very unforgiving' nature of the Bar and 'not just towards women'. Rosalind recalls sadly that one barrister of about 15 years' call, out of practice for eight months with a severe medical problem, returned to find that his practice had disappeared into the coffers not only of other chambers but into the pockets of his fellow tenants; his eight month illness left him in the financial position of someone at the beginning of his career.

Leaving the Bar

Partly because of the uncertainty of income and partly because of a sense of general hazard Rosalind left the Bar and joined the civil service which promised a more stable income and more regular working hours.

She had also begun to find the Bar a very difficult career to combine, logistically and to some extent emotionally, with motherhood. Young and physically strong, she had while at the Bar been able to have her first baby, a daughter, on a Sunday and return to court on the Tuesday. When her second child, also a daughter, was born she was found by her visiting head of chambers sitting up in bed breast-feeding her baby surrounded by divorce petitions. Her strength had already been severely tested by having to travel up to Consett in Northumberland when eight months' pregnant for a court appearance. There were no buses from Newcastle to Consett so she walked for three miles lugging her papers and wig and gown for the princely sum of 15 guineas, out of which she had to pay her return fare between London and Newcastle.

Rosalind undoubtedly had a marketable skill to add to the income of her husband who was a hospital registrar, and a passion for what she was doing, but combining that with family life became increasingly difficult. She had a 'terrible problem' with childcare not because she would not have been a good employer, but because in common with many other young barrister mothers she simply did not have a sufficiently regular, guaranteed income to enable her to employ a nanny. Consequently she would take her children not only to chambers but also to court. She found that in the county courts, secretaries would be happy to mind a carrycot and a toddler for half an hour; in the magistrates' court the Matron for Women Prisoners would perform the same office in return for a ten shilling tip; and for her High Court appearances she would often be accompanied by her mother acting as nursemaid for the children. The school holidays found her constantly 'boxing and coxing' in order to perform her job and to ensure adequate supervision for her children.

Her decision to leave the Bar was also partially hastened by doing family work because, as a young wife and mother with a very rosy view of marriage, she found divorce and fighting over children very dispiriting indeed.

The office of the Director of Public Prosecutions

The move to the office of the Director of Public Prosecutions (DPP) gave her financial security, produced a regular income for regular hours worked but, to someone with a great fondness for children, was not without its emotional problems.

At the DPP she did miss the forensic side of the Bar but found that this was compensated for by the new regularity of her life and in some ways an organisation with only 60 employees did not feel so very different from chambers. The murder cases that she was given as a new member of the department were 'not particularly distressing provided that they did not involve children'. What she found most harrowing were cases involving children and especially the abuse of children. It is easy, she considers, to become very cynical about human nature working in such an environment and she would find herself looking at a man in the street holding a child's hand, who was probably the child's father, and wondering whether in fact the child was being abducted. She had to tell herself very firmly that 'not everyone is like my cases'.

Rosalind very much prefers small organisations where she can know most if not all of the staff. Over the next few years the office of the DPP metamorphosed into the Crown Prosecution Service, its character inevitably changing as it increased from a very small and specialised unit to its new incarnation as the headquarters of an enormous department of 6,000. By the time she felt that she was ready for her next move Rosalind had for four years been head of the Fraud Investigation Group, which was a springboard to leaving the civil service and joining the Stock Exchange where she had a dual contract with the Securities Association (TSA).

New legislation

She realised that she had become 'very interested' in fraud. It was a 'new thing' because of the Financial Services Act 1986 and the thought of being 'on the edge of something quite new' was very exciting. It is very much 'an intellectual pursuit', and although involvement in the legal side can make one cynical about financial investments ('no one should be investing in anything that they do not understand'), this is altogether easier to deal with than becoming cynical about people's personal relationships.

So in 1987 and at the age of 44, which she thought was 'a good age to be moving in another direction', Rosalind found herself at the Stock Exchange legal department with 'the people who started off the new regulatory regime'. She was extraordinarily impressed with the ability of her colleagues at the Stock Exchange, both lawyers and policy makers who were at the forefront of changing the regulatory expectations of Stock Exchange members. Until then brokers had had no external regulation and probably no recognised framework of regulation. Now a new regime required that they should be 'fit and proper' to conduct investment business which meant that they had to satisfy three separate tests of solvency, competence and integrity. This was a huge new institutional change whose implementation fascinated her. It was clear that the City did not see itself as a homogeneous entity, and that some members were more comfortable hiding behind the 'extended lunch type of self-regulation' rather than submitting to the regulatory requirements of the new legislation. When TSA amalgamated with the Association of Futures Brokers and Dealers (AFBD) to form the Securities and Futures Authority (SFA), there was resistance from old Stock Exchange brokers who were suspicious of the 'chaps in white socks', who they felt were one up from the barrow boys.

Rosalind's work at the SFA, where she became general counsel, concerned legal policy and disciplinary cases so that it was not surprising that she was subsequently headhunted by the Serious Fraud Office (SFO). The investigation of financial malpractice had always fascinated her, particularly when there was evidence of rigging a market in shares or the role of advisers in certain high profile cases required scrutiny.

Moving to the Serious Fraud Office (SFO)

In an interview with *Business Week* before she had been invited to apply for the SFO directorship she was asked what she thought of the SFO. She told her interviewer firmly that she felt that the SFO had been the subject of extremely unfair press. 'After all they had had only two or three big failures but the press published only negative comments and did not give equal publicity to their successes.'

Rosalind welcomed the opportunity to change the 'bad image' of the SFO and she had little hesitation in putting her name forward, because 'I really wanted to make it work'. She was amused by the suggestion at her interview that if appointed it would be so easy for the press to call her 'Rosalind Wrong'. She subsequently found, and particularly after the recent *Wickes* case that much newspaper comment was not only very personal, but also biased and misinformed. 'The judge did not throw the case out, so there was a case to answer, and it was perfectly proper for us to bring the case. But it was the jury which, as it was entitled to do, found the defendants not guilty.' She also points out that insufficient coverage has been given to the success of the SFO in the *BCCI* case. 'This was the biggest fraud case ever with six trials, six defendants and six convictions involving a dedicated team of 60 people. This involved a massive effort, huge dedication and rated hardly a mention in the press.'

It is just as well that Rosalind is able to rely on her cheerful, positive nature and her constructive family life when the media assessment of the efficacy of her organisation can be so critical. Her own perception of the SFO is of a very cohesive organisation with a strong ethos and culture where people are 'very fair minded, dedicated, work very hard and have a clear vision of what they are meant to do'. With perhaps particularly female self-deprecation she says 'Whether I have had anything to do with this I'm not sure. But this is what I tell my mother'.

Rosalind feels that she left an organisation which is highly respected internationally, knowing that 'similar organisations in other countries look to us as a role model and many countries have copied us'. She will admit that being director was 'quite a big job and quite stressful', but her 'retirement' did not mean a sudden cessation of work and involvement, as she has taken over from George Staple as chairman of the Fraud Advisory Panel, a voluntary post 'but as busy as you want to make it'. She is also looking forward to spending more time with her husband, a retired microbiologist, and with her three daughters, none of whom is a lawyer, and six grandchildren.

Objectivity

Rosalind looks back with clear-sighted affection at her life as a young mother, because her family is clearly as central to her life as her career, and interweaving these two strands of her life has not always been easy. She certainly sees it as progress that she has moved from having a cleaning lady for two hours a week and no washing machine to a life where she has a proper 'daily lady', can confine shopping to the weekends and applauds the advent of catalogue and internet shopping, where goods can be delivered to the office.

Rosalind probably would not have done anything very differently. 'Everything I have done I have enjoyed enormously, and I feel that there has been tremendous serendipity in my life.' Proper domestic help when she was younger 'would have been a bonus if we could have afforded it'. For the last few years she has been much more active on the Bar Council and is now on the scholarship committee of Middle Temple, which interviews every single person who applies for scholarship. She emphasises that the committee looks for 'potential as barristers, which means young people who are outgoing and have a sufficient degree of persuasive gravitas'. They are as likely, she feels, to come from the old polytechnics as from Oxbridge. 'These are the people who will be the stars of tomorrow.'

She herself is a graduate of University College London where, 'I was not very academic. I managed a 2.2'. Her parents were also UCL graduates, her mother who is now 94, obtaining a First in French. 'Now she is very academic,' Rosalind states firmly. There was serendipity in her own education when she found that at age 17 she was too young to study history but not too young to be accepted by the law faculty, which at that time operated a ruthless system of taking on huge numbers in the first year, without real academic requirements, then rejecting almost 50 per cent of those after the first year examinations.

Rosalind considers that it is important for young people to try to find out as much as they possibly can about the law before deciding to join the legal profession or, more particularly, whether to become solicitor or barrister. 'You should find out what aspects interest you before jumping in one direction or the other. Lots of people do make decisions without adequate knowledge, and although solicitors can now become and do make good advocates young people should remember that advocacy is the Bar's speciality.' On the other hand if a young person feels more comfortable working in an organisation then her advice would be to become a solicitor, because in chambers 'you are on your own and you have to look after yourself'. She has no regrets about the direction of her professional life. 'The law is a great profession because it has so many routes to career fulfilment and a lawyer fills a very important role in society.' Management training she considers is more readily available to solicitors, because the Bar certainly does not train individuals to be managers. 'What it does give you is lots of self-confidence and analytical skills which are important if you are to run an organisation, although,' she smiles 'most barristers can't run themselves let alone an organisation.'

So, what qualities are necessary to be head of the SFO?

There must be public credibility and as far as she is concerned this means the public both inside and outside the office. The people inside must be able to respect the Director as a lawyer who could actually carry out the prosecutions and investigations required of them. To some extent this is the credibility required of the Director as the public face of the SFO, to be able to stand up and with understanding explain and defend the actions and policies of SFO staff. The Director is in effect the SFO's highest ranking public relations officer.

Obviously leadership skills are required in managing a department of about 230 people. To Rosalind leadership equates with people skills, having an ease of communication, being approachable and being able to say that she knew the people in her office, and that they knew her. It is perhaps illustrative of this point that the male receptionist introduced me to Rosalind's secretary as 'a Mrs Cruickshank here to see Ros'.

As accounting officer she was required to 'manage the nuts and bolts' of the SFO, understanding the budget and ensuring its financial well-being, being able to plan for the future and able to make decisions about expansion or contraction of services.

She needed to have 'very strong control' over the cases being investigated by the SFO. There are so few, only about 80 at one time (the SFO takes on probably about 25 new cases each year) that she was required to understand and be able to comment on almost all of them at any particular time. To help her she would read carefully all the case conference minutes on every current case 'whether it reflects something good or bad or just generally something I should know about'.

The word 'dedication' has appeared many times in her conversation. It is obviously a quality which she values in other people but which she may not have recognised as so obvious in herself: Someone who is dedicated to her family, to her colleagues and to the law.

Part Three
Advice

As in most other occupations mere mastery of the technical subject matter may not be enough to ensure success. As one senior partner said, 'We take technical excellence for granted'.

This section deals with the other skills that need to be acquired or honed in order to ensure success. Richard Payne demonstrates how sharpening presentation and communication skills can make for a more effective and relaxed demeanour, and Dianna Keel gives guidance on how we can work more efficiently and at less personal cost in her chapters on time and stress management.

Sally Woodward explains that even the most junior member of a legal team can have untapped leadership skills which can enhance the performance of others. She shows why it is important to become a good leader – and that it is never too early to start! As an aide to promotion prospects Tania Martin offers practical guidance on how to meet and encourage potential new clients, because the ability to bring in new business so often makes the difference between recognition and anonymity in a legal firm.

Improving Your Soft Skills

Richard Payne

What are soft skills?

Soft skills alone will not a career make but they can enhance technical skills and improve career prospects quite considerably.

The Institute of Training and Occupational Learning (ITOL) defines soft skills as, 'skills where there are many ways to achieve an effective outcome, usually in areas such as human relations training. They are often characterised by the need for each individual learner to find their own best way to unleash their personal talents (as opposed to 'Hard' skills which are often technical skills that can be well defined and predetermined)'.[1]

Is it worth developing these skills? Is the time involved in improving soft skills worthwhile in terms of career advancement?

The answer to this question is a resounding 'it depends'. As individuals we possess different strengths and weaknesses and it is important for each of us to establish how we aim to advance and develop our careers. It goes without saying that each of us should play to our own personal strengths. For every brilliant 'people' person who has climbed the 'greasy pole' using her ability to build and establish rapport there will be an introverted, technically skilled star who has made it to the top without ever managing to look anyone in the eye. The ideal would be a healthy balance!

The best advice is to assess yourself realistically. It is best not to force yourself to become the life and soul of the party or the clients' favourite if it is going to cause sleepless nights. It is far better to identify some small aspect of soft skills to develop and to set realistic goals. Although you may never be able to work a room with consummate ease, flitting like a gadfly from one potential client to another, it is perfectly possible for you to set a target of initiating at least one conversation with a potential client at the next social gathering.

On the other hand, you may be someone with finely developed sensibilities who is already able to communicate extremely effectively. In that case you need to ensure that you are not categorised as someone who is merely charming and lacking gravitas. You need to ensure your technical skills are equally advanced so that you have something of substance to say once the ice is broken.

Although soft skills are interrelated and it is difficult to develop one without the other, they can be categorised as:

- ○ presentation skills.
- ○ influencing and selling skills.
- ○ negotiating skills.

Presentation skills

The main benefit of improving your presentation skills is that you will enhance your profile and visibility within the firm. The ability to be able to explain complex issues, particularly to clients, in an accessible style is usually highly valued.

Presentation skills are often associated with formal occasions, but a moment's reflection will enable you to identify a variety of situations where you are required to present information in some form or other; for most lawyers a significant part of every day is taken up with presenting ideas, concepts and arguments, even if only over the telephone. But perhaps the most highly valued presentation skill is the ability to pitch effectively for new business. Firms will always have a need, at the highest level, for those prepared to develop business by presenting persuasively at so-called 'beauty parades'.

What do you need to remember?

- ○ A presentation is very much intended to show the public face of the firm and it is therefore an opportunity to explain why your firm should be awarded a contract. The message you present needs to be outcome focused rather than process driven. In other words you must explain to the potential client what the outcome of any proposal will be. Use lots of benefit statements during any pitch. There is a rather clichéd saying that 'features tell and benefits sell' but it is never more true than when pitching. Try to identify what is special or unique about your proposal and embed this into your message.

  Ensure the firm's brand is clearly understood by everybody involved in the pitching process. There will be a lack of consistency and cohesion if varying messages are being pitched by different team members.

  Try to avoid becoming cynical about beauty parades because this will show in your demeanour and voice. Some lawyers feel that by the time they get in front of the potential client it is all over and the actual presentation will have little effect upon the outcome, therefore no effort need be made. This approach in itself could ensure that you do not get the business! Try to sound energetic and committed even when you do not feel too positive about securing the contract!

○   Put aside some time to prepare and rehearse your contribution as this will help you to shine. Bear in mind that preparation time is never wasted even if your firm doesn't secure the work! You may well get a name check in the debrief after a failed bid and this will not do your credibility or profile any harm.

Write your presentation first and then decide upon the slides necessary as this will ensure that you do not prepare too many. Time your contribution whilst rehearsing as this helps to avoid running over on the day. Try to rehearse your presentation aloud because what reads well on the page may not be so effective when spoken aloud. Try to anticipate in advance questions that may be asked post pitch. Sit down with a colleague to establish the sorts of concerns or questions the potential client may raise and practise some responses. Schedule at least one team rehearsal with the whole team present as this provides everyone with an opportunity to hear one another's contributions.

○   It is perfectly natural to be anxious and to be affected by nerves in the first few moments of a presentation. If the opening phase goes well this generally helps the nerves to subside. It is imperative that you learn the opening few phrases so that you can look the audience in the eye, enabling you to appear confident. If the opening moments go well nervousness will usually become less noticeable both to yourself and the audience.

Presentations should not be read verbatim as this will make your delivery wooden and there is less likelihood of making appropriate eye contact with the audience. Instead, transfer key points onto cue cards. Alternatively slides may be used as a prompt but this is risky as it means the presentation is likely to be driven by Microsoft PowerPoint®, which in turn means you have less chance of engaging the audience. It also means that the pitch will seem more like a slide show with an accompanying commentary rather than a confident attempt to influence and engage the panel.

○   Ensure that you know who is speaking before and after you so that cues can be agreed and picked up appropriately.

○   Once it is all over put time aside to reflect and review. If the pitch was successful, ask yourself, why did it work? Try to use its strong points as a model to structure subsequent pitches. If it didn't work, think about what went wrong. Analysing the success rate of pitches may enable you to make informed choices about improving future performance or altering pitch strategy.

Finally, think about the non-verbal aspects of your communication when making a presentation. Body language is a major part of the communication process and it is worth spending some time getting it right.

It's not what you say . . .

'Body language (or non-verbal communication) is the means by which humans convey information through conscious or subconscious gestures, bodily movements or facial expression. Body language seems to have three broad uses: as a conscious replacement for speech, to reinforce speech, and as a betrayer of mood.'[2]

It can sometimes be difficult to concentrate on body language when presenting as there seems to be so much to think about. So, rather than aiming for perfection, view the non-verbal aspects of the presentation as a process of constant physiological adjustment. If you realise that you are waving your hands around wildly, you can work on calming them down.

When you are presenting your performance will be improved if you:

○ Stand in the middle of the speaking area. Ensure a balanced and upright posture. Keep your head up when speaking and try not to read a presentation.

○ Take a deep breath before speaking and also at the start of every new phrase as this breath will support the voice, ensuring a more confident sound.

○ Look at the audience rather than out of the window or at the screen. It is easier to build rapport if eye contact is made. Do not stare at one person for too long. It's best to sweep the audience slowly from side to side when speaking.

○ Movement is another crucial aspect of presentation and in moderation helps to keep the audience's attention. But don't distract the audience by unfocused pacing up and down. Move from a still position to another still position and avoid turning your back on the audience whilst talking.

○ Use your face. Facial gestures are an important part of the communication process so look pleased if you are delivering good news, i.e. smile!

○ Do not grip onto props such as lecterns, chairs or tables. Place your hands gently on such items if it helps to give you a sense of balance but do not grip on for grim life!

○ Use hand gestures to emphasise points but avoid aggressive gestures such as pointing or shaking a fist. Try to bring your hands back to a resting position when gestures have been completed as this reduces the temptation to use repetitive, distracting motions.

○ Keep your voice vital and alive. Try to emphasise a few words in each phrase and do not speak too quickly but vary the pace and pitch to create interest.

Adopting all these suggestions will take some practice, but if you really want to improve, rehearse using video playback and ask friends, colleagues and mentors for constructive feedback in relation to personal performance.

Meetings

Personal presentation skills are not just confined to formal situations and they can have a big impact in meetings. Most lawyers are very well versed in presenting at client meetings, and know that contributing effectively in internal meetings is a good way to enhance their profile within the firm.

Women sometimes feel they may be at a disadvantage in male dominated meetings and so it is worth considering some strategies which will enable you to communicate confidently.

Asserting yourself – a commonsense approach

- Try to avoid adopting an adversarial approach in meetings as it rarely works.
- Do not lose your temper or shout.
- Listen more than you talk and try to formulate the first phrase before speaking.
- Watch others' breathing patterns when they are speaking. The majority of human speech is produced by egressive lung air.[3] This means that in order to produce sound a breath is usually taken. If you wish to interject, wait for someone else to take a breath. This is a far more effective strategy than trying to shout over others!
- Use eye contact to indicate that you wish to make a contribution. Identify who is chairing the meeting and establish eye contact with that person. A good chairperson should be looking for such non-verbal cues.
- If possible sit where the person leading the meeting can clearly see you. It will prove much easier for that person to pick up gestures and eye contact indicating your desire to speak.
- Repetition is an excellent way of ensuring that your point is made. Quietly and calmly repeating what has been previously stated without altering or amending the original phrase is a useful device. This is known as the 'broken record' technique.[4] For those old enough to remember, broken records were characterised by the needle becoming stuck, resulting in the same phrase being played repeatedly. Broken records invariably get heard!
- Look for allies prior to a meeting and let them know you have something to contribute. A word of warning – do not tell them the whole story or they may steal your ideas and present them as their own!

At best, your allies should bring you into the discussion and create space for your contribution. The more senior the ally the better!

o   Asking a question is a good way of getting the floor. Once you have asked a question you can proceed with your point.

o   Try to be a problem solver rather than a moaner. You are much more likely to be given space to contribute at meetings if you have gained the reputation of being someone with a positive, flexible attitude.

o   Sound committed and enthusiastic about your suggestions and definitely do not apologise for them in advance.

o   Arm yourself to the teeth. If you are likely to encounter resistance take along information or facts which will enable you to support your argument. For example, 'It'll never work!' could be countered with, 'Several other firms of our size have implemented this successfully and I have an interesting article by the senior partner at XYZ who explains how she has initiated this particular scheme to great effect'.

Once you have created the necessary space to air your opinions, keep your comments brief and insightful. Don't waffle and remember the adage 'less is more'. In other words it is better to make a few effective, insightful comments rather than a lot of unfocused ones for the sake of it. Finally, never be frightened to ask for time. Far from damaging your credibility asking for time will give the impression of being someone who considers their answers before 'shooting from the hip'.

Influencing and selling skills

Robert Louis Stevenson once said 'Everybody is selling something', but professionals, such as lawyers, do not like to view themselves as sales people as this can conjure up images of secondhand car salesmen. Even the word 'influencing' can have Machiavellian connotations.

Although developing your influencing and selling skills can produce substantial benefits, the key is to know when to use them covertly rather than overtly. Bringing people around to a view may involve persuading colleagues to think differently, or explaining to a client why they should take certain advice. A more overt form of selling is involvement in marketing the firm's services in both formal and informal situations.

There is no great secret to improving your influencing and selling skills and indeed a lot of successful lawyers have worked out effective strategies for themselves through a process of trial and error.

The main things to consider are:

o   Knowing and understanding the message. A spoken message should be encapsulated clearly and coherently in a phrase or two.

o   Understanding the target audience. In particular master the art of anticipatory objection handling. Try to put yourself in other people's shoes and attempt to think like them. This is particularly important where clients are concerned as they will not necessarily think in the same way as lawyers. Bear in mind that different sectors have different approaches. For example most advertising agencies pride themselves on their ability to think creatively or 'outside the box'. To an organised lawyer this can appear to be chaotic and disorganised but adjusting your approach and style will be crucial if you are to build long-term rapport with such clients.

○ Tailoring the message to suit the recipient. Language is very powerful so think carefully about the words which are used. The way you speak to colleagues is likely to be very different from the way in which you communicate with a client in a different sector. Effective communication between lawyers can be viewed as jargon to others.

○ The easiest way to be influential is to show people the payoff, i.e. what's in it for them. Demonstrate how your ideas and views will be of benefit. Always try to match the outcomes with needs.

○ Never make a claim without providing evidence or an example. Avoid saying, 'We're the best firm in town!'. Better to say, 'We're the best firm in town and this is borne out by the high rate of successful transactions we completed last year'.

○ Think strategically. We cannot always speak immediately to the person who needs to be influenced. Such a person may be too senior or unavailable. Master influencers always find a way to transmit information to the real decision maker even if they cannot deal directly with that person. First of all establish those who are the decision makers and those who are the decision influencers. If the decision makers are not accessible then concentrate on influencing those who are closest to them, i.e. decision influencers.

○ Try to provide actual examples of how other clients have been assisted as this can prove very persuasive and is the best form of evidence.

○ If you are to sell effectively you need to understand the difference between features and benefits. A feature is merely a descriptor. Most people try to influence others by throwing a list of features at their target audience. 'We're the biggest . . . the brightest . . . the best.' This can come across as rather boastful. It is much more effective to turn feature statements into benefit statements by using a link phrase. 'We're the biggest *which means* that we're able to provide a fully resourced team of specialists around the clock.'

Improve your profile

In a groundbreaking 1987 publication entitled *High Visibility*, Rein, Kotler and Stoller expounded the concept that success is not just about ability but is also about visibility. The book is based on the guiding premise that, 'High visibility is not just a matter of vanity anymore – it's a fact of life. Today, throughout all sections of society, you gain power not because of your ability but your visibility. This feeling has become so strong that professionals of all kinds – business people, lawyers, doctors, entertainers, athletes, politicians and others – are finding out that they are only as successful as they are visible.'[5]

In a male dominated profession such as law it is even more important for women to compile a personal marketing plan (PMP) with the aim of improving their visibility. The traditional advice provided to ambitious career planners was to network like crazy. Whilst this is generally good advice it is extremely time consuming and labour intensive! It is much better to identify activities which provide the maximum exposure with the minimum of effort.

The three activities which are likely to give you the biggest benefit for the least effort are:

1   **Becoming a mastermind**
    Strategic placement of your name, image and expertise, particularly within the media, will do more to improve visibility than anything else. Offer expertise to journalists and reporters, and be ready with relevant quotes. Develop a database of key media contacts and become proactive when you feel you are able to comment on changes in legislation or ground-breaking judgments. It is best to target publications which are read by both clients and your own profession rather than those which have a general readership. Ensure that you have obtained permission from the person responsible for media relations within the firm before contacting publications. It may already have been decided that someone more senior is to be the firm's spokesperson on a particular issue, or indeed there may be a more prestigious publication with which the firm has an established relationship.

2   **Becoming an educator**
    Another useful way to improve visibility is to become involved in educational activities. Consider giving the occasional lecture, seminar or running an in-house training course. This does require a good deal of preparation but usually after you have done the initial planning subsequent sessions can be rolled out quite easily. As you will have a captive audience whilst teaching, this is a great way to get noticed, and again, concentrate on teaching opportunities where the audience members are potentially going to be helpful. If you have little teaching or training experience, observe those you consider to be good teachers and, if possible, undertake a 'training the trainer' course. Teaching is an activity which, when done well, looks easy but requires a good deal of skill and preparation.

3   **Asking for the moon**

Be proactive. Ask for responsibility but 'box clever'. Try to identify activities that will improve your profile. Asking to be in charge of the stationery cupboard is unlikely to do anything for your reputation but putting yourself forward to represent the firm at an important conference will be much more beneficial. Think carefully before asking. Be prepared to explain what's in it for the firm (not just yourself!) and choose your moment. Appraisals are a good time to ask for the moon, as are away days and less formal environments where you may have the attention of a key member of the firm's senior management team.

Negotiation skills

Negotiation involves at least two parties, each of whom has something that the other wants, reaching an agreement to exchange through a process of bargaining.[6]

Lawyers negotiate almost more than any other profession, and negotiation is not just confined to formal 'round table' environments. Lawyers are also involved in this complex process on the telephone, when writing letters and in less formal encounters.

Most standard texts on the subject assume that the parties to a negotiation sit down at a given time and in a given place and commence negotiating until the neat conclusion of affairs. The reality for most lawyers is that negotiations may run over many sessions and may take months or even years to conclude.

Negotiation is a fluid principle of exchange and in order to improve and develop skills it is crucial that the phases of a negotiation are clearly understood.

Preparation

This should involve both goal setting and gathering information about the other party. Establish your position and identify the areas upon which you have a degree of flexibility. It is vital at this stage to identify how much can be given away. Ensure the chains of command are clearly understood; you must know when it will be necessary to refer a point to a higher authority in the firm and how much authority you actually have. It is also extremely important to try to establish the same issues in relation to the other party.

Assess the opposition by asking the following questions:

o   How much do they know?
o   How much authority do they possess?
o   Is the other party under pressure to settle?
o   What are the other party's weaknesses in a particular area?

When preparing, do not be frightened to gather intelligence. People in your own firm or network may have previous experience of the other party which could be helpful.

Proposal

After your preparation has been completed, decide whether you want to speak first or respond to someone else's proposal. This is an important and often overlooked part of negotiating strategy.

The advantage of speaking first is that control of the situation is established and this can put the other party on the back foot. The disadvantage is that little time is available to adjust a proposal, if necessary, after you have heard what the other party has to say.

Make the initial offer unrealistic and compromise from that point onwards. Listen carefully to the other party's proposal and ensure it is clearly understood before responding.

Debate

This is where the fun starts! The debating phase takes place only when both parties have heard the other's offer. The goal is to move to a mutually acceptable outcome or agreement once both of you have reassessed your position. The key is to look for mutual points of interest and to highlight the areas or points on which you can agree and the points you may be prepared to concede or to alter. All options should be explored with the aim of achieving a mutually beneficial outcome.

Keep calm during this phase and do not show too much emotion or attempt to score points.

Bargaining

The key to bargaining is to strengthen your own case and to try to weaken the opposition's. Keep testing the validity of the other party's case and look for errors, but do not attack individuals. Be vigilant at this stage for the other side's weaknesses or errors of fact or logic or their selective use of figures or statistics. Use whatever leverage you have at this juncture to press your points home calmly and assertively.

Closing

Closing is an absolutely crucial aspect of the negotiation process. Before moving towards a close it is important to ensure that terms are confirmed so everyone is sure they are talking about the same thing. Any terminology should be confirmed and if a contract is being drawn up any problems should be ironed out before the close.

Of the many and various methods of closing a deal, the three most common are:

1   **Splitting the difference**. All sides are encouraged to move towards the middle ground in order to conclude the deal.
2   **The alternative close**. Giving one party the choice between two acceptable alternatives.
3   **Introducing new incentives or sanctions**. This can provide the necessary impetus to bring the other party to an agreement.

If the other side is still reluctant to conclude the negotiation, then it is useful to ask hypothetical questions in order to establish the reason for the reluctance to conclude, e.g. 'If we could solve the problem regarding exchange date by allowing you another week to complete, would this put you in a position where you are able to agree to this deal in principle?'. If the other party's response is positive then you have a basis for moving towards a conclusion with some adjustment to terms. If there is still resistance then you will know the point you have been discussing is not the real issue and the other party have been using it as a smokescreen!

Body language during negotiation

Body language can be a betrayer of mood and so it is important to ensure personal presentation is congruent with the image and message you wish to convey:

- Sit upright and lean in towards the discussion as this will make you appear involved.
- Keep your face fairly neutral so that the other party is not able to interpret your true feelings.
- Try not to touch your face too much as this can indicate deceptiveness.
- Show your hands. Those who use their hands during meetings are viewed as trustworthy – so do not tuck them under the table!
- Pace your delivery and try to speak clearly and audibly without raising your voice or shouting. This will ensure that the lower vocal registers are utilised. Authority is transmitted through a lower pitch.
- Make good use of pauses during discussions. This breaks up the other party's rhythm. Pausing before responding makes your contributions seem more considered and provides valuable thinking time.

The interpretation of body language is, of course, not one-sided. Becoming more aware of the giveaway signs can also enable you to gauge the true reactions of the other party during the various phases of the negotiation process through observing their non-verbal responses.

Final thoughts

Developing your presentation skills, influencing skills and negotiation skills is a continuous process. You therefore need to be aware of what has worked for you, how other people have influenced or persuaded you, and which of their strategies you could usefully adopt. If you decide to commission training in these areas, you need to consider your options in a focused and pragmatic manner.

First of all identify the core skills which you need to develop.

Second, examine courses with a sceptical eye. There are some incredibly daft courses with bizarre titles out there! A glance through a recent training journal revealed some rather dotty offerings, such as developing your teamworking skills by walking over hot coals or your interpersonal skills by undertaking some excruciatingly ill prepared socio drama or role play. There are even courses around where delegates are encouraged to chant pointless mantras or sing songs in order to change their mental attitude before concluding with a group hug!

Third, consider second generation training. Many individuals will already have had some experience of soft skills training, and good second generation training builds on what has already been achieved. Second generation training is a more focused, specific and advanced training course which addresses specific needs rather than general ones. First generation training is characterised by being general and unspecific, and may even be delivered by someone who does not have personal experience of your sector or profession, which can sometimes make it appear irrelevant. Second generation training on the other hand should focus on specific topics such as pitches and beauty parades or running conferences with constant and specific reference to your profession.

Remember that to be successful you need the right blend of technical skills and soft skills. Female lawyers need to put themselves in a position where they are able to operate effectively and gain an edge. Be ruthless and selective about yourself and establish which are the weaker areas in your soft skills' armoury and then set about addressing them with as much systematic rigour as you would apply to the development of your hard or technical skills.

Notes

1. Institute of Training and Occupational Learning aims to promote best practices in the development of occupational skills and knowledge to the benefit of individuals, employers and the wider community (**www.itol.co.uk**).
2. Lambert, D. and The Diagram Group (1996) *Body Language*, Collins Gem.
3. Kreidler C.W. (1997) *Describing Spoken English*, Routledge.

4. Clarke, D. and Underwood, J. (1988) *Assertion Training*, National Extension College.
5. Rein, I. Kotler P. and Stoller M. (1987) *High Visibility*, Heinemann.
6. Hindle, T. (1998) *Negotiating Skills*, Dorling Kindersley.

Managing Time Effectively

Dianna Keel

If we are happy and feeling productive, we are making appropriate decisions about life. On the other hand feeling unhappy, frustrated, and stressed or anxious most of the time may be the result of making poor choices in the area often called 'time management'.

In general not making good decisions results in feeling overwhelmed and under accomplished. We don't have personal time, we don't get the proper amount of rest and nor do we have time for leisure activities and the people who are most important to us.

'Time management' difficulties are exacerbated because our society encourages productivity, not happiness. The hallmarks of a successful person are to be hardworking, financially secure and goal oriented. This may represent success but it is not happiness.

What can be done?

Treating the symptoms

Most people start at the symptom end by applying mechanical or external solutions, although proper time management will require delving more deeply to find organic or internal solutions. But even addressing the symptoms will get us started on the correct path.

Work faster and longer. This is the technique most of us adopt first. Workaholism is one of the few socially sanctioned addictions, but it can have a detrimental effect on the rest of our lives. How is it viewed in your workplace? The most enlightened organisations understand that working ever longer and harder may provide quantity but does not necessarily produce quality.

Make a realistic schedule of those tasks that need to be done. We usually drastically underestimate how long most things will take. The most common mechanical reason for 'not enough time' is assigning unrealistically short time frames to what needs to be done.

Build time into the schedule to handle the unexpected. There will always be interruptions for which you should allow – traffic, the weather not co-operating, an appointment cancelled or changed, or a meeting overrunning. On the other hand, you can use unexpected bonus time productively by having a list of short tasks that can be completed quickly or set aside without difficulty. Then if your client phones to say that he has been delayed and is unsure when he will be arriving, or a colleague with whom you have scheduled a meeting will 'have the papers ready in half an hour's time,' you will not be fretting about your time being wasted or be tempted to start something important that you know you cannot finish.

Become more effective. This is the so-called original time management solution of 'working smarter'. This includes going for the greatest gains and least losses as well as paying attention to what can be delegated or dumped. Although you will have to negotiate the warranties on the sale of a multi-million pound business, you could ask a trainee to do the first draft of the article that you have promised to write or a new will on which you have just received instructions.

Do mechanical techniques work?

Mechanical techniques work only for a while since they don't address the source of the problem, which requires thinking outside the box. The truth is that, the more we try to 'manage' time, the less likely we are to succeed. It isn't really possible to make more time, because we each get the same amount every day and it is finite.

It is important to recognise that external solutions are always temporary. When we are struggling to 'manage time' we should really be asking inner questions: Is stress necessary to bring the best out of us? Is dissatisfaction necessary in order to achieve progress? Is it OK to become successful lawyers but not to develop a fraction of our full human potential? Do we really want to live this way?

For many people there is a large gap between what is deeply important to them and the way they spend their time. 'We're getting more done in less time,' people are saying, 'but where are the rich relationships, the inner peace, the balance, the confidence that we're doing what matters most and doing it well?'

This is when we should stand back, think carefully about the personal price involved versus the possible rewards, and make a conscious choice about what it is that we really want. Often the biggest challenge is not to do more things but to stop doing things. It is a sad fact for the profession that women might just be better at taking this decision than men; although more women than men enter the profession every year, more than half leave full-time practice within 10 years.

Intermediate techniques

Using 'intermediate' techniques, which straddle both mechanical solutions and more organic concepts will help us to progress, and there are three main techniques which will help at this stage.

Evaluating our use of time

This requires that we:

- ○ Assess how long tasks take us to do.
- ○ Know how much of our time we have already committed, so that we don't commit more than we have.
- ○ Be aware of how our use of time matches up with our priorities.

By simply becoming more aware of these three factors, without judgment and without pressure to move faster, we can almost effortlessly start to make better use of our time.

Remaining as flexible as possible

According to reports from the Menninger Institute in Kansas City,[1] flexibility is the most important single quality we can develop to survive and thrive in the 21st century. Flexibility entails openness, receptivity and the willingness to try new methods and techniques. Flexibility of this kind is not always encouraged in the legal profession, where so much weight is given to tradition, precedent and individual cleverness. One of the challenges facing the competitive culture of law firms is to persuade its staff to share knowledge and experience in a flexible way through office newsletters, intranets and data and precedent banks.

On a personal level one way to become more flexible is to create objectivity through detachment from the situation. We should be more concerned with *what's* right rather than with *who's* right. The main question should be 'Does it work well?'.

Learning to say no gracefully

Saying 'no' to a colleague, and especially to a partner, requires a degree of courage, but the immediate negative reaction that we meet might be much better than the consequences of trying to do too much in an exhausted state. Buying property for our clients as tenants in common when they wanted to be joint tenants or forgetting to file a crucial document at court is much worse than the momentary annoyance of the person who asked you to take on the additional piece of work.

It will help our sense of perspective and our resolution if we can accept that:

- No one is indispensable.
- No one is irreplaceable.
- No one will thank us if we get sick through stress; and hardest of all.
- No one will remember our contributions in 12 months' time.

If a straight-out 'no' is too difficult, there are alternative strategies which get us to the same destination but by a different route. These should be used at spaced out intervals, making it clear that it is not that we are trying to avoid work per se but rather that being so overworked means that re-prioritisation is necessary in order to keep up our present high standards:

- I'm really over-committed right now and if I take this on I can't do it justice.
- I appreciate your confidence in me. I wouldn't want to take this on knowing that the other tasks and responsibilities I have right now would prohibit me from doing an excellent job.
- I'd be happy to do this for you but realistically I cannot do it without foregoing some other things I'm working on. Is it more important to finish the lease for Joe Bloggs today or to discuss the Rent Review with Muddles Ltd? Which can I leave until later?
- I can do that for you, but not now. Will it be okay if I get back to you in the middle of next week? I currently have work for three other partners in the queue.

How we say 'yes' can be just as important as how we say 'no'. Sometimes we have very little choice about accepting a time-constraining request, because a very sick client wishes to change her will or because half your colleagues have gone down with 'flu. In this situation it is important to re-prioritise your work, to carry out the work cheerfully but to make it clear to your colleagues that your own work priorities have had to be reordered.

The temptation when accepting work on apparently unfair terms is to focus on the resentment rather than getting clear instructions. In fact ensuring that the instructions that you receive are clear is a paramount objective in any situation, but when your focus has been diverted by tiredness or feelings of injustice it is even more important. At the very least go back to your room, sit down quietly, write down what you have been asked to do and ask yourself if you understand the instructions. If you find after a little thought that you don't understand them, go back as soon as possible and ask for further and better particulars. Don't waste time speculating on what the person instructing you *might* have meant.

Following these mechanical and intermediate techniques will enable us to get a measure of control over our lives. However, addressing even more fundamental issues will enable us to achieve more leverage; this is like a longer fulcrum allowing heavier loads to be manoeuvred. Here we go beyond the mechanical aspects of time management to address what may be at the root of our difficulties. Managing our priorities and managing ourselves are the final challenges.

Priority management

People short of time tend to find themselves majoring in minor things. That is not to say that small tasks do not lead to larger accomplishments. But spending large amounts of time on lower priority tasks drains the amount of time and energy left for important tasks.

To establish priorities we need to ask ourselves 'Is this really the most important thing I need to do?'. One technique which is of immense help is the classic Covey quadrant[2]. The first step is to divide a square into four equal squares or boxes marked:

o   Urgent and important.
o   Urgent but not important.
o   Important but not urgent.
o   Not important and not urgent.

The second step is to allocate our tasks to these four smaller squares or boxes.

And the third step is to look carefully at what the boxes contain.

Obviously we should turn immediately to the contents of the first box, those tasks that are *urgent and important*, but most of us do in fact spend too much of our time in the last box doing those things which are not important and not urgent! A simple recognition of this and a refusal to permit this behaviour to continue is what is required here.

The next most common time-user is the second box for tasks that *are urgent but not important*. These include answering ringing telephones, speaking to co-workers who have initiated the conversation, and dealing with incoming mail. These tasks appear pressing but in terms of consequences they are not important at all. Many of them could be delegated to someone else. With a competent secretary there is no need to dictate letters declining or accepting invitations or acknowledging receipt of documents; if you have agreed pro-forma letters in advance, a simple 'yes' or 'no' scribbled on the letter should be sufficient indication of how your secretary is to reply.

Too often lawyers are unable or unwilling to spend time on tasks in the box marked *important but not urgent*. This may be because of inadequate support staff or facilities or because too many transactions have been dumped on us with inadequate guidance. But as this is the box which is the most valuable for our future, so we should consciously allocate more time to it. Focusing sharply on completing all urgent and important work followed by concentration on activities that are important but not urgent is a major key to high productivity. If partnership prospects depend on marketing success, it is important to set aside time to work out what we are going to do and then to arrange our diaries and to set up meetings to advance this. Meanwhile all other tasks should be deferred, delayed, delegated or discontinued. What we need is the discipline to stop doing the things that are urgent but not important and those that are neither urgent nor important. We should keep asking ourselves 'Why am I doing this at all?'.

Self-management

Our self-image controls the way we 'manage time'. Take a minute to think about that. It is simply that the internal picture we have of ourselves affects our ability to make the best use of our lives.

We may question other things about life, but we don't readily question the validity of our self-image. We simply behave as if it were an unalterable fact. But our self-image regulates our behaviour just as a thermostat controls room temperature. It determines how we use our knowledge, skills and experiences. And it affects how well we spend our time.

It is very illuminating to ask, 'How would I act if I were already an excellent time manager?'. If we were offered £200,000 to play the part of an excellent time manager in a movie, how would we behave? Well, we would have our desks organised. We would move quickly. We would work on one thing at a time. In an ideal world it would be finished before we started on the next task. We would work from a prioritised list. We would anticipate and plan for interruptions.

What is the difference between acting and reality? Probably only the image of ourselves that we retain in our heads.

Change

Fortunately our attitude to ourselves can change. It takes about two months to create a specific behaviour and to practise it daily until it becomes a habit. Adopting any of the techniques and strategies above will make a difference. Incorporating half a dozen (phased in over time) can transform our lives.

However, at the deepest level what is required is clarity about life purpose, because fuzziness about this is usually at the root of time management difficulties. Although it may be a surprise to some, studies reveal that having direction (or purpose) in life has astonishing benefits. According to the Canadian Institute of Stress, the ability to clarify and express one's values and goals is the most powerful single factor for retaining good health, slowing down the ageing process and increasing happiness. The most important thing is to think outside the box and even outside Covey's quadrant, in terms of time management.

Have a clear purpose if you want to get the most out of your life

If we don't know where we are headed, we are probably going to wind up somewhere other than where we want to be. If we don't know where we are going, what destination will we ask for when buying our ticket?

To discern what we really want, we must constantly ask ourselves 'Do I really want to do this?'. It isn't possible to answer this accurately unless we have a vision for our lives, which springs from our deepest, long term desires which should be vibrant, dynamic and alive.

Having a clear vision will empower us to find an effective direction and to achieve real accomplishment. Keeping to this vision can provide release from the weight and confusion of local problems and concerns, because it will allow us to see the overview – rather like standing at the top of a mountain and looking at the general view. This also enables us to see the general direction and the road that will take us to our destination.

It's easy to forget that our personal values should be what are most important to us about life. Having clarity of values will enable us to make choices that really matter to us. Ensuring that our choices are aligned with both our vision and our values will make it more likely that we make wise choices about our use of time. Studies have found that when people take all their needs, values, and priorities into account when setting goals, their happiness levels increase substantially.

Knowing what you really want will make the biggest difference for successful 'time management'. Only then can the other techniques I have outlined truly help to create more powerful results and achieve a fulfilling life.

One last (bonus) tip: enjoy the process!

Notes

1. Source: Society for Neuronal Regulation 2000 Conference Scientific Papers.
2. Covey, S.R. (1990) *The Seven Habits of Highly Effective People: Powerful Lessons in Personal Change*, Simon and Schuster.

Dealing With Stress

Dianna Keel

Lawyers, especially women, are prone to 'toxic success syndrome'. The symptoms are a lack of delight in daily living and a susceptibility to illnesses caused by too much juggling, too much work and too little play. The result is astonishingly high levels of career dissatisfaction, depression and substance abuse. How do we know this, why does it happen and what can be done?

Some facts and figures

Surveys reveal that 75 per cent of lawyers suffer from work-related stress and that they have a greater level of stress than the average population. Other studies show that lawyers have the highest incidence of both substance abuse and depression among 105 leading occupations and 70 per cent of lawyers say they would start a new career if they could.

Although there are twice as many men as women in the profession, slightly more women than men are presently entering the profession. In 2001, about 72 per cent of the trainee solicitors who called LawCare for support and advice were women. Following just one mention in the *Gazette*, over 750 people visited the LawCare website to check out *100 Other Things a Solicitor Can Do*. A further 200 people called LawCare's helplines for a copy and 190 of them were women!

The three areas most commonly identified by lawyers as causing work-related stress are: too much work, not enough time for family or social life, and excessively long hours. The Law Society research from 1997 showed that more than half the country's qualified solicitors (then numbering 71,000) were working at least 48 hours a week. And statistics suggest that people who regularly work more than 48 hours a week have a higher risk of ill health, including a proven higher risk of heart attacks, than the rest of the population.

Why are lawyers so stressed?

Partly it is to do with the workplace ethos and partly it is to do with those personal qualities that motivated us to become lawyers in the first place. There is a widespread belief that anyone who has spare time at work is not working hard enough and therefore needs to be given more to do, with the result that the really effective people do not get recognition or kudos and that stress in the workplace is actually rewarded. The practice of law encourages this because transactions are often charged by the hour and lawyers are increasingly judged by just two criteria: how much time they can tot up during the year and their total annual billing figures.

Furthermore, the particular internal traits and values of lawyers make us more susceptible to distress. Studies have identified a higher desire for achievement and excellence than the norm. We value leadership, dominance and status versus subordination and deference; and we display a tendency to be much more conscientious and competitive. All of these traits are linked to higher levels of distress. Lawyers are also more pessimistic – a trait linked to depression. Indeed, lawyers generally are more pessimistic than the clinically depressed!

Stress itself does not necessarily produce problems, but certain kinds of stress do. The stress that causes problems is better defined as dis-stress. Distress is directly linked to our attitude. It is about how we respond to what happens to us, and those who choose law already possess a greater propensity to distress-creating traits. Law students, compared to undergraduates generally, score badly on measures of health potential, vocational satisfaction, driven behaviour, achievement ethic, relaxation potential, anxiety, hostility, total stress, and subjective stress.

To make this even worse women's stress appears to be caused more by personal than by academic pressures. For example, first-year female law students reported more strain – attributable to sexism, lack of free time, and lack of time to spend with one's partner, as well as more depression and negative physical symptoms – than either first-year male law students or undergraduates generally. Before starting law school, women did not have more negative physical symptoms or depression than men, so the results were not simply the result of expectable gender differences in willingness to report problems.

What causes workplace stress?

One aspect which is often singled out as producing stress is the long hours' culture of many law firms. Research indicates that lawyers work long hours both because they are internally driven to do so and also externally forced to do so by excessive work demands. The actual number of hours worked in a day is dictated by three factors: first an individual's internally derived commitment to work, actual work overload, and in the case of women, having preschool children. Actual work overload was seen as most significant, producing feelings that work invaded one's non-work life, although lawyers who believe they have a future in their firm or those who gain intrinsic social rewards from working with clients are less likely to view long hours negatively.

Among lawyers with 10 or fewer years of experience, female lawyers were found to have lower job satisfaction than males, primarily because of the lack of influence and opportunity for promotion. Another study found female lawyers to have higher levels of testosterone than non-lawyers. Higher testosterone levels are associated with energy, dominance, persistence and focused attention but also with antisocial behaviour, drug and alcohol use, marital discord, violent crime – and fewer smiles!

The result of prolonged over-stress is 'burnout'. It is interesting that the same study found that burnout did not occur randomly throughout organisations. Instead, it seemed to occur in clusters of workers with a common supervisor or manager. The study's conclusion: the boss is responsible for the lion's share of burnout in organisations.

So, why isn't more being done?

The beliefs that we should work hard past the point of suffering, that there is no gain without pain and that second best is last have come to be seen as formulae for success. This leads many people to deny or attempt to conceal the existence and effects of stress in their own lives.

Many do not believe that they can do anything about workplace stress, yet in 1997 extensive research (using 3,000 interviews) identified workplace stress as the primary cause of home stress, and not the other way around. In fact, this study found that stress tends to originate at work, spread to the home, then boomerang back to the workplace in an intensified form.

What can be done?

To some extent an individual's ability to deal with stress depends on personality type. People appear to use two different styles to deal with their stress: active and passive. Passive individuals who reach the stage of burnout, need extended vacations or personal leave in order to restore their emotional resources and sense of worth. By contrast, active individuals benefit more from workshops, self-help materials and wellness programmes.

It's important to realise that you are the only one who can determine the amount of work or stress that is comfortable for you. Some people thrive on 60 hours' work per week, others are exhausted after 35. Even for workaholics, however, the long hours' culture is a chronic or drip-by-drip source of stress, and in the long term stress is debilitating for most, if not all of us.

There are ways to prevent this. Using effective time management principles (covered elsewhere in this book) can help, as can following sports' psychology principles developed by studying why some people thrive and gain strength when stressed while others in the same circumstances get weaker. What makes the difference?

Burnout and balance

We often use the term 'burnout' to describe exhaustion so severe that it forces individuals to give up or change their careers completely. Another way to describe the condition is shutting down. You don't feel like doing anything so you don't. But instead of being destructive this 'I don't want to do anything' feeling is protective. It may be exactly what you need. Burnout is a forced 'time out' because you wouldn't take the time voluntarily.

Somewhat surprisingly, it is not stress of itself that is dangerous. Actually, we all need some stress. Stress strengthens our muscles and our minds. We humans would die without any stress to challenge and interest us, but it is being able to balance the stress in our lives with other activities which will make the difference as to whether we are dealing with stress or distress.

According to a number of top sports' coaches and psychologists, burnout is caused by the failure to seek relief periodically. High stress rhythmically balanced with intermittent recovery is no problem. But a combination of high stress, poor sleep, inadequate nutrition, no exercise, no humour, too much alcohol, too little (or no) personal time and alienation from friends and family is lethal.

We need work. We need play. We need rest. Oscillating between them is nature's way of balancing our needs. It is very similar to the cycles of day and night and the cycles of the seasons that constantly balance a rest phase with an active phase.

In other words, recognising that we need to oscillate between cycles of stress and recovery is the first step to managing ourselves and our work situation.

Adaptation

Once we have recognised the factors which create undesirable stress (distress), we can consider how to alleviate or prevent them in the first place. Much can be done to transform the attitudes that create an over-stressed life. Have you noticed that after being knocked off track by disruptive change, people who do well on stress follow a similar pattern of actions and reactions? They can be seen to:

- ○ regain emotional balance quickly.
- ○ cope during the transition.
- ○ adapt quickly to the new reality.
- ○ recover to a stable condition.
- ○ thrive by learning to be better and stronger than before.

These individuals have developed 'coping strategies' which increase the likelihood that they will respond constructively to adverse circumstances. The first step in developing such strategies is to strengthen our 'personal foundations'. We can do this by raising our standards, strengthening our boundaries and increasing our reserves. This may require some explanation.

Raising standards. Standards are how we behave (and, to some extent, how we don't behave). They are the way of setting targets of excellence that we naturally adhere to. We need to be clear about what are the minimum standards we will accept without becoming self-righteous or rigid.

Strengthening boundaries. Boundaries are external whereas standards are internal. They are the clear limitations we set on what other people may say or do around us. We need to use boundaries to protect our time, energy and spirit.

Increasing reserves. Humans are animals, and like all animals are genetically coded for survival, not for quality of life. We will reduce stress if we can find ways to reduce risk and at the same time to increase our reserves, especially of time, space and money.

Good news for women

These are practical steps that can be taken to reduce distress but recent research has shown that women could have the edge on men after all in their ability to cope with stress. A landmark UCLA study by two female professors suggests that women respond to stress quite differently from men, because stress produces a cascade of chemicals in the female brain that cause us to seek and maintain friendships with other women.[1] It's a stunning finding that has turned five decades of stress research upside down.

Until this study was published, because nearly 90 per cent of stress research had previously used male subjects, it was generally believed that when people experience stress a hormonal cascade is inevitably triggered which creates the 'cave-dweller reaction', including taking blood away from the brain and sending it to the extremities in readiness for immediate action. The classic 'fight or flight' response. But, as a result of this study, the researchers now believe that women have a larger behavioural repertoire than just this classic 'fight or flight' response.

This is related to the hormone oxytocin which is released as part of the stress response in a woman and which dilutes the fight/flight response.

Instead she is encouraged to tend children and to seek other women. When a woman actually does engage in tending or befriending, it seems that even more oxytocin is released, which further counters stress and produces a calming effect.

This calming response does not occur in men because testosterone, which men produce in high levels when they are under stress, reduces the effects of oxytocin. Oestrogen, on the other hand, seems to enhance it, and even women with higher than usual testosterone levels produce more oestrogen than men. Women's different response to stress has significant implications for their health, and this 'tend and befriend' notion may explain why women consistently outlive men.

So the bad news is that women lawyers appear to be more liable to suffer stress and distress than men; the good news is that we are naturally endowed with more protection.

Take a look at your job

It is probably as important for the employer as the employee to recognise that poor working conditions are in fact more stressful than poor pay and benefits, and that job stress has a greater negative effect on productivity than stress caused by childcare or caring for the elderly.

The most important single determinant of an individual's state of stress at work is job satisfaction or the lack of it. Real job satisfaction is created by four positive factors:

1   Job autonomy.
2   Learning opportunities.
3   Supportive supervisors.
4   Flexible work arrangements.

Job autonomy. Analyse your role and see what aspects of it you can take responsibility for. Make positive suggestions as to how it could be improved. Would it help if you had a dedicated trainee? Do you want to be involved in marketing your department? Would it be better if precedent meetings took place at lunchtime rather than after work? Would it be more efficient if you concentrated on only one type of client work rather than several?

Learning opportunities. Find out what courses are being run in your specialism and ask if you can go on them. Join professional organisations such as Society of Trusts and Estates Practitioners (STEP) or Solicitors Family Law Association (SFLA) which are focused on your specialist areas. Look for self-development courses which will enhance your self-esteem and improve your effectiveness. If these are expensive and your firm is unwilling to pay course fees for only one individual, explore the possibility of training providers coming to your workplace. Most courses do after all attract continuing professional development (CPD) hours.

Supportive supervisors. This may be beyond your immediate control, although if supervisors are consistently negative, this may be an indicator that you should seek alternative employment. However, each of the others may to a greater or lesser extent may be within your control. The operative word is control.

Flexible work arrangements. The Employment Act 2002 gives an employee the right to ask for flexible working arrangements, although the employer is required only to consider the request and not necessarily to implement it. The request is more likely to be given serious consideration if you have produced a reasonable case first. If you want to begin work earlier so that you can leave earlier, or if it would help if you worked part time, find some aspect of your work that would benefit from being carried out in peace and quiet to support your case.

Structuring your day

While at work remember that your efficiency can be improved by attention to some very simple rules.

Take strategic pauses. Laboratory experiments have shown that working too long at mental tasks can increase problem-solving time by up to 500 per cent. Every 20 to 30 minutes take a brief strategic pause of 10 to 60 seconds' duration to disengage yourself from work by changing your mental focus, shifting your gaze and loosening up your neck and shoulders.

Take short breaks at mid-morning and mid-afternoon. Numerous experiments on work productivity have demonstrated that rest pauses and work breaks should amount to at least 15 per cent of working time. This actually speeds up the work and more than makes up for any time spent on breaks. Step outside into some natural light, walk on your own, breathe deeply, sip some water. You will feel more relaxed and not so overwhelmed, your concentration will increase and you will be able to achieve more in less time.

Take frequent physical activity throughout the day. Light physical activity is one of the best ways to raise energy and reduce tension, increase creativity, and promote hardiness. Just spend a few key minutes being active after meals, and in pauses and breaks throughout the day. Get up and get moving again, go for a brief walk, take a flight of stairs, do a few muscle-toning exercises or easy, enjoyable flexible movements.

Enhance your work environment. Amazing improvements come from turning up the lights (this can immediately increase alertness and attentiveness), paying attention to posture and ergonomics, introducing music, colours and scents, and whatever else makes your personal work environment feel more relaxing and energising.

Clean up your work space. Find a way to eliminate the piles of paper-work! Working in an environment that is clean and organised will free up your mind and reduce distractions. When our space feels cluttered, our minds also feel cluttered.

Outside the workplace

Eat nutritious meals and snacks. Research suggests that moderate-sized meals plus small (healthy) between-meals' snacks may increase your energy and metabolic rate.

Be lighthearted. Humour enhances the body's own painkillers and relieves stress. This is a universal wellspring for boosting energy and busting tension. Research suggests that laughter can actually enhance workplace productivity too.

Create reserves. Make sure that you have at least a little extra time, money, space, friends and support. Without reserves, anxiety and stress will stalk you closely. Save 15 per cent of your income (gross or net, your choice) to give you a greater sense of financial security and control over your life even if it means reducing your standard of living.

Build a support network. Talk to those you trust. Ask for help and allow yourself to be helped. Remember that this is the oxytocin hormone in action. Even a close relationship with a pet will relieve stress and improve health.

Have enough deep sleep. On most days large numbers of people with no clinical sleep problems did not get enough sleep the previous night and are therefore not alert. Research shows that negative mood states are inevitable consequences of sleep deficits.

Enjoy family meals. In today's world this can be difficult to achieve but if at all possible eat one meal each day as a family. Make it a rule that only positive news and expressions of appreciation are spoken during that meal. Your life and attitude will improve when you make the effort to focus on the things that work for you and feel good now, rather than only on your problems.

Take some exercise. Ideally exercise for a minimum of 30 minutes three times weekly, but remember that physical activity that lasts just 15 minutes, if done often enough, may be as physically beneficial as longer work-outs and is just as effective in bringing stress levels down. The total amount of time spent exercising, not the length of each session, appears to be what is most important. Walking is particularly good. Walking is not only more beneficial physically than non-aerobic stretching and toning exercise, but has also been shown to improve cognitive function. It is the time spent walking, not necessarily the pace, which matters.

Have something enjoyable to do every day. Develop a hobby or find outside interests that take your mind far away from your stress and engage at least 15 minutes daily in these interests.

And it's good to bear two things in mind

1 Take responsibility for your actions. These are always a result of choices that you've made. When you accept this, you will realise that you are able to make different choices. The 'no choice' attitude will always create stress and anxiety. Get over it.
2 Expect the best but have a plan in case the worst happens. Adopting this strategy helps overcome that pessimistic trait that creates so much stress – even depression – in lawyers.

And if the worst happens

If life is just too much there are professional organisations which can help.[2]

Notes

1. Source: Taylor, S.E., Klein, L.C., Lewis, B.P., Gruenewald, T.L., Gurung, R.A.R. and Updegraff, J.A. (2000) 'Female Responses to Stress: Tend and Befriend, Not Fight or Flight', *Psychological Review* 107(3): 41–429.
2. Contact details for LawCare, Support and Advice for Lawyers: Website: **lawcare.org.uk**
   An Anti-Stress Desk Workbook is available free by calling the Helpline:
   For barristers in England and Wales 0800 018 4299;
   For solicitors in England and Wales 0800 279 6888;
   For solicitors in Scotland 0800 279 6869.

Chapter 3.4
Leadership

Sally Woodward

Introduction

Why is leadership important?

This chapter deals with the nature and role of leadership. One of the myths to dispel is that being a leader becomes important only much later on in your career and that all leaders are people like those whose fascinating stories are recorded elsewhere in this book. As the famous 'management guru', Charles Handy, once put it: 'Leadership is far too important to be left only to those at the top of organisations'. Of course, some leaders have a much bigger group of people to lead and some have a much bigger part to play in setting the direction of their firms or departments than others. Nonetheless in most of the important areas of leadership – at least in the context of legal practice – the majority of you already need to demonstrate, and are already developing, skills as a leader. The aim of this chapter is to help you to learn more effectively from your experience so that, if you want to, you may eventually follow the examples of the women in this book.

Even if you have no aspirations to become a 'leader' in that sense, by being more aware and confident about your day-to-day leadership role and skills, you will produce greater job satisfaction both for yourself and for those with whom you work. And before you say that 'this won't bring in the clients or the fees', remember that most recent research into successful professional services' firms suggests that the level of job satisfaction amongst those who work in them is in fact the most important factor in explaining relative long term success. Of course there are examples of law practices that appear to be very successful but where job satisfaction is far from high (at least in some quarters). The question is whether that success is sustainable in competitive markets where both prospective recruits and clients are looking to gain more from their relationships than 'merely' money and/or competent legal advice.

This chapter will:

- ○   Set out some ideas about what effective leaders do and are – especially in the context of legal practice.
- ○   Identify what are the key leadership skills that should and can be learned through formal training and/or on-the-job experience.
- ○   Point out other useful sources of advice and insights about leaders and leadership.

The ideas and insights in this chapter come from my own experience in creating and leading a team of people in a large law firm; from my formal business education (both as a student and teacher); from talking to many leaders (and their 'followers') in legal practice and industry; and from working with them and their younger colleagues on 'leadership development' programmes. I shall also refer to some useful books and stories – the key is to work out what is transferable from the experience of others into your own environment, and what approaches are meaningful for you. You have to find your own way of demonstrating leadership and one that is right for the people who might look to you for 'leadership'. There is no magic formula and no one right approach. There are, however, some traps for the unwary.

You will get most benefit from reading this chapter if you write down your reactions, ideas and queries as you read through it. Remember that reading a book can be a very passive form of learning. I can present my own views on 'What' leadership is about. For you to learn anything worthwhile as a result, you need to ask yourself 'So what are the implications of these stories, research and opinions for me?' and more importantly 'Now what am I going to do about them?'. This is the essence of being a 'reflective practitioner'.

In what follows the examples used come mainly from the context of private practice, but the fundamental leadership issues do not vary much from one type of organisation to the next. In some companies and government departments people who hold specific positions and have certain job titles, may have more 'authority' to tell others what to do than in the average law firm. In barristers' chambers formal positions and job titles may confer even less authority in themselves. Whatever the context, the most successful 'leaders' of professionals (and probably of everybody else too) will achieve superior results by virtue of abilities and behaviours that are nothing to do with the power vested in them by the organisational hierarchy. This said, the culture and other aspects of the environment in which you are trying to 'lead people' will of course influence how you can and should behave, as we shall see later on when looking at the idea of 'situational leadership'.

Case study: the newly appointed practice leader

Although leadership is not the preserve of senior or managing partners or 'heads' of department, let's have a look at the first six months in post for a newly appointed practice group head; many of you may have been on the receiving end of this approach to leadership and perhaps see yourself in this role one day. This summary, written by Tony Reiss, is based on a mixture of real examples, and while the practice sector may change – in one sense 'e-commerce' is yesterday's news, the leadership issues remain the same.

Jill left Jack's office feeling elated and yet strangely nervous. Jack, the managing partner had just told her that the board wanted her to run a new group in the firm. It would have four other partners and six assistants and its brief would be to get to grips with all the commercial opportunities in the new technology sector.

As she walked along the corridor to her own office, many thoughts whizzed through her head. Could she get a bigger corner office now? How was she going to get on with Ben and Bill, the two more senior partners in the group? Jack had said that the board had explained to Ben and Bill that the two of them had too important a role in looking after major clients of the firm to be given the position of group leader, and apparently they were happy about this.

The other junior partners had not been told the news yet, because the board thought that it would be best coming from her. She was pleased about her appointment partly because she had thought for some time that the firm had been indecisive about exploiting new opportunities. She would show them how to do it.

One month later

Jill's first group meeting seemed to go well. Her copy of the business plan had been circulated beforehand and there seemed to be a good discussion about some of the detail. If anything, Jill thought that the changes suggested by others made the plan even better. There was some disagreement about whether to present the plan to the assistants. Jill and Bill both thought that this was a good idea, but Ben and the two junior partners were concerned that the assistants had less loyalty to the firm and would take the plan to their competitors if they left. They agreed to compromise and to give the assistants only the main messages but not the detail.

Six months later

Jill hadn't had much of a break during her first six months. There had been that long weekend in Amsterdam with her husband, Sam, and the weekend at the spa hotel in the Cotswolds with her sister when Sam went off on his golf tour. She was starting to feel tired, but on the other hand she felt pleased that her figures looked so good. As well as taking on the role of practice group leader she had managed to keep virtually all her client work. That was probably why she now felt in need of a break.

The business plan seemed to have gone down well. Jack was using it as an example to other practice groups. Although she knew that only a few actions specified in the plan had actually been taken, she appreciated that most people were pretty busy. The key thing that pleased her was that no one was actually griping about it. Jill saw this as a huge success.

One of the highlights of the first six months had been the enquiries that came in as a result of setting up, together with a leading management consulting firm, a sort of club of companies interested in using e-commerce as a channel for distributing their products and services. The contact with the consulting firm had come from one of the senior assistants, Dorothy Comme, whom everyone called Dot. Jill was pleased that she had remembered to send a memo to Dot thanking her for the suggestion.

Dot had volunteered to do most of the organising of the club's first meeting. Despite being really busy, Jill thought she had supported Dot well, mainly by coming up with good practical suggestions. She felt that Dot would have learned a lot from this experience.

Another success was the extra data that Jill had requested from accounts to help her spot what was really happening on the money side. Her hours of pouring over these printouts reaped dividends because she could ensure that appropriate action took place, such as getting bills out and chasing debtors.

Nine months later

Jill was keen to know how she was doing. She asked for a review with Jack, the managing partner. Jack looked at the figures. They looked pretty good. He also decided to meet the other partners in the group and to talk to the assistants and secretaries to see what they had to say. There the position looked more mixed. Jill was in for some surprises at this review, Jack thought.

Questions for your reflection

o   What do you think Jill did well?
o   Why do you think that the feedback from many of the people in the group was less than enthusiastic?
o   What would you have done differently if you had been in Jill's shoes, and why?

At the end of the chapter you will find some answers that came from groups of lawyers (at all levels) when we put the same case study to them. How do they compare with yours?

Perhaps it would be interesting to compare what Jill did against some sort of checklist of 'leadership best practice'. In the second half of the 20th century there was a growing realisation that the scientific management techniques of Taylor and others (Taylor, 1947), that had so transformed manufacturing operations in the first half of the century, did not have so much to offer in the post-war economies of the capitalist world, with the shift first to services and now to the 'knowledge economy'. A new 'holy grail' in the search for improved productivity and profitability (along with 'IT') was seen to be 'effective leadership', on which vast amounts of time and money have been expended. Let's have a look at the fruits of all this investment.

What are effective leaders and what do they do?

Some of the ideas that have come out of the research are based on 'theoretical' approaches, such as sociology or psychology, but most derive from empirical research. Such research tends to look either at those individuals who are generally regarded as 'good leaders' by their peers and/or by those whom they lead, and to analyse what it is that might explain this assessment; or it looks at organisations that on a number of criteria seem to outperform similar organisations, and tries to establish the way in which people in those organisations behave that might explain the superior success.

Before reading on, write down your own views on these questions:

o   What leaders do you know that you admire – in business generally, in your own organisation or elsewhere?
o   Why do you admire them?
o   What are they like? How do they behave?
o   Do they have any traits or patterns of behaviour in common?

Leadership, management and administration

When new partners are asked what is the main difference in their roles when they become partners, and even more so when they become heads of practice groups, they frequently say something along the lines of 'we are expected to be leaders now'. In fact they have already been (or should have been) 'leading others' as assistants, but it is interesting that most consider that their new role means much more than 'merely' being an effective manager. So is leadership different from management? If it is, what is the difference? And does it matter?

In an interview for Director magazine in 1988,[4] John Adair, one of the first academics to attempt to clarify the distinction between managing and leading, said:

> Leadership is about sense of direction. The word lead comes from the Anglo Saxon word that means a road. . . It's knowing what the next step is. Managing is from the Latin 'Manus', a hand. It tends to be closely linked with machines and the idea of controlling, particularly financial control and administration.

Warren Bennis, a leading American writer who occasionally took a rather dim view of managers, makes the following distinctions between leaders and managers (Bennis 1989):

Manager	Leader
Driven by context	Masters context
Administers	Innovates
Maintains	Develops
Focuses on systems and structures	Focuses on people
Relies on control	Inspires trust
Short-range view	Long-term perspective
Asks how and when?	Asks what and why?
Has eye on the bottom line	Has eye on the horizon
Imitates	Originates
Accepts status quo	Challenges status quo
Does things right	Does right thing

You will find suggestions for further reading on this type of research in the bibliography at the end of the chapter. It is clear that these researchers consistently consider that the most effective leaders not only seem to spend a lot of time and energy on the following areas, but are viewed as being successful in doing so:

Creating – or at least communicating – a 'vision'

Although the word 'vision' is overused and often abused, the underlying idea is sensible. Broadly it means that successful leaders give people a sense of purpose and direction, which goes beyond that of spelling out objectives for the immediate task. A 'vision' meets our psychological need for some significance in our efforts. Many of us may not be at the forefront of creating the 'vision' for the organisation or group of which we are part, but if we don't know what it is, if we don't believe in it, can't explain it to others, or don't embody it in the way we behave, we will not be effective leaders. A 'vision' can exist on many levels. It can be there for a whole firm, for a practice group, a department or for a team. It is even important in relation to helping particular clients achieve something for their businesses or families which may add meaning and significance to the specific tasks that we may be asking others to help us do for them.

Communicating and coaching

Vision apart, effective leaders place a big emphasis on two-way communication, especially face-to-face communication. Research also stresses that communication lies in deeds as well as words, and that effective leaders say what they mean, mean what they say and do what they say. There is consistency (sometimes called 'integrity') in the way they behave. Note that this does not however mean always behaving in the same way. Effective communication also implies excellent questioning and listening skills to gather information and to check reactions and understanding. One useful definition of effective communication is that 'the message received' matches the message you want to send. More recent research also shows that the best leaders spend a lot of time 'coaching' people to set themselves stretching goals and encouraging them to perform even better, which goes far beyond more traditional ideas of coaching as being some form of 'remedial' treatment for inexperienced or underperforming people.

Motivating others

Making the time to find out what really motivates people and trying to align their individual interests with those of the relevant organisation or group or project team is also a key task for a leader. Good leaders get not simply *compliance* from people to do what is asked of them, but their active *commitment* to the objectives and job in hand. Other research shows that levels of motivation rather than innate abilities or levels of experience are the best predictors of high performance in any group of people.

Sometimes mere compliance is enough, but for most law firms (and increasingly for most businesses) more than this is required from people for the firm to be consistently better than the rest. In some situations, leaders have no alternative but to seek active commitment in order to get the job done – for they have no 'power' to command people. Surprisingly, many managing partners of law firms find that in fact they have no 'real power' over their partners in the sense of being able to tell them what to do despite their job titles, and any power they do have does not derive simply from their position or title. But even where they do have power by virtue of their position or the resources they can give or withhold, the best leaders will seek willing co-operation from their followers. Charles Handy puts it well when he says that leadership is 'the ability to inspire follow-ership'. One exception to this may be that in a true crisis people will fol-low a leader who 'takes the helm' and tells them what to do with no or minimal debate. However, often their willingness to do that is based on the trust and credibility that has been built up by very different behaviour in the past.

The question 'how do I motivate people' is another one to which there is no easy or short answer. Suffice it to say that we are all different. We all have different needs – for money, status, social interaction, recognition by others, responsibility, personal development or some combination of them. These needs, and hence what will encourage us to put time and energy into doing something to satisfy them, are constantly changing. There is thus no substitute for getting to know what makes 'your people' tick and adjusting how you deal with them accordingly – while of course balancing the needs of the client, and the group as a whole. Inevitably there will be some difficult trade-offs to make, but if you are known as someone who invariably takes no account of the individual's concerns or who always puts the interests of the organisation or client first, you will not succeed in this area of leadership.

Self-awareness and learning

This may seem a surprising item on the list. Self-awareness is more a state than a 'task'; but to be self-aware you do need to ask for feedback from others as to how you are perceived by them, to respond to it positively, even if it is painful, and to reflect on the consequences of what you do. You may then need to adjust your behaviour accordingly; you need to be good at learning from your experience. More generally, the best leaders are constantly looking to improve, asking others for new ways and ideas, and are prepared to admit and learn from their own mistakes and to encourage others to do the same while not ignoring sensible risk manage-ment processes. How many lawyers do you know who are comfortable in this area?

Day-to-day leadership

These leadership 'tasks' or behaviours are of course closely linked. The leadership role exists at all levels of an organisation and is probably already part of your day-to-day work. Even if only 'managing' one person, you will need to be doing the things in the checklist to get the best from that person. Where a group of people is being managed the scale and com-plexity of the leadership task increases, but the essence remains the same.

Sometimes people draw a distinction between 'strategic leadership' and other aspects of leadership. The first is more about creating or changing the 'vision'; this is necessary but is not sufficient for success. The necessary further element is to be able to motivate people and to give them the confidence and ability to do what it takes to follow the new direction. That is what makes the real difference between superior success and being one of the, albeit relatively successful, crowd. Increasingly, research shows that this is what makes the difference over the long term in all types of business – even in manufacturing companies. How much more true should it be in the legal services' sector?

A longer-term view

This is not a leadership 'task' or behaviour as such but a perspective that effective leaders tend to bring to the judgments and decisions they have to make. At its simplest, it means being aware of the trade-offs that often exist between short-term wins and the investment that must be made now in terms of energy, time or money in order to achieve greater returns in the longer term. In day-to-day work a manager may go for the short-term win by choosing to give a task to a 'safe pair of hands' who has done the job before or she could plan for the longer term by giving it to someone who will need extra coaching or support but who will learn and develop as a result. Or when delegating a job, it is the choice between telling the delegate exactly what steps to take versus leaving them to find their own way, consistent with meeting the overall objectives of the task.

The focus of 'ordinary' managers is on the current task, on getting the job done at the lowest cost and the lowest risk. The manager who is also an effective leader will consciously make a judgment as to whom and how to delegate a job that takes into account the longer-term opportunities, even if in some cases he still chooses the 'short-term' route.

Making the time

So finally, is there a difference between 'leadership and management' and does it matter? Resources can be managed and tasks can certainly be planned and managed. But where people can choose whether or not to commit to you their full know-how, energy and enthusiasm, leadership is required. We all recognise those who 'go the extra mile' when we see them – and paradoxically, they often get all the credit for doing so. But perhaps there should be far more recognition and kudos given to the leaders who create the environment in which self-starters can flourish.

One thing is clear to those who work in and with law firms. Far too much time and energy of 'lawyer-leaders' is spent on administration and crisis management, somewhat less time is spent on proactive management and far too little on leadership as defined above. Perhaps that is one reason why Jill got the feedback that she did at the end of her first six months. The challenge for firms is to ensure that time spent on leadership tasks, and success achieved, is both recognised and 'rewarded' (in the broadest sense of the word). It is also important that firms encourage people to use and develop the relevant skills and behaviours as early as possible in their careers. For many people like Jill, it is a little late and very demoralising to discover that the job of 'practice group leader' demands different things from those that have made her successful to date. Which brings us to the next question.

Are good leaders born or can they be made?

The answer to this has changed over time and with prevailing fashions, and also with discoveries in different areas of academic research. In the 1950s and 1960s, 'trait' theorists looked for those personality features that marked out the most successful business and military leaders. The unsurprising conclusion was that such leaders had three traits in common; they were white, Anglo-Saxon and male!

Many attempts to identify the behaviours and skills that marked out the most successful leaders followed, and these were identified as especially important in the new 'knowledge economy'. Key elements are clearly superb communication skills and the ability to develop effective working relationships with a variety of different people.

Another group of researchers explored the idea that there is no 'one size fits all' recipe for success and that the behaviours required for success depend on a variety of factors. These could be situational (for example, whether there is a crisis or not), the preferences of the leader, the aspirations and abilities of the people involved or the complexity of the task.

John Adair, Ken Blanchard and others have promoted ideas of 'situational leadership'. They were adamant that leaders could learn to adapt their behaviour provided that they really wanted to do so, and if they used the right tools for analysing the situation. Some suggested that the type of approach required to lead through a crisis 'revolutionary change' is so very different from that required to rebuild relationships and trust afterwards that another key requirement for leadership success is 'to know when it is time to hand over'. The essence of this idea which Charles Handy summarises as the 'best-fit' approach is that leaders need to be able and willing to analyse the situation and to adjust their behaviour to suit the different needs of the group, the task and the environment within which they are operating. Figure 3.4.1 summarises this idea of situational or 'best fit' leadership.

One notable absence from the lists of important traits or skills found in the research literature is 'charisma'. Although 'charismatic' leaders may get the most publicity, there are plenty of examples of effective leaders who are not by any means larger than life characters.

More recently there has been a swing back in favour of the view that some people do find it easier to acquire relevant skills – especially communication skills, and to be flexible in their approach than do others. The

Figure 3.4.1 The 'best fit' approach to leadership.
Source: Adapted from Handy, C. (1993), with permission.

work on emotional intelligence (EQ) is a good example; the best leaders are said to have higher levels of EQ than IQ. EQ is defined as the ability to manage ourselves and our relationships effectively. EQ consists of four fundamental capabilities:

o   Self-awareness.
o   Self-management (sometimes called self-discipline).
o   Social awareness (sometimes called empathy).
o   Social skills (closely linked with communication skills).

Common sense and observation may suggest that these features are found more in some people than others; whether this is a product of 'nature or nurture' is probably a sterile debate. The proponents of EQ as an explanatory factor in leadership success certainly believe that it is never too late to help individuals improve their EQ. This said, some clinical psychologists say that recent neurological research suggests that most of us acquire a degree of 'hardwiring' in our brain patterns, and hence in our emotions and behaviours, some time between the ages of puberty and our early 30s. And occupational psychologists have been telling us for years that we can be categorised according to how 'task orientated' or 'people orientated' we are and whether we use all our senses to collect data about situations or just a few.

Professor Nigel Nicholson, writing in the FT (mainly about leadership at the 'top' of organisations) said: 'personality has returned to the forefront of management and leadership, exploding the myth that social engineering and investment alone can produce great leaders . . . while we can equip people with skills and ways of behaving, it is more difficult to engineer their motives and interests'. He goes on to reiterate the point made by others that what makes for leadership success is contingent on the situation – including the culture of the organisation and even the society of which it is part. 'Embattled businesses in tough markets promote macho managers; . . . The greedy and unethical leaders who made the headlines in 2002 were the product of the reciprocal chemistry between their own personality profiles and their business cultures'. He also points out that many characteristics that make people successful, when overused, carry the seeds of destruction within them, whether this be the driving decisive leader who becomes a tyrant or the nurturing caring leader who becomes incapable of getting anything done. His comments also confirm that your own motivation to be an effective leader is a critical ingredient of success.

In the end, as in so many debates, the answer probably lies in a mixture of many perspectives; effectiveness as a leader is a function both of nature and nurture and of opportunity and experience. But one thing seems clear – the earlier you start to think about and do something about your leadership potential the more likely you are to create or take the right opportunities to develop it and to avoid becoming 'hardwired' in those behaviours that are less successful in inspiring others to follow you.

Do you have to be good at everything?

Certain leaders may be very effective at all aspects of the job but some may be looking to other people to help them. In fact, some of the best leaders (i.e. those with that job title) recognise their limitations and share leadership tasks with others who have complementary skills. Sometimes those who are best at strategic thinking and at creating the vision may feel less comfortable with the day-to-day people aspects of leadership. But they certainly encourage and reward those who are good at communicating with and motivating others, for they recognise that these are essential requirements for turning good strategic thinking into action.

So what, now what . . . ?

So where does all this research leave us? Perhaps with a few more perspectives on the subject, but still with no straightforward comprehensive definition of leadership, still less a recipe for success. The reality is that we have to make up our own minds about what sort of organisation we want to work in, and what aspects of leadership will be important for us to be happy and successful in it, bearing in mind that the world around is constantly changing.

The following leadership roles are likely to be increasingly important in many law firms, and indeed in any business that depends for success on the commitment and know-how of its people, and which is facing an increasingly complex and competitive climate:

o   Having yourself, and helping others to have, a sense of purpose and direction for both the group of which they form part and for themselves as individuals.

o   Building relationships with a variety of people – including those who are not like you and certainly don't think the same way as you do!

o   Being willing to balance short and longer term issues and to invest time and energy in helping others succeed as well as yourselves, and to do so in ways that make sense to them as well as to the organisation.

o   Being 'ethical' – in the broadest sense of the word (i.e. not linked to any specific code of ethics or set of professional rules). In essence this means acting consistently with the fundamental purpose and values of the group of people to and for whom you may be accountable. It also means 'walking the talk' and 'talking the walk'.

What would you add to this list? Or do you disagree fundamentally with some of these ideas? What is important is that you should form your own view in order to help make choices about your career, about the context in which and the people with whom you will be happy working; and about what you will put first in your day-to-day work from now on.

If any of the above ideas does strike a chord, you should be investing in the following skills and activities sooner rather than later:

o   Becoming more self aware – reflecting on what you do, considering how others respond to you and asking for feedback (and not just on your technical competence).

o   Developing good basic communication skills – especially skills of questioning and listening.

o   Developing a flexible style for delegating work to others, of giving constructive feedback, and for providing on the job training. Your style will need to respond to the needs of individuals as well as to the time, cost and risk involved. You need to be able to move along a spectrum between being highly directive (controlling) and very 'hands-off' in your approach. Being able to use a coaching (questioning) style is an excellent way of trying to balance managing risk with involving others in decisions, and encouraging them to take responsibility and to think for themselves, and hence to learn faster from the work they do.

o   Talking to your colleagues about their aspirations and concerns beyond what is required simply to get the next job done.

o   Using the work allocation process in a conscious way to help promote the learning and development of those for whom you are responsible (i.e. not always giving work to those you find easiest to work with and who have already learned how to do the job).

- Being prepared to 'manage upwards' where necessary – this means developing a variety of influencing styles to tackle different people and situations.
- Reading (selectively) books and articles about management and leadership. Not all of them are full of management gobbledygook.

Traps for the unwary

Many of these are the mirror image of the behaviours above, but there are others:

- Assuming that everyone else is (or should be) like you (and is motivated by the same things that you are).
- Assuming that if people are not taking responsibility or initiative, or 'going the extra mile' that this is entirely 'their fault'. Bad managers or leaders sometimes get the behaviour they deserve.
- Assuming that the firm and not you, can and should sort out issues of low morale, lack of training or other people problems. However good or bad the environment and the HR systems, individual managers have the greatest influence on the motivation and hence the performance of those who work for them.
- Assuming that money is always the cause of, or a cure for, lack of commitment; it is not, though it is often used as an easy rationalisation for what are far more complex factors undermining morale or prompting a move.
- Assuming that if you know that 'no news is good news' and are happy with that, everyone else will be too.
- Failing to 'grasp nettles', confronting those individuals whose behaviour is generating resentment or conflict or cynicism, or whose negative attitudes are draining the energy and commitment of others.
- Treating as role models those whose behaviour is very different but who 'got to the top' anyway. In many legal practices the criteria for success are now very different from those that operated even just a few years ago.
- Consciously or unconsciously thinking that 'I survived this lack of good management, so why can't they'?
- Assuming that 'nodding donkeys' (people who say 'yes', or who don't say 'no') to ideas or plans will do what it takes to put them into practice.
- Assuming that having excellent people skills is a substitute for the other skills that good managers need, including planning and project management.
- Assuming that because you understand the problem and have the solution that you can shortcut the need to get others on board too and to ask them for alternatives.

- ○ Giving up too soon, especially when trying to get people to change their behaviour in some way or to adapt to a new role or environment. However, much time you spend on getting their 'buy-in', people will still resist being asked to change their ways when the time comes.
- ○ Assuming that others see you in the way you see yourself.
- ○ Expecting to be liked – effective leaders are rarely universally popular!

In the observations on the case study in the Appendix that follows, you will see that Jill had some of these failings which undermined her effectiveness even though she was someone who was genuinely trying to involve others and to be a 'good leader'. It is important that if we do find good leaders in our organisations, or experience examples of effective leadership in relation to ourselves, that we recognise and encourage them. We lawyers are often very good at pointing out the problems or defects in performance. It is part of our critical training. We need to learn to be more generous with praise.

Finally, apart from relying on self-awareness and self-help, be sure to take advantage of the management development training that many organisations are now providing from an early stage in your career. Do not be put off by partners who have 'learned all this stuff the hard way' or who label it as 'soft skills' and by implication, therefore, less important than technical knowledge and procedural skills. Many such partners have never experienced such training themselves and are naturally sceptical. Ironically, if they can be persuaded to take part, they often become ardent converts. And if there is nothing available within your current organisation, why not make some time to explore what is available outside. That may be the first step in becoming a good leader.

Appendix: some observations on the case study

Tony Reiss

Some of these are more obviously relevant to a private practice law firm but many are universal to any group that sees itself as having a collective purpose, rather than simply providing a context in which everyone is entitled and expected to 'paddle their own canoe'.

These comments focus on the activities of the nominal 'leader', Jill. Her leadership role is to set up the group, to get agreement on what it is going to do, on what will be counted as 'success' and to create the environment in which group members will work well together both to achieve the group's objectives, and also to satisfy their own aspirations. She is trying to provide strategic leadership as well as day-to-day leadership. Clearly other members of the group will also need to demonstrate leadership in relation to the people working with and for them. The other partners will need to work with Jill to create a 'vision' in which they all believe, but they may well not see her as experienced enough to agree to do what she suggests just because she has the title of practice group head.

1   The production of a business plan is usually a good place to start. If it is well structured it should clarify the group's direction and have clear tasks, responsibilities and timescales to increase the chances of the group using all its strengths and pulling together. Jill's approach is flawed because drafting the plan herself and discussing it in a partners' meeting only briefly means that it does not receive everybody else's full commitment. Just because nobody expresses negative thoughts about an idea does not mean that they like the idea and certainly does not mean that they are committed to it and will help to implement it.

Sometimes it is appropriate to lead from the front and to tell people what to do. A platoon leader with a hill to take needs to issue instructions. There is no better way of being a leader when you are in an emergency. But this is not usually the situation in a practice group.

To maximise the chances of people being committed to actions, the ideal approach is to involve them in the process of review and consideration of options. The whole process takes much longer, and it usually goes round in circles, because some people say one thing and others disagree. The leader needs to find ways of resolving these disagreements without causing offence. Many leaders find this frustrating and prefer the faster 'I'll-tell-them-what-to-do approach'. Until they discover that it rarely works.

Another problematic area is the circulation of drafts to assistants by practice group leaders. The leader sees this as a consultation process, and can be surprised to learn that assistant solicitors often have a negative reaction to this. So much so that it would have been better not to circulate the draft, as assistants typically can find this action manipulative or patronising.

2   An alternative approach rarely adopted by leaders, but which can reap great rewards, is to establish at the outset some ground rules or values by which the group agrees to be run. This has the effect of giving the leader a mandate. One way of doing this is to agree what sort of behaviour is going to be encouraged and what behaviour is not going to be tolerated. In some groups it may help performance if it is agreed that, for example, all partners are expected to support actions agreed by 80 per cent of the group even if they personally did not agree with the action.

3   Jill might have spent longer getting a clearer idea of what the board expected of her. This would have helped her to decide where she was going to focus her efforts. Too many practice group leaders try to achieve too much on too many initiatives and end up achieving very little. As an eminent commentator on leadership says, 'it is better to attempt some foothills first before tackling Everest'. There is no better way of building team morale than getting some successes under your belt.

Practice group leaders can feel somewhat stuck in the middle, between the board on one side and the group members on the other. One of the challenges of the leader is to align the talents and motivations of the group members with what the firm wants to achieve. Not easy this one!

4   It is almost impossible to be a truly effective leader and maintain the same level of fee earning work. It may be tempting to try; after all, chargeable hours are the common benchmark in firms and maintaining a high billing level is very much to lead from the front. However, a leader will achieve more through others by allowing personal chargeable hours to drop. Again, this should be agreed with the group and the board.

5   The vision contained in the business plan is unlikely to be clear in everyone's mind, which means that the group will not pull together as Jill hopes. Effective leaders find activities to reinforce the vision so that it is well understood by everyone. Assistants and support staff frequently comment that they hear partners saying one thing and see them doing another. Messages become blurred and members of staff become cynical. The leader can play a vital role in ensuring consistency of communication by walking the talk and talking the walk. Michael Hammer advocates that 'The same thing must be communicated seven times in seven different ways before anyone will believe it'.

6   There are other benefits from the leader finding time to walk the floors. There is no evidence from what we know of Jill's first nine months that she has had time to find out about the position of everyone in her group – whether her staff are fulfilled and happy with their workload or career prospects. Research studies show time after time that the biggest single factor that determines a person's performance is whether they are motivated. If some time is not spent in finding out if all staff are fulfilled, the chances are that some issues are not being dealt with. Leaders cannot simply hope and expect people to come to them if they need to. People usually need some extra encouragement to express their thoughts. An effective leader is one who recognises that all this takes time and reduces the potential for doing as much fee earning.

7   The effective leader tends to spend more time praising the effort of partners and staff. Jill does well to pass on some praise to Dot, but this would have had an even bigger impact if it had been done face-to-face, rather than sending off a memo. Practice group leaders often fail to appreciate the value of praise and personal communication. They choose to take the short-term benefit of chargeable work now rather than investing their time in raising the motivation of staff for the longer-term benefit of the business.

8   Coaching is a very powerful way of enhancing the capability of other people. Jill has chosen to be directive in supporting Dot on the e-commerce club initiative. This approach would be more appropriate if Dot were inexperienced, but she is a senior assistant. A less directive style would have been more appropriate. This approach would have taken a bit longer, but the learning would have been deeper. Dot would be more capable of organising the next event if she had been encouraged to think it through for herself. In other words, if she had been coached. Senior assistants often comment that they are not given enough responsibility or not respected sufficiently for the experience that they have. This can have a serious demotivating effect.

9   Many practice group leaders see their role as getting to grips with the group's financial position. There can obviously be benefits for someone to look closely at this information and to chase partners to bill work in progress. But Jill could have been doing many other more useful things with her time. Reviewing the financial information is an administrative task and would be better performed by an administrator at a lower cost. If partners need chasing, all the administrator has to do is tell the practice group leader. If the group is large enough, this role can usefully be delegated to another partner so that the group leader shares the role of leadership and is not seen to be cracking the whip all the time.

10 Virtually all the writers on leadership agree that one of the traits of
an effective leader is the ability to be self-aware and to learn from
experiences. Jill does well to ask for a review with Jack, the managing partner. But she should also have asked members of her team
for comments on how well they thought she was doing. The 360
degree feedback is invaluable in obtaining an accurate picture of
personal performance. When such feedback is obtained, the majority of leaders discover that there is a difference between their own
perception of their leadership style and how others experience it.
One practice group leader was really quite proud of what he saw as
his democratic style. He was surprised to discover that his team all
perceived him to be autocratic. Typical reactions were along the
lines of 'he does ask us what we think – but he always seems to go
ahead and do whatever he wanted anyway'.

Bibliography

Bennis, W. (1989) *On becoming a Leader,* Random House.

Bennis, W., Spreitzer, G.M., Cummings, T.G. (2001) *The Future of Leadership: Today's Top Leadership Thinkers Speak to Tomorrow's Leaders,* Jossey Bass.

Blanchard, K., Zigarmi, P., and Zigarmi, D. (2000) *Leadership and the One Minute Manager,* Harper Collins Business.

Covey, S.R. (1999) *Principle-Centred Leadership,* Simon & Schuster.

Financial Times 'Features on Business' pages and its on-line 'Mastering Management' materials are also an excellent source for expanding your understanding about business generally.

Goleman, D. (1996) *Emotional Intelligence: Why it can matter more than IQ,* Bloomsbury.

Goleman, D. (1999) *Working with Emotional Intelligence,* Bloomsbury.

Goleman, D., Boyatzis, R. and McKee, A. (2003) *The New Leaders: Transforming the Art of Leadership,* Times Warner.

Handy, C. (1993) *Understanding Organisations,* Penguin Business.

Kotter, J. (1996) *Leading Change,* Harvard Business School Press.

Mayson, S.M. (1997) *Making Sense of Law Firms,* Blackstone (especially Chapter 23).

Maister, D.H. (2002) *Practise what you Preach,* Free Press.

McKenna, P.J. and Maister, D.H. (2002) *First among Equals: How to manage a group of professionals,* Free Press.

Taylor, F.W. (1947) *The Principles of Scientific Management,* Scientific Management, Harper.

Notes

1. See for example Maister, D. (2002) *Practise what you Preach*, Free Press.
2. The concept of 'reflective practice' is one that underpins ideas about how adults learn from their experience – i.e. how we 'learn by doing'. In essence being a 'reflective practitioner' means being good at experimenting with new ideas and techniques, reviewing and analysing what happens, drawing conclusions about the effectiveness of our actions and adjusting our behaviour to achieve better results next time. We all learn in this way, whether we are conscious of it or not. But some of us are more effective at going through this 'learning cycle' than others. Many of us tend to get stuck on 'having a go' and don't spend enough time thinking first and reviewing afterwards; others may spend so much time planning or analysing that they risk never getting anything done, or never learning new things.
3. This case study was written by my Sherwood colleague, Tony Reiss. Tony is a principal consultant in Sherwood PSF Consulting Ltd. This case study has previously been published by Tony Reiss in *Managing Partner* magazine, Ark publishers.
4. Bickerstaffe, G, (1988) 'Take me to your Leader', *Director Magazine,* November, p. 101.
5. First widely publicised by Daniel Goleman and others – see bibliography.
6. On 8 November 2002; and see **www.ft.com**

Rainmaking and Networking

Tania Martin

Introduction

As law firms, like other commercial enterprises, require business in order to turn a profit, individuals who are able to bring in new business for their firms are very valuable. Many a partnership has been earned by the revenue value to a firm of new business introductions. The popular term applied to the process of generating new paying business is 'rainmaking' and people who bring in the work are called 'rainmakers'. They are often partners, or senior associates knocking on the door of partnership, but need not be so. Lawyers at any level can bring new work into a firm, and usually increase their standing by doing so.

It is important to understand the distinction between cold-calling and networking, as both might be considered to be rainmaking activities. In essence cold-calling, a much used tool of commission-based salespeople, is calling someone you haven't been introduced to. Life insurance salespeople, who have obtained your name and office number from the roll of solicitors, may attempt to sell you insurance in this way. Headhunters, who have been asked to fill specialised legal vacancies also cold-call although the research that they have first carried out is somewhat more detailed than merely looking up a directory.

Lawyers, on the other hand, do not usually indulge in cold-calling as it is seen as unprofessional and perhaps even unethical depending on the jurisdiction and the nature of the cold-calling. In England and Wales, cold-calling by solicitors is governed by section 1(d) of the Solicitors' Publicity Code 2001 which in essence prohibits unsolicited visits or telephone calls by solicitors to anyone other than current or former clients or to another solicitor or an existing or potential professional connection or a commercial organisation or public body.

On the other hand, legal firms positively advocate networking by their staff in order to bring in new business. Networking can be loosely defined as taking every possible opportunity to introduce your firm and its strengths by ensuring that you yourself present a favourable image to those that you encounter in professional and even social situations. It can thus be used to identify potential targets of new business, to win new business and to keep new business, as well as having other subsidiary benefits which will be discussed in the networking section below.

Rainmaking

There are four steps in the rainmaking process:

- ○ targeting new business.
- ○ pitching for new business.
- ○ winning new business.
- ○ keeping new business.

Targeting new business

As the saying goes, if you want to catch fish you need to fish where the fish are. But you also need to decide which fish you want to catch, where they are likely to be located, whether travelling to that location is a good use of your resources and whether you have the skills necessary to catch the fish you want.

Targeting new business operates on the same principles. First, you need to decide what your target is. It may seem obvious that targeting should relate to your current practice, but this is not always the case. If you are a defendant insurance lawyer, targeting insurance companies is an obvious source of new work, just as targeting property developers is an obvious step for commercial property practitioners. However, expertise in trusts can be re-channelled to build up a pensions' practice, which would make your firm's company clients or external pension providers a clear focus of your efforts.

It is always important to remember that if your goal is to be a successful rainmaker, you should not waste too much energy on businesses which are unlikely to use your services. On the other hand, in the context of networking, for reasons which will be discussed further below, there are very few people on whom you deploy your skills, who will represent a total waste of your time. At the very least you should always be aware of the possibility of referrals. You may find that your potential property developer client does not want your services as a property lawyer, but that he is about to embark on a complicated dispute over responsibility for dilapidations and may require a good litigator. In the world of private client practice time spent with accountants and foreign lawyers may pay substantial dividends in the referral to you of work that they are not qualified to do themselves.

After identification comes research. This is necessary both in order to speak knowledgeably to your target about his business, but also so that you can think creatively about what his legal needs might be. This can be time-consuming, but is greatly aided by the number of research tools that are now available. The Internet can provide company reports, up-to-date news on share prices and the advertised aims of companies together with comment and industry gossip. Reading daily financial newspapers and regular industry journals will give you some idea of the general marketplace for your target and also the ambitions and weaknesses of its competitors. And a slightly off-the-wall suggestion that shows that you are interested in the target as a well-rounded entity is to note whether your target is one of the sponsors of theatres, opera companies or sporting events.

More specific questions to consider

○ Is your target currently using a lawyer who is charging much more for the service that you could provide? For companies this is relatively easy to identify by reading company reports, where the lawyer will be identified. You will then be in a position to decide whether it is likely that what they want could be provided more inexpensively by you. If, for example, you are based in Manchester, they operate from Chester and they are currently using a London City firm the answer is likely to be yes. For individuals this is likely to be more difficult to determine.

○ Is your target's business such that a new law will be an issue on which you are in a position to advise them to their advantage?

○ Can you find out who is the real decision-maker in the organisation, and can you influence that person? This may be difficult if you are relatively junior, but listening to your junior counterparts in a target organisation can often provide you with exactly the information that you require to pass on to the right senior person in your firm.

Locating your target

Having researched your target you now need to make contact. How do you find your target in order to present yourself? Consider:

○ Is there an industry body to which your target belongs which holds functions that you could attend?

○ Does your target attend functions at the Chamber of Commerce or other local organisation?

○ Does the in-house legal counsel attend functions at networking organisations which you could join such as the Association of Women Solicitors, Association of Women in Property, the City Women's Network or the International Bar Association?

○ Is your target a foreign company or an organisation which sends representatives to events focused on the home country, such as Australian Business in Europe events?

○ Do you know someone who could introduce you to a decision-maker (a director or in-house counsel) at your target?
○ Do any of the decision-makers attend a gym, squash club, race course or other club in their spare time? And do you have some not entirely spurious reason for being there?

Getting access to your target sometimes requires some lateral thinking, but it is essential in order to proceed to the next step in rainmaking, namely pitching for new business.

Pitching for new business

Once you have made contact with your target, remember that the object of meeting the target is eventually to be able to pitch for legal work. 'Pitching' is a term usually used in legal circles to mean a formal attempt to win work, often by giving a presentation. But you should think of it as encompassing much more informal contacts which you can turn into an opportunity to attract new business. You 'pitch' your ideas to the target and hope that he catches them. Even if the first contact is very informal you should still remember a few basic rules because first impressions count! In brief:

○ Be well presented in your appearance. The target won't be interested if you don't *look like* a competent lawyer.
○ Exhibit good manners. A simple gesture like holding open a door or offering the target wine first can improve your likeability; contrast this with eating with your mouth open, which can put people off or make you a subject of ridicule.
○ Communicate clearly. The target won't be interested if you can't string a sentence together.
○ Get on before you sell. For many people there is nothing more off-putting than the hard sell, particularly at an informal meeting. By contrast, someone who likes you, or at least gets on with you, is more likely to give you business. Be prepared to chat and discuss other matters before moving in to any discussion of what you can do for the target. Don't however ask about personal matters (like children or holidays) unless you are genuinely interested. Insincerity kills pitching.
○ Remember that the goal is to get business. You are not talking to the target in order to have a good time, you are there with an objective and should retain your focus on achieving that objective.
○ Listen to the target, and don't talk too much. The target will feel that you are interested if you ask questions and listen attentively to answers. At the same time you can gain valuable information about the target or his major issues of concern by listening.
○ Remember that you will need to know the issues that affect the target in order to define what it is you can do, as you will only get

business if you can give the target reason to give it to you. This reason may be:

(i) An economic benefit. You may be able to provide the same services as the existing legal representatives for less money. It might cost the target a lot of money in the long run if the target doesn't take your advice on, say, an emerging legal issue now. Alternatively, you might point out that litigating now might cost £30,000 but that this would recover £200,000 of lost funds.

(ii) A problem resolution. There may be an existing problem which you or your firm can resolve, either on a strictly legal basis or because your commercial approach to a legal problem will solve an adverse commercial situation faced by the target.

(iii) A more personal reason. Perhaps simply that you get on with the target. People like to feel important and perhaps you have demonstrated that you recognise that the target is important and merits attention.

o If the target is buying, stop pitching – don't keep trying to sell your services to someone who has agreed to use them. Not only is this a waste of energy, but it might look as though you aren't paying attention.

Pitching is a fundamental part of the rainmaking process. If it is done well it may lead to new business; if it is done badly, it certainly won't.

The ultimate outcome of pitching is to get new business. It is rare, however, that someone will agree at first contact to give you work. So the first time you pitch, all you may be seeking is an agreement to meet again.

Winning new business

Once you have pitched (and this may involve more than one conversation with the target) whether or not you 'win' the new business will be up to the target. This may depend on how well you have pitched, the target's attitude to you and your firm, how confident the target is that you will provide a useful service to a professional standard, and the target's attitude to your competition.

Your target may really like, or have a very successful business relationship with, another lawyer at another firm. If you are making any headway at all with the target you should be able to ascertain directly or indirectly during the conversation what firm and even what other individual lawyer is being used. It's unwise to criticise that other firm or lawyer openly; not only does it appear unprofessional but it goes against the confident impression that you are trying to provide. It's much better to use implied comparison – 'I hear that they are very good at personal injury. Do they also do medical negligence?'. You know that they don't, but that your firm does!

Accordingly, when you pitch you must make sure that the target understands all the benefits you can provide, whether that is value for money, commercially viable legal solutions, or quality of advice, as well as believing that you will treat the target as the target wishes to be treated.

Winning new business from an existing client is usually easier than winning new business from a target who is not an existing client. If you and your firm have worked well for existing clients before, they will be grateful, loyal, and be well disposed towards you. You can win new business from an existing client by targeting a different type of work. For example you presently do a client's commercial work, but it could be possible to take on the employment work as well. You should always try to be aware of how you can help your client by suggesting other ways to assist in the existing area of legal advice you provide. If you presently provide intellectual property advice to that client, and a new right arises, such as the concept of moral rights being incorporated into copyright law, you may be able to amend your client's business practices to take account of that new legal right.

Keeping new business

To maximise the time that you have spent acquiring new business, you must ensure that you keep it. Obtaining new work from an existing client or obtaining work from a new client will not be of benefit if the client quickly ceases to be a client of the firm, or moves the new work to another firm. Even if this is not strictly speaking the province of rainmaking, you should bear in mind how important it is to ensure that your client gets at least what you have led him to expect. This may involve monitoring the service and attitudes of those who are actually doing the work, as it may not be you.

You must be sure that you know what the client wants in terms of price, quality, accessibility, reliability, timeliness, and attitude – and then ensure that it is delivered. Finding out what the client wants is not a trite statement. Not every client has the same requirements, and an aspect of legal service which is trivial to one client may destroy the relationship with another client. Some clients are not price sensitive and do not mind paying provided the service is delivered yesterday, while others, who are more cost conscious will trade off expeditiousness against lower fees. Some clients will be happy to pay for unrequested tax advice, if you consider that it is a necessary part of the service; others will have retained their own tax advisers and so will see this as an unwelcome intrusion. It goes without saying that you should constantly be monitoring your clients' attitudes to your service and endeavouring to provide the level of service they require. If you or your firm cannot meet the expectations of your new client or of a particular type of client, then perhaps you should re-think how you are identifying potential targets.

Networking

As noted at the beginning of this chapter, networking is one of the primary tools of a rainmaker. Whilst networking can have a very direct application in rainmaking, networking also has a number of subsidiary benefits, which can assist a lawyer in other less obvious ways, such as:

○ Attracting new clients and business through market recognition, reputation enhancement and improved focus.
○ Making useful contacts.
○ Increasing knowledge.
○ Learning of new opportunities.

Attracting new clients and business

Attracting new clients and business should be the primary motivation of networking as a rainmaking tool, and there are several general outcomes that you should look to achieve from networking.

Market recognition

Ensuring that people in the marketplace recognise your name or your firm's name for your professional capabilities in your field is a good first step in attracting new clients and business. This is similar to consumers recognising a brand name, such as Marks and Spencer, and making certain assumptions about the quality of the product by virtue of the brand name. If a firm or lawyer has acquired market recognition, it is not necessary for the lawyer or firm to go to potential clients – potential clients will seek out the lawyer or firm on the strength of their reputation.

Accordingly, the mere fact of networking, by putting a lawyer's or firm's name in the marketplace as often as possible in positive circumstances will assist in attracting new business.

Reputation enhancement

Every time you represent yourself and your firm in a positive way your reputation will improve, and, as people tend to talk to each other about other people, your good reputation is likely to spread. Every networking opportunity is an opportunity to improve your reputation in a potential market. Remember, however, that this works both ways and that if you present yourself badly, your reputation will be diminished.

Improved focus

Every time you pitch your legal services you should note whether the subsequent reaction is positive or negative. The responses you receive may cause you to alter some of the aspects or focus of your pitch or even of your services so as to assist in future efforts at pitching for new business. At the same time, the increased practice in presentation, communication and sales skills will enhance your pitching.

Making useful contacts

Chain letters operate on the principle of rapid multiplication. In theory if the chain is not broken sending a letter to 10 friends should quickly ensure that the original missive is read by 1,000 people. Networking can be like that. The more people you meet the more you will be introduced to others, who will in turn introduce you to even more people. As your network grows so does your opportunity for selling business and learning new things.

Increasing knowledge

As has often been said, knowledge is the path to power. Every time you speak to someone you have the opportunity to acquire more knowledge about something. You have to accept that sometimes this is useful and sometimes it is not. Think of it as similar to panning through buckets of river dust; this can sometimes produce nuggets of gold or in your case worthwhile information. In the context of networking the types of information of particular use are:

- ○ information about your clients, actual or prospective;
- ○ information about your competitors; and
- ○ information on topical matters in your sector.

Even if you do not glean anything which is immediately useful you may find something of general conversational utility in another context.

Learning of new opportunities

A saying that is often heard is that 'it's not what you know, it's who you know'. This can be true, even if it's just because expanding who you know and speak to will expand what you know. Networking can lead to finding out about opportunities which you otherwise wouldn't know were available. This may be for a new job, to join a mentoring scheme, to become a committee member of an industry body where you might get to meet many more prospective new clients, or the opportunity to speak at an important event. Be aware of the potential for finding new opportunities as you network.

Networking in practice

Most networking is done at functions, whether they are hosted by your firm, hosted by a client or are external, such as industry or locally specific functions. They can range from small meetings attended by a very few people to grandiose affairs with hundreds of guests. No matter who hosts or how big the event is, there are some fundamental rules to follow. These apply before the event, at the event and following the event.

Before the event – preparation

The first step in any networking situation is to be prepared. This includes:

- Finding out the details of the event.
- Understanding why you are attending the event and who you wish to target.
- Obtaining some background information on your targets.
- Knowing the services that you and your firm can provide.
- Preparing yourself.
- Preparing for conversation.
- Where more than one lawyer from your office is attending, considering how best to deploy your resources.

Details of the event

Make sure you are clear about:

- The location of the event, how you will get there and how long it will take.
- When the event commences.
- When the event concludes.
- The order of proceedings (if say there are to be drinks followed by lunch followed by a speaker).

If there is a speaker, do some background research on the speaker and the advertised topic so that you can discuss them intelligently should any of your targets raise them in conversation following the speech.

The purpose of attending

The purpose of attending should be to achieve one of the networking outcomes noted above. No matter what is your prime motivator, you should identify who may be at the function that you intend to speak to. If you don't know the precise attendees in advance, you may be able to identify a likely category of people it would be helpful for you to speak to, for example, directors of commercial enterprises.

Obtaining background information on targets

By the time you attend a networking function, you should already have identified the clients or types of client you would like to attract. Then, at any function, you should seek out those prospective clients.

Where possible, find out before the function who will be attending. Sometimes you can obtain a guest list before the event starts. This can give you a head start. Examine the guest list and identify whom you wish to meet. If there are to be many suitable guests you may have to prioritise, or bring a colleague or colleagues along and split the targets between you. If a guest list is not provided in advance, but guests are wearing name tags, doing a discreet reconnoitre of the room before launching into conversation is perfectly acceptable. Where neither an advance list nor name tags are provided, you will have to 'work the room' by moving from group to group to find your targets.

Where you are able to identify who will be attending (particularly easy if your firm is hosting the function!) and whom you wish to target, try to determine the following in advance:

o   Whether the target already has a business relationship with your firm.
o   Whether any particularly pertinent issues are currently facing the target's business or industry.
o   What is the target's business style.

Knowing your own services

When you are networking you are trying to sell your services to potential users of those services. It is therefore essential that you are able to discuss your services and answer any questions a potential user of your services might have. This can include questions such as:

o   What do you do? Try and have an accurate but interesting response to this question. Saying 'I'm a lawyer' is often a conversation stopper. Saying that you specialise in fraud litigation, chasing company directors around the world and recovering the money they have acquired through fraud, is likely to elicit a great deal more interest and conversation. Think in advance how you might answer this question; lawyers often find it difficult to provide a conversation-continuing answer.
o   What areas of law does your firm practice in? What areas doesn't your firm cover, and why not?
o   How long have you (and your firm) been practising in this area?
o   Are you (or your firm) noted for any particular achievements in this area?
o   What is your fee structure?
o   Have you acted for anybody whom I might know?

You should also anticipate questions which are designed to assess you against your competition. Knowing the other firms in your area would be useful in this regard. You can expect questions like:

o   Who else practises in this area?
o   Which is the biggest firm that does this work?
o   Why should I use you?

You must know your profession, and more importantly understand the points of distinction between your firm and yourself and your competition. In conversation with potential clients you must be able to point out the positive points of distinction. For example, perhaps you have not practised in an area for as long as Messrs Smith & Jones, but you provide a more rapid and commercially oriented response.

And should you receive some immediate positive reaction from the potential new client you must know your firm's new business procedures, so that you can answer questions such as: 'Where do we go from here?'.

Be able to tell the prospective client whom to call to arrange an appointment and which partner (if you are not one yourself) they are likely to see. Even better, arrange for someone in the firm to call the target to arrange an appointment.

You should also be prepared for any doubts raised by the targeted prospective client, such as concerns about your experience or your fees, or the target's favoured relationship with another firm, and be able to deal with these in a positive manner. Remove the concerns and the target will be much more amenable to using your services.

You should be aware of current trends, events, scandals and developments in the legal world. Commercial people who deal regularly with lawyers are bound to bring up such things in conversation, and if you are unfamiliar with them they may not think of you as being very switched on.

Preparing yourself

There are a number of things you can do to prepare yourself to maximise the networking opportunity.

o   Consider beforehand the type of impression you wish to create and then ensure that you wear the right clothes, makeup, jewellery and hairstyle to promote that image. Leave enough time prior to the event to check each aspect of your appearance — for example, that you don't have dog hair on your clothes, smudged lipstick and a windblown hair-do.
o   Make sure that you are appropriately attired. It is acceptable to stand out because of your smart appearance but not because you are the one wearing casual clothes to a black tie function. Contact the event organisers beforehand to check the applicable dress code.

○ If you are carrying a handbag, take one which can be slung over your shoulder – if you have to carry it in your hand you won't be able to hold a drink and shake hands at the same time. Sling it over your left shoulder so that it doesn't fall and dangle from your arm whilst you are shaking someone's hand.

○ If you are attending a long event which involves alcohol try to eat beforehand. This will slow the effect of the alcohol and also discourage you from trying to eat, drink and meet new people at the same time (try shaking someone's hand whilst holding a drink and a sandwich!). The point of the event for you is to meet new people, not to have a good meal.

○ Don't forget to go to the loo beforehand.

○ Always have a tissue handy.

Preparing for conversation

Functions can be very dull, and people who attend them regularly often have very low expectations of them. In particular, where attendees at functions just want to chat about their own work, it can be boring in the extreme. So be prepared to discuss non-work topics that may be of interest. These could include:

○ Current affairs and world news.

○ Current local affairs.

○ Industry developments in the client's industry;

○ Current sporting news.

○ Subjects that interest the target (if you have targeted specific people, try to find out what their interests are, whether it be golf or stamp collecting, as this can provide a useful ice-breaker).

This is definitely something you can prepare for and just a few minutes of preparation can produce substantial rewards, although the weather, whilst a rather unexciting traditional stand-by, can at least get the conversation going, particularly if it is unusual for the time of year. But also consider your surroundings:

○ Is the building or other setting of the event of architectural or unusual interest?

○ Are the wines, drinks or food being served unusual or of particular note?

○ Do you know anything interesting about the speaker or the subject of the event?

○ Did anything unusual occur on your journey to the event?

○ Have you recently had any unusual or interesting experiences (whether that be an adventure holiday or a good movie)?

○ Is there any interesting art or craftwork at the venue?

Topics like these can break the ice very easily and in a refreshingly non-business way.

Team preparation

If more than one member of your firm is attending the function, you should consider beforehand how you will target prospective clients:

- Are there so many targets that you should split up and take a few each?
- Should you operate a tag team approach whereby one of you meets a new target and then introduces the target to another member of the team and so on?
- Should you approach targets in pairs or singly?

You should also share your background knowledge of the targets as individuals and as players in a particular industry as well as any other useful information you have which will help each team member to get successfully through the event, such as breaking news in big current affairs.

At the event

When you arrive at the function, whether it is taking place in a room, a restaurant, a gallery, or any other setting, take a moment to examine the venue and the people who are already there.

Look out for practical points such as:

- The layout of the room, in particular where you can stand so that it is easy to mingle rather than being trapped in a corner.
- Where the drinks are.
- Where the loos are.

Also see if you can identify:

- Anyone you know.
- Any potential target.
- Anyone you don't want to get trapped talking to!

The first few minutes of arriving at an event are often the most daunting for those who are shy or new to networking. You will be faced with a room full of people and you will have to walk up to someone and initiate a conversation. Once you have been practising networking for a while, especially where you frequently attend events with regular attendees whom you come to know, you should find this an easy and fun thing to do. But recognise that it can be difficult at first when you don't know a soul and you haven't had much experience of working a room.

Breaking into a group

At large functions people stand in small groups and then move between them. The first thing you will have to do on arriving at a function is 'break into' a group. The ideal group size to break into consists of three people. If you walk up to one person it may be easy to engage in conversation (after all you are both relieved to be talking to someone rather than standing on your own), but it may be difficult to get away again. If you walk up to two people, you may be breaking into a strong conversation and they may go on conversing with each other while excluding you completely. A group of two will also usually be standing toe to toe which makes it more difficult to make eye contact with one of them to draw you into the group. Three people will be standing at an angle to each other and it will therefore be easier to catch someone's eye as you enter the group. If you break into a group of four people you may split the group, although as groups mix and merge the sub-group numbers can soon change.

Breaking into a group is often the challenge most new networkers dislike the most about networking. It is easily done when there is someone in the group whom you know and who you are confident likes you enough to welcome you into the group. Where you don't know anyone in the group then follow this approach for entering the group:

- ○   Walk up to the group, fix one member of the group with eye contact, smile, hold out your hand and introduce yourself, then introduce yourself to the other members of the group. If you have heard a little of the conversation of the group beforehand and are able to carry on in that vein that will make your entrance appear a little less abrupt.
- ○   Do not hang indefinitely on the edge of the group, as you will be ignored, or worse still, seen as behaving rather strangely.
- ○   Try not to approach just when one member of the group is deeply engaged in recounting a story which engrosses the others.

Attitude

Attitude is important. Be courteous, sincere, friendly and open. Remember that body language often says considerably more than words, and in a much shorter space of time. Apart from being well presented, make sure that you have an easy and genuine smile, a firm handshake, that you use appropriate eye contact, and open body language (for example, don't cross your legs and arms).

Eye contact

You should maintain an appropriate amount of eye contact. Staring at the floor or over the head of the person you are speaking to will appear unduly shy, but you should break eye contact from time to time, otherwise it may look as though you are trying to outstare the person you are speaking to which may appear aggressive. Your eyes should be focused on the area between mouth and forehead taking care to meet and hold the eyes frequently. Looking around the room as you are speaking to someone will make you seem totally uninterested in them and what they are saying, but when in a group do move your eye contact from one person to another as they speak and as you speak so that you include everyone in the group.

Smile

Think of the saying 'smile, and the world smiles with you'. People are always more attracted to a smile. The smile must, however, be sincere. Remember that a plastered-on fake smile doesn't fool anybody, and that a quick insincere smile won't endear you to the person you are addressing.

Handshake

A handshake should be:

- Confident. Don't hesitate or linger in offering your hand.
- Full. Don't offer the tips of your fingers, which seems weak and suggests a distrust or dislike of the person shaking your hand.
- Firm. Don't offer a limp hand, but don't crush the other person's hand either.
- Of one to three short pumps' duration, lasting only a couple of seconds.
- Not too vigorous. Don't pull someone's arm out of the socket;
- Offered with a clean and dry hand.
- Accompanied by good eye contact and a genuine smile.
- With the hand shakers standing comfortably apart so that neither person has to lean in to shake hands or have his elbow crushed into his side when shaking.

Having a clean and dry hand can be tricky at an event where food and drink are being served, particularly if you are nervous. Remember the following:

- Keep your right palm lightly touching your clothing so that any nervous perspiration can transfer to your skirt or trousers rather than stay on your palm, giving you a clammy handshake. But don't wipe your hand on your clothes just before you shake someone's hand as that will not create a favourable impression.
- Drinks' glasses are often wet on the outside, either from the drink itself or from condensation. Keep your glass in your left hand so that your right hand remains both dry and free to shake hands.
- Don't hold food in your right hand. If you are holding food at the time someone greets you or is introduced to you, you won't be able

to shake hands. Whilst it is acceptable to take bite-sized food with the right hand and pop it straight into your mouth, be careful not to pick up greasy, sticky or messy food that will leave a residue on your hand (eating before the event may discourage you from doing so at the event).

Body language

Eye contact, smiling, and a firm handshake are all elements of appropriate body language for a networking event. They each indicate courtesy, friendliness, sincerity and openness. In addition you should consider the rest of your body language, such as your posture, where your arms and legs are placed, and how you move whilst you are speaking to someone.

You should stand upright, but not rigidly, which might suggest nerves or a wish to get away. You should not cross your legs or arms as this can seem defensive. Remember to nod occasionally, but not excessively, when the other person is speaking, as this indicates empathetic listening. Stand an appropriate distance from the other person – not so close as to invade his personal space but not so far away as to appear distant.

Listening

You should employ 'active listening', which means 70 per cent listening and 30 per cent speaking on your part.

For a start, you want information about the business and interests of the people you are speaking to, particularly where they are targets, so let them speak and tell you all of this. People like to speak about themselves and generally will have a more favourable impression from a conversation with you if they have done more of the talking and you have been listening attentively. Show you are attentive by asking relevant questions and 'echoing' back some of what they are telling you. If you are being ignored in a group, you can insinuate yourself by asking questions – if you launch into a monologue you will be seen as a bore, and probably a cocky one at that.

The sorts of questions that keep a conversation flowing well, in addition to eliciting the most information, are open questions such as 'Describe to me . . .'; 'Tell me about . . .'; 'I'm interested in why you took that particular approach to . . .'. Closed questions, namely those that elicit 'yes' or 'no' responses, tend to stifle conversations and can have the effect of turning you into an interrogator as you keep asking more and more questions to try to get a conversation going.

Remember that a great part of any decision on the allocation of business depends upon whom the giver of the business likes the most. Engaging in a conversation which is interesting to the target will produce a more favourable impression of the conversation and of you. Also remember that very few people like a hard sell, especially at social events. Talk about things of interest to the target in order to build a rapport, and discuss business later, unless, of course, the target wants to discuss business immediately. The business discussion could even be on a subsequent occasion; you need to judge the mood of the target at the time. Meeting someone for the first time and immediately launching into a sale of your services and why that person should use them is likely to result in his refusing and even avoiding you at subsequent events. People won't even listen to the benefits of using your services if they are on the defensive from a marketing onslaught.

You should also be on the lookout for indications that the target or other members of the group are getting bored or restless or wish to move on for some reason. Don't overstay your welcome. If they are looking around the room, for example, it is time to make your exit.

Breaking out of a group

Breaking out of a group can be even more difficult for some than breaking into a group in the first place, because there are often misplaced fears about insulting the group. If you are at a function, it is unlikely anyone will be offended because functions are for mixing and mingling. When breaking out of a group you need to:

o   Excuse yourself.
o   Say goodbye to everyone in the group.

Excusing yourself

There are a number of things you can say which are appropriate reasons for leaving a group:

o   'I must speak with my colleague X before she departs, it's been a pleasure to meet you.'
o   'I promised to speak with Y whilst I was here, it's been a pleasure to meet you.'
o   'On that note, it has been a pleasure to meet you A, B and C. I hope you enjoy the rest of the evening.'
o   Where you are the host, 'It's been lovely to see you here, but I must go and introduce some other people around.'
o   Or simply 'Well, it's been a pleasure to meet you all.'

Saying goodbye to everyone in the group

When you leave the group you must say goodbye to everyone there. Having made your general departure comment to the group, you should then shake each of their hands, making eye contact with and smiling at each of them, before walking away.

If you have ended up speaking to just one person on his own, then do not leave that person all alone. To 'break away' from one other person you should either introduce them to someone you know who is already in another group, or take them with you to join a new group, which you then leave and move on.

After the event – following up

You will usually find that the place at which you first made contact with your prospective new client is not the place where your services will be engaged. For a start most networking environments are not conducive to discussing the nitty-gritty of what it is that you or your firm can do for the target, and even less what it will cost! Possibly the person you spoke to may not be in a position to use your services but he may know someone else who may wish to, to whom he could pass on your contact details after the event. Even if there is no likelihood of immediate business either directly or indirectly, you may still have encountered a useful future target or a useful source of future introductions or information. It is therefore critical that you follow up your new contact. This could be by:

- A telephone call, either to get some further information or to arrange a meeting, or to arrange an introduction to someone else.
- Sending some information that was requested by the contact at the event or which might be useful to him.
- Meeting over a coffee, drink, lunch or dinner as arranged at the event or subsequently.
- Seeking out the contact at the next event.
- Visiting the contact's office (if invited) or inviting the contact to your office.

For a successful or aspiring rainmaker, networking isn't a sometime activity. It is an all-the-time activity.

Networking is about connecting people. Every time you speak to someone you have a networking opportunity – to obtain new business, to portray your business in a positive light in anticipation of a referral, to have him introduce you to someone else, or perhaps just to increase your knowledge. It is all useful. It may appear daunting at first but networking is the sort of activity at which you can improve very quickly with very basic tips and tricks, some of which you will have read in this chapter. The more you do, the easier, and the more fun, it becomes. You'll notice a difference in your business, and probably in yourself too.